The World-Ending Fire

The World-Ending Fire
The Essential Wendell Berry

Selected and with an Introduction
by Paul Kingsnorth

COUNTERPOINT

BERKELEY, CALIFORNIA

The World-Ending Fire

First published in the UK in 2017 by Allen Lane, an Imprint of Penguin Books
First Counterpoint hardcover edition: 2018
First Counterpoint paperback edition: 2019

Cover photograph by James Baker Hall: *Wendell Berry, Forty Panes,
Henry County, Kentucky, 1970s.*

Library of Congress has cataloged the hardcover as follows:
Names: Berry, Wendell, 1934– author. | Kingsnorth, Paul, 1972– writer of introduction.
Title: The world-ending fire : the essential Wendell Berry /
selected and introduced by Paul Kingsnorth.
Description: First Counterpoint edition. | Berkeley, CA : Counterpoint Press, 2018.
Identifiers: LCCN 2017060544 | ISBN 9781640090286
Subjects: LCSH: Agriculture—United States. | Farm life—United States. | Authors, American—
Kentucky. | Sustainable agriculture—United States. | Sustainable agriculture—Industrial
capacity. | Agriculture—Moral and ethical aspects.
Classification: LCC PS3552.E75 W66 2018 | DDC 818/.5409—dc23
LC record available at https://lccn.loc.gov/2017060544

Paperback ISBN: 978-1-64009-197-9

Cover design by Nicole Caputo

COUNTERPOINT
2560 Ninth Street, Suite 318
Berkeley, CA 94710
www.counterpointpress.com

Printed in the United States of America

7 9 10 8

Contents

Contents

Introduction

In tribute to Wendell Berry, I am writing this introduction long-hand, in pen, in a small hardback notebook. It seems appropriate. Berry has never upgraded his writing tools from a pencil even to a typewriter, let alone to anything more complex, as he explains in his short but high-impact essay 'Why I am Not Going to Buy a Computer' (pp. 236–43). As with all his decisions, this one seems to have been taken after a good deal of thinking. In his writing, as in his farming, Wendell Berry's readers get the impression that this man does not do anything lightly, and that he chooses his words as carefully as his actions.

With that in mind, and now that I think about it, I see that he would probably take issue with the way I have just lazily used the word 'upgraded'. Not just because of the word's ugliness, but because of its implication: that a pencil is a lesser tool than a laptop, simply because it is older and less complex. Older and less complex, in Berry's world, are often virtues. Now in his eighties, he still uses horses to work his Kentucky farm, not for the nostalgia value but because horses do a better job than tractors, and are more satisfying to work with, as he explains in 'Horse-Drawn Tools and the Doctrine of Labor Saving' (pp. 152–9).

As with all thinkers who choose to set their face against both fashion and power, Wendell Berry is regularly caricatured for the crime of thinking things through – accused of 'living in the past', 'wanting to turn the clock back' and various other predictable insults grabbed at random from the progressive toolbag. From one angle he can certainly appear, as he acknowledges himself, a relic from the past. Born at the height of the Great Depression into a farming family which, like all its neighbours, still worked their land the preindustrial way, he is a unique figure in modern American letters. Brought up as a farmer, he left the land as a young man to study and travel, eventually moving to New York City to 'be a writer'. Writers, then as now, in the long shadow of Modernism, were supposed to ensconce themselves in the metropolis and live as placeless chroniclers of its unease.

But it wasn't long before Berry felt drawn back to rural Kentucky, where he had grown up. The place was pulling him. Places, in my experience, often do that. I think that some places want writers to tell their stories. Wendell Berry was never meant to tell the stories of New York City; there were quite enough people doing that already. So, as his fellow scribes looked at him aghast, some of them trying to persuade him of his foolishness, he left the city and went back to the land, buying a farm five miles from where he had grown up, in the area where both his mother and father had grown up before him. This is the place in which he has lived, worked and written for the last half-century. This is the place whose story he has told, and through it he has told the story of America, and through that the story of modern humanity as it turns its back on the land and lays waste to the soil.

Soil is the recurring image in these essays. Again and again, Berry worries away at the question of topsoil. This is both a writer's metaphor and a farmer's reality, and for Wendell Berry, metaphors always come second to reality. 'No use talking about getting enlightened or saving your soul,' he wrote to his friend, the poet Gary Snyder, in 1980, 'if you can't keep the topsoil from washing away.' Over the last century, by some estimates, over half the world's topsoil has been washed away by the war on nature that we call industrial farming. We may have perhaps fifty or sixty years of topsoil left if we continue to erode, poison and lay waste to it at this rate. As the human population continues to burgeon, the topsoil in which it grows its food continues to collapse. It is perhaps the least sexy environmental issue in the world, but for the future of human civilization, which continues to depend upon farmers whether it knows it or not, it may be the most important.

Wendell Berry knows this, because he sees it every day, and because he works with it. I have spent the last several months read-ing every book of essays he has ever published, and the image which has stayed with me above all others comes at the beginning of his 1988 essay 'The Work of Local Culture' (pp. 103–18). An old galvanized bucket hangs on a fence post near a hollow, in a wood on what was once his grandfather's farm. In the bucket, slowly and over many decades, soil is being born:

> The old bucket has hung there through many autumns, and the leaves have fallen around it and some have fallen into it. Rain and snow have fallen into it, and the fallen leaves have held the moisture and so have rotted. Nuts have fallen into it, or been carried into it by squirrels; mice and squirrels have eaten the meat of the nuts and left the shells; they and other animals have left their droppings; insects have flown into the bucket and died and decayed; birds have scratched in it and left their droppings and perhaps a feather or two. This slow work of growth and death, gravity and decay, which is the chief work of the world, has by now produced in the bottom of the bucket several inches of black humus. I look into that bucket with fascination because I am a farmer of sorts and an artist of sorts, and I recognize there an artistry and a farming far superior to mine, or to that of any human.

In patience, in slowness, there is hope. In the places where we often deposit our hopes, meanwhile, there is less. Berry's questing thoughtfulness challenges traditional political categories; challenges notions of activism, of movements, of politics itself on a national and global scale. All this makes liberating reading for those who enjoy thinking for themselves. To the 'right' he shows the consequences of a love of money and markets, of government by corporation, of an economic growth unmoored from place, which eats through nature and culture and leaves ruins. To the 'left' he shows the consequences of a rootless individualism, of rights without rites, of the rejection of family and tradition, of the championing of the cosmopolitan over the rooted and the urban over the rural.

In place of these tired labels, and for those who still insist on categories, Berry suggests two alternatives, originally coined by his mentor, the writer Wallace Stegner: 'boomers' and 'stickers'.

'Boomers' are those who rush through and past, chasing the green grass or concreting it for money, the acolytes of growth-n-progress™. 'Stickers' are those who find a place and make it home, stay in it and try to leave it a little better than they found it. Wendell Berry's formula for a good life and a good community is simple and pleasingly unoriginal. Slow down. Pay attention. Do good work. Love your neighbours. Love your place. Stay in your place. Settle for less, enjoy it more.

Wendell Berry has been an extremely prolific writer, and this selection is chosen from hundreds of essays written over five decades. This means it is necessarily partial and personal and incomplete, and I have probably given everybody something to complain about. Still, to me, the essays between these covers represent some of the best of the writing and thoughts of a remarkable man – farmer, poet, novelist, philosopher – who deserves to be better known outside America than he is. I hope this volume will win him some new admirers in a time when voices like his are urgently needed.

Paul Kingsnorth
County Galway, Ireland
May 2016

The World-Ending Fire

A Native Hill

Pull down thy vanity, it is not man
Made courage, or made order, or made grace,
Pull down thy vanity, I say pull down.
Learn of the green-world what can be thy place . . .

Ezra Pound, Canto LXXXI

1

The hill is not a hill in the usual sense. It has no 'other side.' It is an arm of Kentucky's central upland known as The Bluegrass; one can think of it as a ridge reaching out from that center, progressively cut and divided, made ever narrower by the valleys of the creeks that drain it. The town of Port Royal in Henry County stands on one of the last heights of this upland, the valleys of two creeks, Gullion's Branch and Cane Run, opening on either side of it into the valley of the Kentucky River. My house backs against the hill's foot where it descends from the town to the river. The river, whose waters have carved the hill and so descended from it, lies within a hundred steps of my door.

Within about four miles of Port Royal, on the upland and in the bottoms upriver, all my grandparents and great-grandparents lived and left such memories as their descendants have bothered to keep. Little enough has been remembered. The family's life here goes back to my mother's great-great-grandfather and to my father's great-grandfather, but of those earliest ones there are only a few vague word-of-mouth recollections. The only place antecedent to this place that has any immediacy to any of us is the town of Cashel in County Tipperary, Ireland, which one of my great-grandfathers left as a boy to spend the rest of his life in Port Royal. His name was James Mathews, and he was a shoemaker. So well did he fit his life into this place that he is remembered, even in the family, as having belonged here. The family's only real memories of Cashel are my own, coming from a short visit I made there five years ago.

And so, such history as my family has is the history of its life here. All that any of us may know of ourselves is to be known in relation to this place. And since I did most of my growing up here, and have had most of my most meaningful experiences here, the place and the history, for me, have been inseparable, and there is a sense in which my own life is inseparable from the history and the place. It is a complex inheritance, and I have been both enriched and bewildered by it.

I began my life as the old times and the last of the old-time people were dying out. The Depression and World War II delayed the mechanization of the farms here, and one of the first disciplines imposed on me was that of a teamster. Perhaps I first stood in the role of student before my father's father, who, halting a team in front of me, would demand to know which mule had the best head, which the best shoulder or rump, which was the lead mule, were they hitched right. And there came a time when I knew, and took a considerable pride in knowing. Having a boy's usual desire to play at what he sees men working at, I learned to harness and hitch and work a team. I felt distinguished by that, and took the same pride in it that other boys my age took in their knowledge of automobiles. I seem to have been born with an aptitude for a way of life that was doomed, although I did not understand that at the time. Free of any intuition of its doom, I delighted in it, and learned all I could about it.

That knowledge, and the men who gave it to me, influenced me deeply. It entered my imagination, and gave its substance and tone to my mind. It fashioned in me possibilities and limits, desires and frustrations, that I do not expect to live to the end of. And it is strange to think how barely in the nick of time it came to me. If I had been born five years later I would have begun in a different world, and would no doubt have become a different man.

Those five years made a critical difference in my life, and it is a historical difference. One of the results is that in my generation I am something of an anachronism. I am less a child of my time than the people of my age who grew up in the cities, or than the people who grew up here in my own place five years after I did. In my acceptance of twentieth-century realities there has had to be a certain deliberateness, whereas most of my contemporaries had them simply by being born to them.

In my teens, when I was away at school, I could comfort myself by recalling in intricate detail the fields I had worked and played in, and hunted over, and ridden through on horseback – and that were richly associated in my mind with people and with stories. I could recall even the casual locations of certain small rocks. I could recall the look of a hundred different kinds of daylight on all those places, the look of animals grazing over them, the postures and attitudes and movements of the men who worked in them, the quality of the grass and the crops that had grown on them. I had come to be aware of it as one is aware of one's body; it was present to me whether I thought of it or not.

When I have thought of the welfare of the earth, the problems of its health and preservation, the care of its life, I have had this place before me, the part representing the whole more vividly and accurately, making clearer and more pressing demands, than any *idea* of the whole. When I have thought of kindness or cruelty, weariness or exuberance, devotion or betrayal, carelessness or care, doggedness or awkwardness or grace, I have had in my mind's eye the men and women of this place, their faces and gestures and movements.

I have pondered a great deal over a conversation I took part in a number of years ago in one of the offices of New York University. I had lived away from Kentucky for several years – in California, in

Europe, in New York City. And now I had decided to go back and take a teaching job at the University of Kentucky, giving up the position I then held on the New York University faculty. That day I had been summoned by one of my superiors at the university, whose intention, I had already learned, was to persuade me to stay on in New York 'for my own good.'

The decision to leave had cost me considerable difficulty and doubt and hard thought – for hadn't I achieved what had become one of the almost traditional goals of American writers? I had reached the greatest city in the nation; I had a good job; I was meeting other writers and talking with them and learning from them; I had reason to hope that I might take a still larger part in the literary life of that place. On the other hand, I knew I had not escaped Kentucky, and had never really wanted to. I was still writing about it, and had recognized that I would probably need to write about it for the rest of my life. Kentucky was my fate – not an altogether pleasant fate, though it had much that was pleasing in it, but one that I could not leave behind simply by going to another place, and that I therefore felt more and more obligated to meet directly and to understand. Perhaps even more important, I still had a deep love for the place I had been born in, and liked the idea of going back to be part of it again. And that, too, I felt obligated to try to understand. Why should I love one place so much more than any other? What could be the meaning or use of such love?

The elder of the faculty began the conversation by alluding to Thomas Wolfe, who once taught at the same institution. 'Young man,' he said, 'don't you know you can't go home again?' And he went on to speak of the advantages, for a young writer, of living in New York among the writers and the editors and the publishers.

The conversation that followed was a persistence of politeness in the face of impossibility. I knew as well as Wolfe that there is a certain *metaphorical* sense in which you can't go home again – that is, the past is lost to the extent that it cannot be lived in again. I knew perfectly well that I could not return home and be a child, or recover the secure pleasures of childhood. But I knew also that as the sentence was spoken to me it bore a self-dramatizing sentimentality that was absurd. Home – the place, the countryside – was still there, still pretty much as I left it, and there was no reason I could not go back to it if I wanted to.

As for the literary world, I had ventured some distance into that, and liked it well enough. I knew that because I was a writer the literary world would always have an importance for me and would always attract my interest. But I never doubted that the world was more important to me than the literary world; and the world would always be most fully and clearly present to me in the place I was fated by birth to know better than any other.

And so I had already chosen according to the most intimate and necessary inclinations of my own life. But what keeps me thinking of that conversation is the feeling that it was a confrontation of two radically different minds, and that it was a confrontation with significant historical overtones.

I do not pretend to know all about the other man's mind, but it was clear that he wished to speak to me as a representative of the literary world – the world he assumed that I aspired to above all others. His argument was based on the belief that once one had attained the metropolis, the literary capital, the worth of one's origins was canceled out; there simply could be nothing *worth* going back to. What lay behind one had ceased to be a part of life, and had become 'subject matter.' And there was the belief, long honored among American intellectuals and artists and writers, that a place such as I came from could be returned to only at the price of intellectual death; cut off from the cultural springs of the metropolis, the American countryside is Circe and Mammon. Finally, there was the assumption that the life of the metropolis is *the* experience, the *modern* experience, and that the life of the rural towns, the farms, the wilderness places is not only irrelevant to our time, but archaic as well because unknown or unconsidered by the people who really matter – that is, the urban intellectuals.

I was to realize during the next few years how false and destructive and silly those ideas are. But even then I was aware that life outside the literary world was not without honorable precedent: if there was Wolfe, there was also Faulkner; if there was James, there was also Thoreau. But what I had in my mind that made the greatest difference was the knowledge of the few square miles in Kentucky that were mine by inheritance and by birth and by the intimacy the mind makes with the place it awakens in.

What finally freed me from these doubts and suspicions was the insistence in what was happening to me that, far from being bored and diminished and obscured to myself by my life here, I had grown more alive and more conscious than I had ever been.

I had made a significant change in my relation to the place: before, it had been mine by coincidence or accident; now it was mine by choice. My return, which at first had been hesitant and tentative, grew wholehearted and sure. I had come back to stay. I hoped to live here the rest of my life. And once that was settled I began to *see* the place with a new clarity and a new understanding and a new seriousness. Before coming back I had been willing to allow the possibility – which one of my friends insisted on – that I already knew this place as well as I ever would. But now I began to see the real abundance and richness of it. It is, I saw, inexhaustible in its history, in the details of its life, in its possibilities. I walked over it, looking, listening, smelling, touching, alive to it as never before. I listened to the talk of my kinsmen and neighbors as I never had done, alert to their knowledge of the place, and to the qualities and energies of their speech. I began more seriously than ever to learn the names of things – the wild plants and animals, the natural processes, the local places – and to articulate my observations and memories. My language increased and strengthened, and sent my mind into the place like a live root system. And so what has become the usual order of things reversed itself with me; my mind became the root of my life rather than its sublimation. I came to see myself as growing out of the earth like the other native animals and plants. I saw my body and my daily motions as brief coherences and articulations of the energy of the place, which would fall back into it like leaves in the autumn.

In this awakening there has been a good deal of pain. When I lived in other places I looked on their evils with the curious eye of a traveler; I was not responsible for them; it cost me nothing to be a critic, for I had not been there long, and I did not feel that I would stay. But here, now that I am both native and citizen, there is no immunity to what is wrong. It is impossible to escape the sense that I am involved in history. What I am has been to a considerable extent determined by what my forebears were, by how they chose to treat this place while they lived in it; the lives of most of them diminished it, and limited its possibilities, and narrowed its future. And every day I am confronted by the question of what inheritance I will leave. What do I have that I am using up? For it has been our history that each generation in this place has been less welcome to it than the last. There has been less here for them. At each arrival there has been less fertility in the soil, and a larger inheritance of destructive precedent and shameful history.

I am forever being crept up on and newly startled by the realization that my people established themselves here by killing or driving out the original possessors, by the awareness that people were once bought and sold here by my people, by the sense of the violence they have done to their own kind and to each other and to the earth, by the evidence of their persistent failure to serve either the place or their own community in it. I am forced, against all my hopes and inclinations, to regard the history of my people here as the progress of the doom of what I value most in the world: the life and health of the earth, the peacefulness of human communities and households.

And so here, in the place I love more than any other and where I have chosen among all other places to live my life, I am more painfully divided within myself than I could be in any other place.

I know of no better key to what is adverse in our heritage in this place than the account of 'The Battle of the Fire-Brands,' quoted in Collins's *History of Kentucky* 'from the autobiography of Rev. Jacob Young, a Methodist minister.' The 'Newcastle' referred to is the present-day New Castle, the county seat of Henry County. I give the quote in full:

The costume of the Kentuckians was a hunting shirt, buckskin pantaloons, a leathern belt around their middle, a scabbard, and a big knife fastened to their belt; some of them wore hats and some caps. Their feet were covered with moccasins, made of dressed deer skins. They did not think themselves dressed without their powder-horn and shot-pouch, or the gun and the tomahawk. They were ready, then, for all alarms. They knew but little. They could clear ground, raise corn, and kill turkeys, deer, bears, and buffalo; and, when it became necessary, they understood the art of fighting the Indians as well as any men in the United States.

Shortly after we had taken up our residence, I was called upon to assist in opening a road from the place where Newcastle now stands, to the mouth of Kentucky river. That country, then, was an unbroken forest; there was nothing but an Indian trail passing the wilderness. I met the company early in the morning, with my axe, three days' provisions, and my knapsack. Here I found a captain, with about 100 men, all prepared to labor; about as jovial a company as I ever saw, all good-natured and civil. This was about the last of November, 1797. The day was cold and clear. The country through which the company passed was delightful; it was not a flat country, but, what the Kentuckians called, rolling ground – was quite well stored with lofty timber, and the undergrowth was very pretty. The beautiful canebrakes gave it a peculiar charm. What rendered it most interesting was the great abundance of wild turkeys, deer, bears, and other wild animals. The company worked hard all day, in quiet, and every man obeyed the captain's orders punctually.

About sundown, the captain, after a short address, told us the night was going to be very cold, and we must make very large fires. We felled the hickory trees in great abundance; made great log-heaps, mixing the dry wood with the green hickory; and, laying down a kind of sleepers under the pile, elevated the heap and caused it to burn rapidly. Every man had a water vessel in his knapsack; we searched for and found a stream of water. By this time, the fires were showing to great advantage; so we warmed our cold victuals, ate our suppers, and spent the evening in hearing the hunter's stories relative to the bloody scenes of the Indian war. We then heard some pretty fine singing, considering the circumstances.

Thus far, well; but a change began to take place. They became very rude, and raised the war-whoop. Their shrill shrieks made me tremble. They chose two captains, divided the men into two companies, and commenced fighting with the firebrands – the log heaps having burned down. The only law for their government was, that no man should throw a brand without fire on it – so that they might know how to dodge. They fought, for two or three hours, in perfect good nature; till brands became scarce, and they began to violate the law. Some were severely wounded, blood began to flow freely, and they were in a fair way of commencing a fight in earnest. At this moment, the loud voice of the captain rang out above the din, ordering every man to retire to rest. They dropped their weapons of warfare, rekindled the fires, and laid down to sleep. We finished our road according to directions, and returned home in health and peace.

The significance of this bit of history is in its utter violence. The work of clearing the road was itself violent. And from the orderly violence of that labor, these men turned for amusement to disorderly violence. They were men whose element was violence; the only alternatives they were aware of were those within the comprehension of main strength. And let us acknowledge that these were the truly influential men in the history of Kentucky, as well as in the history of most of the rest of America. In comparison to the fatherhood of such as these, the so-called 'founding fathers' who established our political ideals are but distant cousins. It is not John Adams or Thomas Jefferson whom we see night after night in the magic mirror of the television set; we see these builders of the road from New Castle to the mouth of the Kentucky River. Their reckless violence has glamorized all our trivialities and evils. Their aggressions have simplified our complexities and problems. They have cut all our Gordian knots. They have appeared in all our disguises and costumes. They have worn all our uniforms. Their war whoop has sanctified our inhumanity and ratified our blunders of policy.

To testify to the persistence of their influence, it is only necessary for me to confess that I read the Reverend Young's account of them with delight; I yield a considerable admiration to the exuberance and extravagance of their fight with the firebrands; I take a certain pride in belonging to the same history and the same place that they belong to – though I know that they represent the worst that is in us, and in me, and that their presence in our history has been ruinous, and that their survival among us promises ruin.

'They knew but little,' the observant Reverend says of them, and this is the most suggestive thing he says. It is surely understandable and pardonable, under the circumstances, that these men were ignorant by the standards of formal schooling. But one immediately reflects that the American Indian, who was ignorant by the same standards, nevertheless knew how to live in the country without making violence the invariable mode of his relation to it; in fact, from the ecologist's or the conservationist's point of view, he did it *no* violence. This is because he had, in place of what we would call education, a fully integrated culture, the content of which was a highly complex sense of his dependence on the earth. The same, I believe, was generally true of the peasants of certain old agricultural societies, particularly in the Orient. They belonged by an intricate awareness to the earth they lived on and by, which meant that they respected it, which meant that they practiced strict economies in the use of it.

The abilities of those Kentucky road builders of 1797 were far more primitive and rudimentary than those of the Stone Age people they had driven out. They could clear the ground, grow corn, kill game, and make war. In the minds and hands of men who 'know but little' – or little else – all of these abilities are certain to be destructive, even of those values and benefits their use may be intended to serve.

On such a night as the Reverend Young describes, an Indian would have made do with a small shelter and a small fire. But these road builders, veterans of the Indian War, 'felled the hickory trees in great abundance; made great log-heaps . . . and caused [them] to burn rapidly.' Far from making a small shelter that could be adequately heated by a small fire, their way was to make no shelter at all, and heat instead a sizable area of the landscape. The idea was that when faced with abundance one should consume abundantly – an idea that has survived to become the basis of our present economy. It is neither natural nor civilized, and even from a 'practical' point of view it is to the last degree brutalizing and stupid.

I think that the comparison of these road builders with the Indians, on the one hand, and with Old World peasants on the other, is a most suggestive one. The Indians and the peasants were people who belonged deeply and intricately to their places. Their ways of life had evolved slowly in accordance with their knowledge of their land, of its needs, of their own relation of dependence and responsibility to it. The road builders, on the contrary, were *placeless* people. That is why they 'knew but little.' Having left Europe far behind, they had not yet in any meaningful sense arrived in America, not yet having *devoted* themselves to any part of it in a way that would produce the intricate knowledge of it necessary to live in it without destroying it. Because they belonged to no place, it was almost inevitable that they should behave violently toward the places they came to. We *still* have not, in any meaningful way, arrived in America. And in spite of our great reservoir of facts and methods, in comparison to the deep earthly wisdom of established peoples we still know but little.

But my understanding of this curiously parabolic fragment of history will not be complete until I have considered more directly that the occasion of this particular violence was the building of a road. It is obvious that one who values the idea of community cannot speak against roads without risking all sorts of absurdity. It must be noticed, nevertheless, that the predecessor to this first road was 'nothing but an Indian trail passing the wilderness' – a path. The Indians, then, who had the wisdom and the grace to live in this country for perhaps ten thousand years without destroying or damaging any of it, needed for their travels no more than a footpath; but their successors, who in a century and a half plundered the area of at least half its topsoil and virtually all of its forest, felt immediately that they had to have a road. My interest is not in the question of whether or not they *needed* the road, but in the fact that the road was then, and is now, the most characteristic form of their relation to the country.

The difference between a path and a road is not only the obvious one. A path is little more than a habit that comes with knowledge of a place. It is a sort of ritual of familiarity. As a form, it is a form of contact with a known landscape. It is not destructive. It is the perfect adaptation, through experience and familiarity, of movement to place; it obeys the natural contours; such obstacles as it meets it goes around. A road, on the other hand, even the most primitive road, embodies a resistance against the landscape. Its reason is not simply the necessity for movement, but haste. Its wish is to *avoid* contact with the landscape; it seeks so far as possible to go over the country, rather than through it; its aspiration, as we see clearly in the example of our modern freeways, is to be a bridge; its tendency is to translate place into space in order to traverse it with the least effort. It is destructive, seeking to remove or destroy all obstacles in its way. The primitive road advanced by the destruction of the forest; modern roads advance by the destruction of topography.

That first road from the site of New Castle to the mouth of the Kentucky River – lost now either by obsolescence or metamorphosis – is now being crossed and to some extent replaced by its modern descendant known as I–71, and I have no wish to disturb the question of whether or not *this* road was needed. I only want to observe that it bears no relation whatever to the country it passes through. It is a pure abstraction, built to serve the two abstractions that are the poles of our national life: commerce and expensive pleasure. It was built, not according to the lay of the land, but according to a blueprint. Such homes and farmlands and woodlands as happened to be in its way are now buried under it. A part of a hill near here that would have caused it to turn aside was simply cut down and disposed of as thoughtlessly as the pioneer road builders would have disposed of a tree. Its form is the form of speed, dissatisfaction, and anxiety. It represents the ultimate in engineering sophistication, but the crudest possible valuation of life in this world. It is as adequate a symbol of our relation to our country now as that first road was of our relation to it in 1797.

•

But the sense of the past also gives a deep richness and resonance to nearly everything I see here. It is partly the sense that what I now see, other men that I have known once saw, and partly that this knowledge provides an imaginative access to what I do not know. I think of the country as a kind of palimpsest scrawled over with the comings and goings of people, the erasure of time already in process even as the marks of passage are put down. There are the ritual marks of neighborhood – roads, paths between houses. There are the domestic paths from house to barns and outbuildings and gardens, farm roads threading the pasture gates. There are the wanderings of hunters and searchers after lost stock, and the speculative or meditative or inquisitive 'walking around' of farmers on wet days and Sundays. There is the spiraling geometry of the rounds of implements in fields, and the passing and returning scratches of plows across croplands. Often these have filled an interval, an opening, between the retreat of the forest from the virgin ground and the forest's return to ground that has been worn out and given up. In the woods here one often finds cairns of stones picked up out of furrows, gullies left by bad farming, forgotten roads, stone chimneys of houses long rotted away or burned.

Occasionally one stumbles into a coincidence that, like an unexpected alignment of windows, momentarily cancels out the sense of historical whereabouts, giving with an overwhelming immediacy an awareness of the reality of the past.

The possibility of this awareness is always immanent in old homesites. It may suddenly bear in upon one at the sight of old orchard trees standing in the dooryard of a house now filled with baled hay. It came to me when I looked out the attic window of a disintegrating log house and saw a far view of the cleared ridges with wooded hollows in between, and nothing in sight to reveal the date. Who was I, leaning to the window? When?

It broke upon me one afternoon when, walking in the woods on one of my family places, I came upon a gap in a fence, wired shut, but with deep-cut wagon tracks still passing through it under the weed growth and the fallen leaves. Where that thicket stands there was crop ground, maybe as late as my own time. I knew some of the men who tended it; their names and faces were instantly alive in my mind. I knew how it had been with them – how they would harness their mule teams in the early mornings in my grandfather's big barn and come to the woods-rimmed tobacco patches, the mules' feet wet with the dew. And in the solitude and silence that came upon them they would set to work, their water jugs left in the shade of bushes in the fencerows.

As a child I learned the early mornings in these places for myself, riding out in the wagons with the tobacco-cutting crews to those steep fields in the dew-wet shadow of the woods. As the day went on the shadow would draw back under the feet of the trees, and it would get hot. Little whirlwinds would cross the opening, picking up the dust and the dry 'ground leaves' of the tobacco. We made a game of running with my grandfather to stand, shoulders scrunched and eyes squinched, in their middles.

Having such memories, I can acknowledge only with reluctance and sorrow that those slopes should never have been broken. Rich as they were, they were too steep. The humus stood dark and heavy over them once; the plow was its doom.

Early one February morning in thick fog and spattering rain I stood on the riverbank and listened to a towboat working its way downstream. Its engines were idling, nudging cautiously through the fog into the Cane Run bend. The end of the head barge emerged finally like a shadow, and then the second barge appeared, and then the towboat itself. They made the bend, increased power, and went thumping off out of sight into the fog again.

Because the valley was so enclosed in fog, the boat with its tow appearing and disappearing again into the muffling whiteness within two hundred yards, the moment had a curious ambiguity.

It was as though I was not necessarily myself at all. I could have been my grandfather, in his time, standing there watching, as I knew he had.

2

I start down from one of the heights of the upland, the town of Port Royal at my back. It is a winter day, overcast and still, and the town is closed in itself, humming and muttering a little, like a winter beehive.

The dog runs ahead, prancing and looking back, knowing the way we are about to go. This is a walk well established with us – a route in our minds as well as on the ground. There is a sort of mystery in the establishment of these ways. Anytime one crosses a given stretch of country with some frequency, no matter how wanderingly one begins, the tendency is always toward habit. By the third or fourth trip, without realizing it, one is following a fixed path, going the way one went before. After that, one may still wander, but only by deliberation, and when there is reason to hurry, or when the mind wanders rather than the feet, one returns to the old route. Familiarity has begun. One has made a relationship with the landscape, and the form and the symbol and the enactment of the relationship is the path. These paths of mine are seldom worn on the ground. They are habits of mind, directions and turns. They are as personal as old shoes. My feet are comfortable in them.

From the height I can see far out over the country, the long open ridges of the farmland, the wooded notches of the streams, the valley of the river opening beyond, and then more ridges and hollows of the same kind.

Underlying this country, nine hundred feet below the highest ridgetops, more than four hundred feet below the surface of the river, is sea level. We seldom think of it here; we are a long way from the coast, and the sea is alien to us. And yet the attraction of sea level dwells in this country as an ideal dwells in a man's mind. All our rains go in search of it and, departing, they have carved the land in a shape that is fluent and falling. The streams branch like vines, and between the branches the land rises steeply and then rounds and gentles into the long narrowing fingers of ridgeland. Near the heads of the streams even the steepest land was not too long ago farmed and kept cleared. But now it has been given up and the woods is returning. The wild is flowing back like a tide. The arable ridgetops reach out above the gathered trees like headlands into the sea, bearing their human burdens of fences and houses and barns, crops and roads.

Looking out over the country, one gets a sense of the whole of it: the ridges and hollows, the clustered buildings of the farms, the open fields, the woods, the stock ponds set like coins into the slopes. But this is a surface sense, an exterior sense, such as you get from looking down on the roof of a house. The height is a threshold from which to step down into the wooded folds of the land, the interior, under the trees and along the branching streams.

I pass through a pasture gate on a deep-worn path that grows shallow a little way beyond, and then disappears altogether into the grass. The gate has gathered thousands of passings to and fro that have divided like the slats of a fan on either side of it. It is like a fist holding together the strands of a net.

Beyond the gate the land leans always more steeply toward the branch. I follow it down, and then bear left along the crease at the bottom of the slope. I have entered the downflow of the land. The way I am going is the way the water goes. There is something comfortable and fit-feeling in this, something free in this yielding to gravity and taking the shortest way down.

As the hollow deepens into the hill, before it has yet entered the woods, the grassy crease becomes a raw gully, and along the steepening slopes on either side I can see the old scars of erosion, places where the earth is gone clear to the rock. My people's errors have become the features of my country.

It occurs to me that it is no longer possible to imagine how this country looked in the beginning, before the white people drove their plows into it. It is not possible to know what was the shape of the land here in this hollow when it was first cleared. Too much of it is gone, loosened by the plows and washed away by the rain. I am walking the route of the departure of the virgin soil of the hill. I am not looking at the same land the firstcomers saw. The original surface of the hill is as extinct as the passenger pigeon. The pristine America that the first white man saw is a lost continent, sunk like Atlantis in the sea. The thought of what was here once and is gone forever will not leave me as long as I live. It is as though I walk knee-deep in its absence.

The slopes along the hollow steepen still more, and I go in under the trees. I pass beneath the surface. I am enclosed, and my sense, my interior sense, of the country becomes intricate. There is no longer the possibility of seeing very far. The distances are closed off by the trees and the steepening walls of the hollow. One cannot grow familiar here by sitting and looking as one can up in the open on the ridge. Here the eyes become dependent on the feet. To see the woods from the inside one must look and move and look again. It is inexhaustible in its standpoints. A lifetime will not be enough to experience it all. Not far from the beginning of the woods, and set deep in the earth in the bottom of the hollow, is a rock-walled pool not a lot bigger than a bathtub. The wall is still nearly as straight and tight as when it was built. It makes a neatly turned narrow horseshoe, the open end downstream. This is a historical ruin, dug here either to catch and hold the water of the little branch, or to collect the water of a spring whose vein broke to the surface here – it is probably no longer possible to know which. The pool is filled with earth now, and grass grows in it. And the branch bends around it, cut down to the bare rock, a torrent after heavy rain, other times bone dry. All that is certain is that when the pool was dug and walled there was deep topsoil on the hill to gather and hold the water. And this high up, at least, the bottom of the hollow, instead of the present raw notch of the streambed, wore the same mantle of soil as the slopes, and the stream was a steady seep or trickle, running most or all of the year. This tiny pool no doubt once furnished water for a considerable number of stock through the hot summers. And now it is only a lost souvenir, archaic and useless, except for the bitter intelligence there is in it. It is one of the monuments to what is lost.

Wherever one goes along the streams of this part of the country, one is apt to come upon this old stonework. There are walled springs and pools. There are the walls built in the steeper hollows where the fences cross or used to cross; the streams have drifted dirt in behind them, so that now where they are still intact they make waterfalls that have scooped out small pools at their feet. And there used to be miles of stone fences, now mostly scattered and sifted back into the ground.

Considering these, one senses a historical patience, now also extinct in the country. These walls were built by men working long days for little wages, or by slaves. It was work that could not be hurried at, a meticulous finding and fitting together, as though reconstructing a previous wall that had been broken up and scattered like puzzle pieces. The wall would advance only a few yards a day. The pace of it could not be borne by most modern men, even if the wages could be afforded. Those men had to move in closer accord with their own rhythms, and nature's, than we do. They had no machines. Their capacities were only those of flesh and blood. They talked as they worked. They joked and laughed. They sang. The work was exacting and heavy and hard and slow. No opportunity for pleasure was missed or slighted. The days and the years were long. The work was long. At the end of this job the next would begin. Therefore, be patient. Such pleasure as there is, is here, now. Take pleasure as it comes. Take work as it comes. The end may never come, or when it does it may be the wrong end.

Now the men who built the walls and the men who had them built have long gone underground to be, along with the buried ledges and the roots and the burrowing animals, a part of the nature of the place in the minds of the ones who come after them. I think of them lying still in their graves, as level as the sills and thresholds of their lives, as though resisting to the last the slant of the ground. And their old walls, too, reenter nature, collecting lichens and mosses with patience their builders never conceived.

Like the pasture gates, the streams are great collectors of comings and goings. The streams go down, and paths always go down beside the streams. For a while I walk along an old wagon road that is buried in leaves – a fragment, beginningless and endless as the middle of a sentence on some scrap of papyrus. There is a cedar whose branches reach over this road, and under the branches I find the leavings of two kills of some bird of prey. The most recent is a pile of blue jay feathers. The other has been rained on and is not identifiable. How little we know. How little of this was intended or expected by any man. The road that has become the grave of men's passages has led to the life of the woods.

> And I say to myself: Here is your road
> without beginning or end, appearing
> out of the earth and ending in it, bearing
> no load but the hawk's kill, and the leaves
> building earth on it, something more
> to be borne. Tracks fill with earth
> and return to absence. The road was worn
> by men bearing earth along it. They have come
> to endlessness. In their passing
> they could not stay in, trees have risen
> and stand still. It is leading to the dark,
> to mornings where you are not. Here
> is your road, beginningless and endless as God.

Now I have come down within the sound of the water. The winter has been rainy, and the hill is full of dark seeps and trickles, gathering finally, along these creases, into flowing streams. The sound of them is one of the elements, and defines a zone. When their voices return to the hill after their absence during summer and autumn, it is a better place to be. A thirst in the mind is quenched.

I have already passed the place where water began to flow in the little streambed I am following. It broke into the light from beneath a rock ledge, a thin glittering stream. It lies beside me as I walk, overtaking me and going by, yet not moving, a thread of light and sound. And now from below comes the steady tumble and rush of the water of Camp Branch – whose nameless camp was it named for? – and gradually as I descend the sound of the smaller stream is lost in the sound of the larger.

The two hollows join, the line of the meeting of the two spaces obscured even in winter by the trees. But the two streams meet precisely as two roads. That is, the stream*beds* do; the one ends in the other. As for the meeting of the waters, there is no looking at that. The one flow does not end in the other, but continues in it, one with it, two clarities merged without a shadow.

All waters are one. This is a reach of the sea, flung like a net over the hill, and now drawn back to the sea. And as the sea is never raised in the earthly nets of fishermen, so the hill is never caught and pulled down by the watery net of the sea. But always a little of it is. Each of the gathering strands of the net carries back some of the hill melted in it. Sometimes, as now, it carries so little that the water flows clear; sometimes it carries a lot and is brown and heavy with it. Whenever greedy or thoughtless men have lived on it, the hill has literally flowed out of their tracks into the bottom of the sea.

There appears to be a law that when creatures have reached the level of consciousness, as men have, they must become conscious of the creation; they must learn how they fit into it and what its needs are and what it requires of them, or else pay a terrible penalty: the spirit of the creation will go out of them, and they will become destructive; the very earth will depart from them and go where they cannot follow.

My mind is never empty or idle at the joinings of streams. Here is the work of the world going on. The creation is felt, alive and intent on its materials, in such places. In the angle of the meeting of the two streams stands the steep wooded point of the ridge, like the prow of an up-turned boat – finished, as it was a thousand years ago, as it will be in a thousand years. Its becoming is only incidental to its being. It will be because it is. It has no aim or end except to be. By being, it is growing and wearing into what it will be. The fork of the stream lies at the foot of the slope like hammer and chisel laid down at the foot of a finished sculpture. But the stream is no dead tool; it is alive, it is still at its work. Put your hand to it to learn the health of this part of the world. It is the wrist of the hill.

Perhaps it is to prepare to hear someday the music of the spheres that I am always turning my ears to the music of streams. There is indeed a music in streams, but it is not for the hurried. It has to be loitered by and imagined. Or imagined *toward*, for it is hardly for men at all. Nature has a patient ear. To her the slowest funeral march sounds like a jig. She is satisfied to have the notes drawn out to the lengths of days or weeks or months. Small variations are acceptable to her, modulations as leisurely as the opening of a flower.

The stream is full of stops and gates. Here it has piled up rocks in its path, and pours over them into a tiny pool it has scooped at the foot of its fall. Here it has been dammed by a mat of leaves caught behind a fallen limb. Here it must force a narrow passage, here a wider one. Tomorrow the flow may increase or slacken, and the tone will shift. In an hour or a week that rock may give way, and the composition will advance by another note. Some idea of it may be got by walking slowly along and noting the changes as one passes from one little fall or rapid to another. But this is a highly simplified and diluted version of the real thing, which is too complex and widespread ever to be actually heard by us. The ear must imagine an impossible patience in order to grasp even the unimaginableness of such music.

But the creation is musical, and this is a part of its music, as birdsong is, or the words of poets. The music of the streams is the music of the shaping of the earth, by which the rocks are pushed and shifted downward toward the level of the sea.

And now I find an empty beer can lying in the path. This is the track of the ubiquitous man Friday of all our woods. In my walks I never fail to discover some sign that he has preceded me. I find his empty shotgun shells, his empty cans and bottles, his sandwich wrappings. In wooded places along roadsides one is apt to find, as well, his overtraveled bedsprings, his outcast refrigerator, and heaps of the imperishable refuse of his modern kitchen. A year ago, almost in this same place where I have found his beer can, I found a possum that he had shot dead and left lying, in celebration of his manhood. He is the true American pioneer, perfectly at rest in his assumption that he is the first and the last whose inheritance and fate this place will ever be. Going forth, as he may think, to sow, he only broadcasts his effects.

As I go on down the path alongside Camp Branch, I walk by the edge of croplands abandoned only within my own lifetime. On my left are the south slopes where the woods is old, long undisturbed. On my right, the more fertile north slopes are covered with patches of briars and sumacs and a lot of young walnut trees. Tobacco of an extraordinary quality was once grown here, and then the soil wore thin, and these places were given up for the more accessible ridges that were not so steep, where row cropping made better sense anyway. But now, under the thicket growth, a mat of bluegrass has grown to testify to the good nature of this ground. It was fine dirt that lay here once, and I am far from being able to say that I could have resisted the temptation to plow it. My understanding of what is best for it is the tragic understanding of hindsight, the awareness that I have been taught what was here to be lost by the loss of it.

We have lived by the assumption that what was good for us would be good for the world. And this has been based on the even flimsier assumption that we could know with any certainty what was good even for us. We have fulfilled the danger of this by making our personal pride and greed the standard of our behavior toward the world – to the incalculable disadvantage of the world and every living thing in it. And now, perhaps very close to too late, our great error has become clear. It is not only our own creativity – our own capacity for life – that is stifled by our arrogant assumption; the creation itself is stifled.

We have been wrong. We must change our lives, so that it will be possible to live by the contrary assumption that what is good for the world will be good for us. And that requires that we make the effort to *know* the world and to learn what is good for it. We must learn to cooperate in its processes, and to yield to its limits. But even more important, we must learn to acknowledge that the creation is full of mystery; we will never entirely understand it. We must abandon arrogance and stand in awe. We must recover the sense of the majesty of creation, and the ability to be worshipful in its presence. For I do not doubt that it is only on the condition of humility and reverence before the world that our species will be able to remain in it.

Standing in the presence of these worn and abandoned fields, where the creation has begun its healing without the hindrance or the help of man, with the voice of the stream in the air and the woods standing in silence on all the slopes around me, I am deep in the interior not only of my place in the world, but of my own life, its sources and searches and concerns. I first came into these places following the men to work when I was a child. I knew the men who took their lives from such fields as these, and their lives to a considerable extent made my life what it is. In what came to me from them there was both wealth and poverty, and I have been a long time discovering which was which.

It was in the woods here along Camp Branch that Bill White, my grandfather's Negro hired hand, taught me to hunt squirrels. Bill lived in a little tin-roofed house on up nearer the head of the hollow. And this was, I suppose more than any other place, his hunting ground. It was the place of his freedom, where he could move without subservience, without considering who he was or who anybody else was. On late summer mornings, when it was too wet to work, I would follow him into the woods. As soon as we stepped in under the trees he would become silent and absolutely attentive to the life of the place. He was a good teacher and an exacting one. The rule seemed to be that if I wanted to stay with him, I had to make it possible for him to forget I was there. I was to make no noise. If I did he would look back and make a downward emphatic gesture with his hand, as explicit as writing: Be quiet, or go home. He would see a squirrel crouched in a fork or lying along the top of a branch, and indicate with a grin and a small jerk of his head where I should look; and then wait, while I, conscious of being watched and demanded upon, searched it out for myself. He taught me to look and to listen and to be quiet. I wonder if he knew the value of such teaching or the rarity of such a teacher.

In the years that followed I hunted often here alone. And later in these same woods I experienced my first obscure dissatisfactions with hunting. Though I could not have put it into words then, the sense had come to me that hunting as I knew it – the eagerness to kill something I did not need to eat – was an artificial relation to the place, when what I was beginning to need, just as inarticulately then, was a relation that would be necessary and meaningful. That was a time of great uneasiness and restlessness for me. It would be the fall of the year, the leaves would be turning, and ahead of me would be another year of school. There would be confusions about girls and ambitions, the wordless hurried feeling that time and events and my own nature were pushing me toward what I was going to be – and I had no notion what it was, or how to prepare.

And then there were years when I did not come here at all – when these places and their history were in my mind, and part of me, in places thousands of miles away. And now I am here again, changed from what I was, and still changing. The future is no more certain to me now than it ever was, though its risks are clearer, and so are my own desires: I am the father of two young children whose lives are hostages given to the future. Because of them and because of events in the world, life seems more fearful and difficult to me now than ever before. But it is also more inviting, and I am constantly aware of its nearness to joy. Much of the interest and excitement that I have in my life now has come from the deepening, in the years since my return here, of my relation to this place. For in spite of all that has happened to me in other places, the great change and the great possibility of change in my life has been in my sense of this place. The major difference is perhaps only that I have grown able to be whole-heartedly present here. I am able to sit and be quiet at the foot of some tree here in this woods along Camp Branch, and feel a deep peace, both in the place and in my awareness of it, that not too long ago I was not conscious of the possibility of. This peace is partly in being free of the suspicion that pursued me for most of my life, no matter where I was, that there was perhaps another place I *should* be, or would be happier or better in; it is partly in the increasingly articulate consciousness of being here, and of the significance and importance of being here.

After more than thirty years I have at last arrived at the candor necessary to stand on this part of the earth that is so full of my own history and so much damaged by it, and ask: What *is* this place? What is in it? What is its nature? How should men live in it? What must I do?

I have not found the answers, though I believe that in partial and fragmentary ways they have begun to come to me. But the questions are more important than their answers. In the final sense they *have* no answers. They are like the questions – they are perhaps the same questions – that were the discipline of Job. They are a part of the necessary enactment of humility, teaching a man what his importance is, what his responsibility is, and what his place is, both on the earth and in the order of things. And though the answers must always come obscurely and in fragments, the questions must be asked. They are fertile questions. In their implications and effects, they are moral and aesthetic and, in the best and fullest sense, practical. They promise a relationship to the world that is decent and preserving.

They are also, both in origin and effect, religious. I am uneasy with the term, for such religion as has been openly practiced in this part of the world has promoted and fed upon a destructive schism between body and soul, Heaven and earth. It has encouraged people to believe that the world is of no importance, and that their only obligation in it is to submit to certain churchly formulas in order to get to Heaven. And so the people who might have been expected to care most selflessly for the world have had their minds turned elsewhere – to a pursuit of 'salvation' that was really only another form of gluttony and self-love, the desire to perpetuate their lives beyond the life of the world. The Heaven-bent have abused the earth thoughtlessly, by inattention, and their negligence has permitted and encouraged others to abuse it deliberately. Once the creator was removed from the creation, divinity became only a remote abstraction, a social weapon in the hands of the religious institutions. This split in public values produced or was accompanied by, as it was bound to be, an equally artificial and ugly division in people's lives, so that a man, while pursuing Heaven with the sublime appetite he thought of as his soul, could turn his heart against his neighbors and his hands against the world. For these reasons, though I know that my questions *are* religious, I dislike having to *say* that they are.

But when I ask them my aim is not primarily to get to Heaven. Though Heaven is certainly more important than the earth if all they say about it is true, it is still morally incidental to it and dependent on it, and I can only imagine it and desire it in terms of what I know of the earth. And so my questions do not aspire beyond the earth. They aspire *toward* it and *into* it. Perhaps they aspire *through* it. They are religious because they are asked at the limit of what I know; they acknowledge mystery and honor its presence in the creation; they are spoken in reverence for the order and grace that I see, and that I trust beyond my power to see.

The stream has led me down to an old barn built deep in the hollow to house the tobacco once grown on those abandoned fields. Now it is surrounded by the trees that have come back on every side – a relic, a fragment of another time, strayed out of its meaning. This is the last of my historical landmarks. To here, my walk has had insistent overtones of memory and history. It has been a movement of consciousness through knowledge, eroding and shaping, adding and wearing away. I have descended like the water of the stream through what I know of myself, and now that I have there is a little more to know. But here at the barn, the old roads and the cow paths – the formal connections with civilization – come to an end.

I stoop between the strands of a barbed-wire fence, and in that movement I go out of time into timelessness. I come into a wild place. The trees grow big, their trunks rising clean, free of undergrowth. The place has a serenity and dignity that one feels immediately; the creation is whole in it and unobstructed. It is free of the strivings and dissatisfactions, the partialities and imperfections of places under the mechanical dominance of men. Here, what to a housekeeper's eye might seem disorderly is nonetheless orderly and within order; what might seem arbitrary or accidental is included in the design of the whole; what might seem evil or violent is a comfortable member of the household. Where the creation is whole nothing is extraneous. The presence of the creation here makes this a holy place, and it is as a pilgrim that I have come. It is the creation that has attracted me, its perfect interfusion of life and design. I have made myself its follower and its apprentice.

One early morning last spring, I came and found the woods floor strewn with bluebells. In the cool sunlight and the lacy shadows of the spring woods the blueness of those flowers, their elegant shape, their delicate fresh scent kept me standing and looking. I found a delight in them that I cannot describe and that I will never forget. Though I had been familiar for years with most of the spring woods flowers, I had never seen these and had not known they were here. Looking at them, I felt a strange loss and sorrow that I had never seen them before. But I was also exultant that I saw them now – that they were here.

For me, in the thought of them will always be the sense of the joyful surprise with which I found them – the sense that came suddenly to me then that the world is blessed beyond my understanding, more abundantly than I will ever know. What lives are still ahead of me here to be discovered and exulted in, tomorrow, or in twenty years? What wonder will be found here on the morning after my death? Though as a man I inherit great evils and the possibility of great loss and suffering, I know that my life is blessed and graced by the yearly flowering of the bluebells. How perfect they are! In their presence I am humble and joyful. If I were given all the learning and all the methods of my race I could not make one of them, or even imagine one. Solomon in all his glory was not arrayed like one of these. It is the privilege and the labor of the apprentice of creation to come with his imagination into the unimaginable, and with his speech into the unspeakable.

3

Sometimes I can no longer think in the house or in the garden or in the cleared fields. They bear too much resemblance to our failed human history – failed, because it has led to this human present that is such a bitterness and a trial. And so I go to the woods. As I go in under the trees, dependably, almost at once, and by nothing I do, things fall into place. I enter an order that does not exist outside, in the human spaces. I feel my life take its place among the lives – the trees, the annual plants, the animals and birds, the living of all these and the dead – that go and have gone to make the life of the earth. I am less important than I thought, the human race is less important than I thought. I rejoice in that. My mind loses its urgings, senses its nature, and is free. The forest grew here in its own time, and so I will live, suffer and rejoice, and die in my own time. There is nothing that I may decently hope for that I cannot reach by patience as well as by anxiety. The hill, which is a part of America, has killed no one in the service of the American government. Then why should I, who am a fragment of the hill? I wish to be as peaceable as my land, which does no violence, though it has been the scene of violence and has had violence done to it.

How, having a consciousness, an intelligence, a human spirit – all the vaunted equipment of my race – can I humble myself before a mere piece of the earth and speak of myself as its fragment? Because my mind transcends the hill only to be filled with it, to comprehend it a little, to know that it lives on the hill in time as well as in place, to recognize itself as the hill's fragment.

The false and truly belittling transcendence is ownership. The hill has had more owners than its owners have had years – they are grist for its mill. It has had few friends. But I wish to be its friend, for I think it serves its friends well. It tells them they are fragments of its life. In its life they transcend their years.

The most exemplary nature is that of the topsoil. It is very Christ-like in its passivity and beneficence, and in the penetrating energy that issues out of its peaceableness. It increases by experience, by the passage of seasons over it, growth rising out of it and returning to it, not by ambition or aggressiveness. It is enriched by all things that die and enter into it. It keeps the past, not as history or as memory, but as richness, new possibility. Its fertility is always building up out of death into promise. Death is the bridge or the tunnel by which its past enters its future.

To walk in the woods, mindful only of the *physical* extent of it, is to go perhaps as owner, or as knower, confident of one's own history and of one's own importance. But to go there, mindful as well of its temporal extent, of the age of it, and of all that led up to the present life of it, and of all that may follow it, is to feel oneself a flea in the pelt of a great living thing, the discrepancy between its life and one's own so great that it cannot be imagined. One has come into the presence of mystery. After all the trouble one has taken to be a modern man, one has come back under the spell of a primitive awe, wordless and humble.

In the centuries before its settlement by white men, among the most characteristic and pleasing features of the floor of this valley, and of the stream banks on its slopes, were the forests and the groves of great beech trees. With their silver bark and their light graceful foliage, turning gold in the fall, they were surely as lovely as any forests that ever grew on earth. I think so because I have seen their diminished descendants, which have returned to stand in the wasted places that we have so quickly misused and given up. But those old forests are all gone. We will never know them as they were. We have driven them beyond the reach of our minds, only a vague hint of their presence returning to haunt us, as though in dreams – a fugitive rumor of the nobility and beauty and abundance of the squandered maidenhood of our world – so that, do what we will, we will never quite be satisfied ever again to be here.

The country, as we have made it by the pretense that we can do without it as soon as we have completed its metamorphosis into cash, no longer holds even the possibility of such forests, for the topsoil that they made and stood upon, like children piling up and trampling underfoot the fallen leaves, is no longer here.

There is an ominous – perhaps a fatal – presumptuousness in living in a place by the *imposition* on it of one's ideas and wishes. And that is the way we white people have lived in America throughout our history, and it is the way our history now teaches us to live here.

Surely there could be a more indigenous life than we have. There could be a consciousness that would establish itself on a place by understanding its nature and learning what is potential in it. A man ought to study the wilderness of a place before applying to it the ways he learned in another place. Thousands of acres of hill land, here and in the rest of the country, were wasted by a system of agriculture that was fundamentally alien to it. For more than a century, here, the steepest hillsides were farmed, by my forefathers and their neighbors, as if they were flat, and as if this was not a country of heavy rains. We haven't yet, in any meaningful sense, arrived in these places that we declare we own. We undertook the privilege of the virgin abundance of this land without any awareness at all that we undertook at the same time a responsibility toward it. That responsibility has never yet impressed itself upon our character; its absence in us is signified on the land by scars.

Until we understand what the land is, we are at odds with everything we touch. And to come to that understanding it is necessary, even now, to leave the regions of our conquest – the cleared fields, the towns and cities, the highways – and reenter the woods. For only there can a man encounter the silence and the darkness of his own absence. Only in this silence and darkness can he recover the sense of the world's longevity, of its ability to thrive without him, of his inferiority to it and his dependence on it. Perhaps then, having heard that silence and seen that darkness, he will grow humble before the place and begin to take it in – to learn *from it* what it is. As its sounds come into his hearing, and its lights and colors come into his vision, and its odors come into his nostrils, then he may come into *its* presence as he never has before, and he will arrive in his place and will want to remain. His life will grow out of the ground like the other lives of the place, and take its place among them. He will be *with* them – neither ignorant of them, nor indifferent to them, nor against them – and so at last he will grow to be native-born. That is, he must reenter the silence and the darkness, and be born again.

One winter night nearly twenty years ago I was in the woods with the coon hunters, and we were walking toward the dogs, who had moved out to the point of the bluff where the valley of Cane Run enters the valley of the river. The footing was difficult, and one of the hunters was having trouble with his lantern. The flame would 'run up' and smoke the globe, so that the light it gave obscured more than it illuminated, an obstacle between his eyes and the path. At last he cursed it and flung it down into a hollow. Its little light went looping down through the trees and disappeared, and there was a distant tinkle of glass as the globe shattered. After that he saw better and went along the bluff easier than before, and lighter, too.

Not long ago, walking up there, I came across his old lantern lying rusted in the crease of the hill, half buried already in the siftings of the slope, and I let it lie. But I've kept the memory that it renewed. I have made it one of my myths of the hill. It has come to be truer to me now than it was then.

For I have turned aside from much that I knew, and have given up much that went before. What will not bring me, more certainly than before, to where I am is of no use to me. I have stepped out of the clearing into the woods. I have thrown away my lantern, and I can see the dark.

The hill, like Valéry's sycamore, is a voyager standing still. Never moving a step, it travels through years, seasons, weathers, days and nights. These are the measures of its time, and they alter it, marking their passage on it as on a man's face. The hill has never observed a Christmas or an Easter or a Fourth of July. It has nothing to do with a dial or a calendar. Time is told in it mutely and immediately, with perfect accuracy, as it is told by the heart in the body. Its time is the birth and the flourishing and the death of the many lives that are its life.

The hill is like an old woman, all her human obligations met, who sits at work day after day, in a kind of rapt leisure, at an intricate embroidery. She has time for all things. Because she does not expect ever to be finished, she is endlessly patient with details. She perfects flower and leaf, feather and song, adorning the briefest life in great beauty as though it were meant to last forever.

In the early spring I climb up through the woods to an east-facing bluff where the bloodroot bloom in scattered colonies around the

foot of the rotting monument of a tree trunk. The sunlight is slanting, clear, through the leafless branches. The flowers are white and
perfect, delicate as though shaped in air and water. There is a fragil-
ity about them that communicates how short a time they will last.
There is some subtle bond between them and the dwindling great
trunk of the dead tree. There comes on me a pressing wish to preserve them. But I know that what draws me to them would not pass
over into anything I can *do*. They will be lost. In a few days none will
be here.

Coming upon a mushroom growing out of a pad of green moss
between the thick roots of an oak, the sun and the dew still there
together, I have felt my mind irresistibly become small, to inhabit
that place, leaving me standing vacant and bewildered, like a boy
whose captured field mouse has just leaped out of his hand.

As I slowly fill with the knowledge of this place, and sink into it, I
come to the sense that my life here is inexhaustible, that its possibilities lie rich behind and ahead of me, that when I am dead it will not
be used up.

Too much that we do is done at the expense of something else, or
somebody else. There is some intransigent destructiveness in us. My
days, though I think I know better, are filled with a thousand irrita-
tions, worries, regrets for what has happened and fears for what may,
trivial duties, meaningless torments – as destructive of my life as if I
wanted to be dead. Take today for what it is, I counsel myself. Let it
be enough.

And I dare not, for fear that if I do, yesterday will infect tomorrow.
We are in the habit of contention – against the world, against each
other, against ourselves.

It is not from ourselves that we will learn to be better than we are.

•

In spite of all the talk about the law of tooth and fang and the struggle for survival, there is in the lives of the animals and birds a great peacefulness. It is not all fear and flight, pursuit and killing. That is part of it, certainly; and there is cold and hunger; there is the likelihood that death, when it comes, will be violent. But there is peace, too, and I think that the intervals of peace are frequent and prolonged. These are the times when the creature rests, communes with himself or with his kind, takes pleasure in being alive.

This morning while I wrote I was aware of a fox squirrel hunched in the sunlight on a high elm branch beyond my window. The night had been frosty, and now the warmth returned. He stayed there a long time, warming and grooming himself. Was he not at peace? Was his life not pleasant to him then?

I have seen the same peacefulness in a flock of wood ducks perched above the water in the branches of a fallen beech, preening and dozing in the sunlight of an autumn afternoon. Even while they dozed they had about them the exquisite alertness of wild things. If I had shown myself they would have been instantly in the air. But for the time there was no alarm among them, and no fear. The moment was whole in itself, satisfying to them and to me.

Or the sense of it may come with watching a flock of cedar waxwings eating wild grapes in the top of the woods on a November afternoon. Everything they do is leisurely. They pick the grapes with a curious deliberation, comb their feathers, converse in high windy whistles. Now and then one will fly out and back in a sort of dancing flight full of whimsical flutters and turns. They are like farmers loafing in their own fields on Sunday. Though they have no Sundays, their days are full of sabbaths.

One clear fine morning in early May, when the river was flooded, my friend and I came upon four rough-winged swallows circling over the water, which was still covered with frail wisps and threads of mist from the cool night. They were bathing, dipping down to the water until they touched the still surface with a little splash. They wound their flight over the water like the graceful falling loops of a fine cord. Later they perched on a dead willow, low to the water, to dry and groom themselves, the four together. We paddled the canoe almost within reach of them before they flew. They were neat, beautiful, gentle birds. Sitting there preening in the sun after their cold bath, they communicated a sense of domestic integrity, the serenity of living within order. We didn't belong within the order of the events and needs of their day, and so they didn't notice us until they had to.

But there is not only peacefulness, there is joy. And the joy, less deniable in its evidence than the peacefulness, is the confirmation of it. I sat one summer evening and watched a great blue heron make his descent from the top of the hill into the valley. He came down at a measured deliberate pace, stately as always, like a dignitary going down a stair. And then, at a point I judged to be midway over the river, without at all varying his wingbeat he did a backward turn in the air, a loop-the-loop. It could only have been a gesture of pure exuberance, of joy – a speaking of his sense of the evening, the day's fulfillment, his descent homeward. He made just the one slow turn, and then flew on out of sight in the direction of a slew farther down in the bottom. The movement was incredibly beautiful, at once exultant and stately, a benediction on the evening and on the river and on me. It seemed so perfectly to confirm the presence of a free nonhuman joy in the world – a joy I feel a great need to believe in – that I had the skeptic's impulse to doubt that I had seen it. If I had, I thought, it would be a sign of the presence of something heavenly in the earth. And then, one evening a year later, I saw it again.

Every man is followed by a shadow which is his death – dark, featureless, and mute. And for every man there is a place where his shadow is clarified and is made his reflection, where his face is mirrored in the ground. He sees his source and his destiny, and they are acceptable to him. He becomes the follower of what pursued him. What hounded his track becomes his companion.

That is the myth of my search and my return.

I have been walking in the woods, and have lain down on the ground to rest. It is the middle of October, and around me, all through the woods, the leaves are quietly sifting down. The newly fallen leaves make a dry, comfortable bed, and I lie easy, coming to rest within myself as I seem to do nowadays only when I am in the woods.

And now a leaf, spiraling down in wild flight, lands on my shirt at about the third button below the collar. At first I am bemused and mystified by the coincidence – that the leaf should have been so hung, weighted and shaped, so ready to fall, so nudged loose and slanted by the breeze, as to fall where I, by the same delicacy of circumstance, happened to be lying. The event, among all its ramifying causes and considerations, and finally its mysteries, begins to take on the magnitude of history. Portent begins to dwell in it.

And suddenly I apprehend in it the dark proposal of the ground. Under the fallen leaf my breastbone burns with imminent decay. Other leaves fall. My body begins its long shudder into humus. I feel my substance escape me, carried into the mold by beetles and worms. Days, winds, seasons pass over me as I sink under the leaves. For a time only sight is left me, a passive awareness of the sky overhead, birds crossing, the mazed interreaching of the treetops, the leaves falling – and then that, too, sinks away. It is acceptable to me, and I am at peace.

When I move to go, it is as though I rise up out of the world.

(1968)

The Making of a Marginal Farm

One day in the summer of 1956, leaving home for school, I stopped on the side of the road directly above the house where I now live. From there you could see a mile or so across the Kentucky River Valley, and perhaps six miles along the length of it. The valley was a green trough full of sunlight, blue in its distances. I often stopped here in my comings and goings, just to look, for it was all familiar to me from before the time my memory began: woodlands and pastures on the hillsides; fields and croplands, wooded slew-edges and hollows in the bottoms; and through the midst of it the tree-lined river passing down from its headwaters near the Virginia line toward its mouth at Carrollton on the Ohio.

Standing there, I was looking at land where one of my great-great-great-grandfathers settled in 1803, and at the scene of some of the happiest times of my own life, where in my growing-up years I camped, hunted, fished, boated, swam, and wandered – where, in short, I did whatever escaping I felt called upon to do. It was a place where I had happily been, and where I always wanted to be. And I remember gesturing toward the valley that day and saying to the friend who was with me: 'That's all I need.'

I meant it. It was an honest enough response to my recognition of its beauty, the abundance of its lives and possibilities, and of my own love for it and interest in it. And in the sense that I continue to recognize all that, and feel that what I most need is here, I can still say the same thing.

And yet I am aware that I must necessarily mean differently – or at least a great deal more – when I say it now. Then I was speaking mostly from affection, and did not know, by half, what I was talking about. I was speaking of a place that in some ways I knew and in some ways cared for, but did not live in. The differences between knowing a place and living in it, between cherishing a place and living responsibly in it, had not begun to occur to me. But they are critical differences, and understanding them has been perhaps the chief necessity of my experience since then.

I married in the following summer, and in the next seven years lived in a number of distant places. But, largely because I continued to feel that what I needed was here, I could never bring myself to want to live in any other place. And so we returned to live in Kentucky in the summer of 1964, and that autumn bought the house whose roof my friend and I had looked down on eight years before, and with it 'twelve acres more or less.' Thus I began a profound change in my life. Before, I had lived according to expectation rooted in ambition. Now I began to live according to a kind of destiny rooted in my origins and in my life. One should not speak too confidently of one's 'destiny;' I use the word to refer to causes that lie deeper in history and character than mere intention or desire. In buying the little place known as Lanes Landing, it seems to me, I began to obey the deeper causes.

We had returned so that I could take a job at the University of Kentucky in Lexington. And we expected to live pretty much the usual academic life: I would teach and write; my 'subject matter' would be, as it had been, the few square miles in Henry County where I grew up. We bought the tiny farm at Lanes Landing, thinking that we would use it as a 'summer place,' and on that understanding I began, with the help of two carpenter friends, to make some necessary repairs on the house. I no longer remember exactly how it was decided, but that work had hardly begun when it became a full-scale overhaul.

By so little our minds had been changed: this was not going to be a house to visit, but a house to live in. It was as though, having put our hand to the plow, we not only did not look back, but could not. We renewed the old house, equipped it with plumbing, bathroom, and oil furnace, and moved in on July 4, 1965.

•

Once the house was whole again, we came under the influence of the 'twelve acres more or less.' This acreage included a steep hillside pasture, two small pastures by the river, and a 'garden spot' of less than half an acre. We had, besides the house, a small barn in bad shape, a good large building that once had been a general store, and a small garage also in usable condition. This was hardly a farm by modern standards, but it was land that could be used, and it was unthinkable that we would not use it. The land was not good enough to afford the possibility of a cash income, but it would allow us to grow our food – or most of it. And that is what we set out to do.

In the early spring of 1965 I had planted a small orchard; the next spring we planted our first garden. Within the following six or seven years we reclaimed the pastures, converted the garage into a hen-house, rebuilt the barn, greatly improved the garden soil, planted berry bushes, acquired a milk cow – and were producing, except for hay and grain for our animals, nearly everything that we ate: fruit, vegetables, eggs, meat, milk, cream, and butter. We built an outbuilding with a meat room and a food-storage cellar. Because we did not want to pollute our land and water with sewage, and in the process waste nutrients that should be returned to the soil, we built a composting privy. And so we began to attempt a life that, in addition to whatever else it was, would be responsibly agricultural. We used no chemical fertilizers. Except for a little rotenone, we used no insecticides. As our land and our food became healthier, so did we. And our food was of better quality than any that we could have bought.

We were not, of course, living an idyll. What we had done could not have been accomplished without difficulty and a great deal of work. And we had made some mistakes and false starts. But there was great satisfaction, too, in restoring the neglected land, and in feeding ourselves from it.

Meanwhile, the forty-acre place adjoining ours on the downriver side had been sold to a 'developer,' who planned to divide it into lots for 'second homes.' This project was probably doomed by the steepness of the ground and the difficulty of access, but a lot of bulldozing – and a lot of damage – was done before it was given up. In the fall of 1972, the place was offered for sale and we were able to buy it.

We now began to deal with larger agricultural problems. Some of this new land was usable; some would have to be left in trees. There were perhaps fifteen acres of hillside that could be reclaimed for pasture, and about two and a half acres of excellent bottomland on which we would grow alfalfa for hay. But it was a mess, all of it badly neglected, and a considerable portion of it badly abused by the developer's bulldozers. The hillsides were covered with thicket growth; the bottom was shoulder high in weeds; the diversion ditches had to be restored; a bulldozed gash meant for 'building sites' had to be mended; the barn needed a new foundation, and the cistern a new top; there were no fences. What we had bought was less a farm than a reclamation project – which has now, with a later purchase, grown to seventy-five acres.

While we had only the small place, I had got along very well with a Gravely 'walking tractor' that I owned, and an old Farmall A that I occasionally borrowed from my Uncle Jimmy. But now that we had increased our acreage, it was clear that I could not continue to depend on a borrowed tractor. For a while I assumed that I would buy a tractor of my own. But because our land was steep, and there was already talk of a fuel shortage – and because I liked the idea – I finally decided to buy a team of horses instead. By the spring of 1973, after a lot of inquiring and looking, I had found and bought a team of five-year-old sorrel mares. And – again by the generosity of my Uncle Jimmy, who has never thrown any good thing away – I had enough equipment to make a start.

Though I had worked horses and mules during the time I was growing up, I had never worked over ground so steep and problematical as this, and it had been twenty years since I had worked a team over ground of any kind. Getting started again, I anticipated every new task with uneasiness, and sometimes with dread. But to my relief and delight, the team and I did all that needed to be done that year, getting better as we went along. And over the years since then, with that team and others, my son and I have carried on our farming the way it was carried on in my boyhood, doing everything with our horses except baling the hay. And we have done work in places and in weather in which a tractor would have been useless. Experience has shown us – or re-shown us – that horses are not only a satisfactory and economical means of power, especially on such small places as ours, but are probably *necessary* to the most conservative use of steep land. Our farm, in fact, is surrounded by potentially excellent hillsides that were maintained in pasture until tractors replaced the teams.

Another change in our economy (and our lives) was accomplished in the fall of 1973 with the purchase of our first wood-burning stove. Again the petroleum shortage was on our minds, but we also knew that from the pasture-clearing we had ahead of us we would have an abundance of wood that otherwise would go to waste – and when that was gone we would still have our permanent wood lots. We thus expanded our subsistence income to include heating fuel, and since then have used our furnance only as a 'backup system' in the coldest weather and in our absences from home. The horses also contribute significantly to the work of fuel-gathering; they will go easily into difficult places and over soft ground or snow where a truck or a tractor could not move.

As we have continued to live on and from our place, we have slowly begun its restoration and healing. Most of the scars have now been mended and grassed over, most of the washes stopped, most of the buildings made sound; many loads of rocks have been hauled out of the fields and used to pave entrances or fill hollows; we have done perhaps half of the necessary fencing. A great deal of work is still left to do, and some of it – the rebuilding of fertility in the depleted hillsides – will take longer than we will live. But in doing these things we have begun a restoration and a healing in ourselves.

I should say plainly that this has not been a 'paying proposition.' As a reclamation project, it has been costly both in money and in effort. It seems at least possible that, in any other place, I might have had little interest in doing any such thing. The reason I have been interested in doing it here, I think, is that I have felt implicated in the history, the uses, and the attitudes that have depleted such places as ours and made them 'marginal.'

I had not worked long on our 'twelve acres more or less' before I saw that such places were explained almost as much by their human history as by their nature. I saw that they were not 'marginal' because they ever were unfit for human use, but because in both culture and character *we* had been unfit to use them. Originally, even such steep slopes as these along the lower Kentucky River Valley were deep-soiled and abundantly fertile; 'jumper' plows and generations of carelessness impoverished them. Where yellow clay is at the surface now, five feet of good soil may be gone. I once wrote that on some of the nearby uplands one walks as if 'knee-deep' in the absence of the original soil. On these steeper slopes, I now know, that absence is shoulder-deep.

That is a loss that is horrifying as soon as it is imagined. It happened easily, by ignorance, indifference, 'a little folding of the hands to sleep.' It cannot be remedied in human time; to build five feet of soil takes perhaps fifty or sixty thousand years. This loss, once imagined, is potent with despair. If a people in adding a hundred and fifty years to itself subtracts fifty thousand from its land, what is there to hope?

And so our reclamation project has been, for me, less a matter of idealism or morality than a kind of self-preservation. A destructive history, once it is understood as such, is a nearly insupportable burden. Understanding it is a disease of understanding, depleting the sense of efficacy and paralyzing effort, unless it finds healing work. For me that work has been partly of the mind, in what I have written, but that seems to have depended inescapably on work of the body and of the ground. In order to affirm the values most native and necessary to me – indeed, to affirm my own life as a thing decent in possibility – I needed to know in my own experience that this place did not have to be abused in the past, and that it can be kindly and conservingly used now.

With certain reservations that must be strictly borne in mind, our work here has begun to offer some of the needed proofs.

Bountiful as the vanished original soil of the hillsides may have been, what remains is good. It responds well – sometimes astonishingly well – to good treatment. It never should have been plowed (some of it never should have been cleared), and it never should be plowed again. But it can be put in pasture without plowing, and it will support an excellent grass sod that will in turn protect it from erosion, if properly managed and not overgrazed.

Land so steep as this cannot be preserved in row crop cultivation. To subject it to such an expectation is simply to ruin it, as its history shows. Our rule, generally, has been to plow no steep ground, to maintain in pasture only such slopes as can be safely mowed with a horse-drawn mower, and to leave the rest in trees. We have increased the numbers of livestock on our pastures gradually, and have carefully rotated the animals from field to field, in order to avoid overgrazing. Under this use and care, our hillsides have mended and they produce more and better pasturage every year.

As a child I always intended to be a farmer. As a young man, I gave up that intention, assuming that I could not farm and do the other things I wanted to do. And then I became a farmer almost unintentionally and by a kind of necessity. That wayward and necessary becoming – along with my marriage, which has been intimately a part of it – is the major event of my life. It has changed me profoundly from the man and the writer I would otherwise have been.

There was a time, after I had left home and before I came back, when this place was my 'subject matter.' I meant that too, I think, on the day in 1956 when I told my friend, 'That's all I need.' I was regarding it, in a way too easy for a writer, as a mirror in which I saw myself. There was obviously a sort of narcissism in that – and an inevitable superficiality, for only the surface can reflect.

In coming home and settling on this place, I began to *live* in my subject, and to learn that living in one's subject is not at all the same as 'having' a subject. To live in the place that is one's subject is to pass through the surface. The simplifications of distance and mere observation are thus destroyed. The obsessively regarded reflection is broken and dissolved. One sees that the mirror was a blinder; one can now begin to see where one is. One's relation to one's subject ceases to be merely emotional or aesthetical, or even merely critical, and becomes problematical, practical, and responsible as well. Because it must. It is like marrying your sweetheart.

Though our farm has not been an economic success, as such success is usually reckoned, it is nevertheless beginning to make a kind of economic sense that is consoling and hopeful. Now that the largest expenses of purchase and repair are behind us, our income from the place is beginning to run ahead of expenses. As income I am counting the value of shelter, subsistence, heating fuel, and money earned by the sale of livestock. As expenses I am counting maintenance, newly purchased equipment, extra livestock feed, newly purchased animals, reclamation work, fencing materials, taxes, and insurance.

If our land had been in better shape when we bought it, our expenses would obviously be much smaller. As it is, once we have completed its restoration, our farm will provide us a home, produce our subsistence, keep us warm in winter, and earn a modest cash income. The significance of this becomes apparent when one considers that most of this land is 'unfarmable' by the standards of conventional agriculture, and that most of it was producing nothing at the time we bought it.

And so, contrary to some people's opinion, it *is* possible for a family to live on such 'marginal' land, to take a bountiful subsistence and some cash income from it, and, in doing so, to improve both the land and themselves. (I believe, however, that, at least in the present economy, this should not be attempted without a source of income other than the farm. It is now extremely difficult to pay for the best of farmland by farming it, and even 'marginal' land has become unreasonably expensive. To attempt to make a living from such land is to impose a severe strain on land and people alike.)

I said earlier that the success of our work here is subject to reservations. There are only two of these, but both are serious.

The first is that land like ours – and there are many acres of such land in this country – can be conserved in use only by competent knowledge, by a great deal more work than is required by leveler land, by a devotion more particular and disciplined than patriotism, and by ceaseless watchfulness and care. All these are cultural values and resources, never sufficiently abundant in this country, and now almost obliterated by the contrary values of the so-called 'affluent society.'

One of my own mistakes will suggest the difficulty. In 1974 I dug a small pond on a wooded hillside that I wanted to pasture occasionally. The excavation for that pond – as I should have anticipated, for I had better reason than I used – caused the hillside to slump both above and below. After six years the slope has not stabilized, and more expense and trouble will be required to stabilize it. A small hillside farm will not survive many mistakes of that order. Nor will a modest income.

The true remedy for mistakes is to keep from making them. It is not in the piecemeal technological solutions that our society now offers, but in a change of cultural (and economic) values that will encourage in the whole population the necessary respect, restraint, and care. Even more important, it is in the possibility of settled families and local communities, in which the knowledge of proper means and methods, proper moderations and restraints, can be handed down, and so accumulate in place and stay alive; the experience of one generation is not adequate to inform and control its actions. Such possibilities are not now in sight in this country.

The second reservation is that we live at the lower end of the Kentucky River watershed, which has long been intensively used, and is increasingly abused. Strip mining, logging, extractive farming, and the digging, draining, roofing, and paving that go with industrial and urban 'development,' all have seriously depleted the capacity of the watershed to retain water. This means not only that floods are higher and more frequent than they would be if the watershed were healthy, but that the floods subside too quickly, the watershed being far less a sponge, now, than it is a roof. The floodwater drops suddenly out of the river, leaving the steep banks soggy, heavy, and soft. As a result, great strips and blocks of land crack loose and slump, or they give way entirely and disappear into the river in what people here call 'slips.'

The flood of December 1978, which was unusually high, also went down extremely fast, falling from banktop almost to pool stage within a couple of days. In the aftermath of this rapid 'drawdown,' we lost a block of bottomland an acre square. This slip, which is still crumbling, severely damaged our place, and may eventually undermine two buildings. The same flood started a slip in another place, which threatens a third building. We have yet another building situated on a huge (but, so far, very gradual) slide that starts at the river and, aggravated by two state highway cuts, goes almost to the hilltop. And we have serious river bank erosion the whole length of our place.

What this means is that, no matter how successfully we may control erosion on our hillsides, our land remains susceptible to a more serious cause of erosion that we cannot control. Our river bank stands literally at the cutting edge of our nation's consumptive economy. This, I think, is true of many 'marginal' places – it is true, in fact, of many places that are not marginal. In its consciousness, ours is an upland society; the ruin of watersheds, and what that involves and means, is little considered. And so the land is heavily taxed to subsidize an 'affluence' that consists, in reality, of health and goods stolen from the unborn.

Living at the lower end of the Kentucky River watershed is what is now known as 'an educational experience' – and not an easy one. A lot of information comes with it that is severely damaging to the reputation of our people and our time. From where I live and work, I never have to look far to see that the earth does indeed pass away. But however that is taught, and however bitterly learned, it is something that should be known, and there is a certain good strength in knowing it. To spend one's life farming a piece of the earth so passing is, as many would say, a hard lot. But it is, in an ancient sense, the human lot. What saves it is to love the farming.

(1980)

Think Little

First there was Civil Rights, and then there was the War, and now it is the Environment. The first two of this sequence of causes have already risen to the top of the nation's consciousness and declined somewhat in a remarkably short time. I mention this in order to begin with what I believe to be a justifiable skepticism. For it seems to me that the Civil Rights Movement and the Peace Movement, as popular causes in the electronic age, have partaken far too much of the nature of fads. Not for all, certainly, but for too many they have been the fashionable politics of the moment. As causes they have been undertaken too much in ignorance; they have been too much simplified; they have been powered too much by impatience and guilt of conscience and short-term enthusiasm, and too little by an authentic social vision and long-term conviction and deliberation. For most people those causes have remained almost entirely abstract; there has been too little personal involvement, and too much involvement in organizations that were insisting that *other* organizations should do what was right.

There is considerable danger that the Environmental Movement will have the same nature: that it will be a public cause, served by organizations that will self-righteously criticize and condemn other organizations, inflated for a while by a lot of public talk in the media, only to be replaced in its turn by another fashionable crisis. I hope that will not happen, and I believe that there are ways to keep it from happening, but I know that if this effort is carried on solely as a public cause, if millions of people cannot or will not undertake it as a *private* cause as well, then it is *sure* to happen. In five years the energy of our present concern will have petered out in a series of public gestures – and no doubt in a series of empty laws – and a great, and perhaps the last, human opportunity will have been lost.

It need not be that way. A better possibility is that the movement to preserve the environment will be seen to be, as I think it has to be, not a digression from the civil rights and peace movements, but the logical culmination of those movements. For I believe that the separation of these three problems is artificial. They have the same cause, and that is the mentality of greed and exploitation. The mentality that exploits and destroys the natural environment is the same that abuses racial and economic minorities, that imposes on young men the tyranny of the military draft, that makes war against peasants and women and children with the indifference of technology. The mentality that destroys a watershed and then panics at the threat of flood is the same mentality that gives institutionalized insult to black people and then panics at the prospect of race riots. It is the same mentality that can mount deliberate warfare against a civilian population and then express moral shock at the logical consequence of such warfare at My Lai. We would be fools to believe that we could solve any one of these problems without solving the others.

To me, one of the most important aspects of the Environmental Movement is that it brings us not just to another public crisis, but to a crisis of the protest movement itself. For the environmental crisis should make it dramatically clear, as perhaps it has not always been before, that there is no public crisis that is not also private. To most advocates of civil rights, racism has seemed mostly the fault of someone else. For most advocates of peace, the war has been a remote reality, and the burden of the blame has seemed to rest mostly on the government. I am certain that these crises have been more private, and that we have each suffered more from them and been more responsible for them, than has been readily apparent, but the connections have been difficult to see. Racism and militarism have been institutionalized among us for too long for our personal involvement in those evils to be easily apparent to us. Think, for example, of all the Northerners who assumed – until black people attempted to move into *their* neighborhoods – that racism was a Southern phenomenon. And think how quickly – one might almost say how naturally – among some of its members the Peace Movement has spawned policies of deliberate provocation and violence.

•

But the environmental crisis rises closer to home. Every time we draw a breath, every time we drink a glass of water, we are suffering from it. And more important, every time we indulge in, or depend on, the wastefulness of our economy – and our economy's first principle is waste – we are *causing* the crisis. Nearly every one of us, nearly every day of his life, is contributing *directly* to the ruin of this planet. A protest meeting on the issue of environmental abuse is not a convocation of accusers, it is a convocation of the guilty. That realization ought to clear the smog of self-righteousness that has almost conventionally hovered over these occasions and let us see the work that is to be done.

In this crisis it is certain that every one of us has a public responsibility. We must not cease to bother the government and the other institutions to see that they never become comfortable with easy promises. For myself, I want to say that I hope never again to go to Frankfort to present a petition to the governor on an issue so vital as that of strip mining, only to be dealt with by some ignorant functionary – as several of us were not so long ago, the governor himself being 'too busy' to receive us. Next time I will go prepared to wait as long as necessary to see that the petitioners' complaints and their arguments are heard *fully* – and by the governor. And then I will hope to find ways to keep those complaints and arguments from being forgotten until something is done to relieve them. The time is past when it was enough merely to elect our officials. We will have to elect them and then go and *watch* them and keep our hands on them, the way the coal companies do. We have made a tradition in Kentucky of putting self-servers, and worse, in charge of our vital interests. I am sick of it. And I think that one way to change it is to make Frankfort a less comfortable place. I believe in American political principles, and I will not sit idly by and see those principles destroyed by sorry practice. I am ashamed that American government should have become the chief cause of disillusionment with American principles.

And so when the government in Frankfort again proves too stupid or too blind or too corrupt to see the plain truth and to act with simple decency, I intend to be there, and I trust that I won't be alone. I hope, moreover, to be there, not with a sign or a slogan or a button, but with the facts and the arguments. A crowd whose discontent has risen no higher than the level of slogans is *only* a crowd. But a crowd that understands the reasons for its discontent and knows the remedies is a vital community, and it will have to be reckoned with. I would rather go before the government with two men who have a competent understanding of an issue, and who therefore deserve a hearing, than with two thousand who are vaguely dissatisfied.

But even the most articulate public protest is not enough. We don't live in the government or in institutions or in our public utterances and acts, and the environmental crisis has its roots in our *lives*. By the same token, environmental health will also be rooted in our lives. That is, I take it, simply a fact, and in the light of it we can see how superficial and foolish we would be to think that we could correct what is wrong merely by tinkering with the institutional machinery. The changes that are required are fundamental changes in the way we are living.

What we are up against in this country, in any attempt to invoke private responsibility, is that we have nearly destroyed private life. Our people have given up their independence in return for the cheap seductions and the shoddy merchandise of so-called 'affluence.' We have delegated all our vital functions and responsibilities to salesmen and agents and bureaus and experts of all sorts. We cannot feed or clothe ourselves, or entertain ourselves, or communicate with each other, or be charitable or neighborly or loving, or even respect ourselves, without recourse to a merchant or a corporation or a public service organization or an agency of the government or a style-setter or an expert. Most of us cannot think of dissenting from the opinions or the actions of one organization without first forming a new organization. Individualism is going around these days in uniform, handing out the party line on individualism. Dissenters want to publish their personal opinions over a thousand signatures.

The Confucian *Great Digest* says that the 'chief way for the production of wealth' (and it is talking about real goods, not money) is 'that the producers be many and that the mere consumers be few . . .' But even in the much-publicized rebellion of the young against the materialism of the affluent society, the consumer mentality is too often still intact: the standards of behavior are still those of kind and quantity, the security sought is still the security of numbers, and the chief motive is still the consumer's anxiety that he is missing out on what is 'in.' In this state of total consumerism – which is to say a state of helpless dependence on things and services and ideas and motives that we have forgotten how to provide ourselves – all meaningful contact between ourselves and the earth is broken. We do not understand the earth in terms either of what it offers us or of what it requires of us, and I think it is the rule that people inevitably destroy what they do not understand. Most of us are not directly responsible for strip mining and extractive agriculture and other forms of environmental abuse. But we are guilty nevertheless, for we connive in them by our ignorance. We are ignorantly dependent on them. We do not know enough about them; we do not have a particular enough sense of their danger. Most of us, for example, not only do not know how to produce the best food in the best way – we don't know how to produce any kind in any way. Our model citizen is a sophisticate who before puberty understands how to produce a baby, but who at the age of thirty will not know how to produce a potato. And for this condition we have elaborate rationalizations, instructing us that dependence for everything on somebody else is efficient and economical and a scientific miracle. I say, instead, that it is madness, mass produced. A man who understands the weather only in terms of golf is participating in a public insanity that either he or his descendants will be bound to realize as suffering. I believe that the death of the world is breeding in such minds much more certainly and much faster than in any political capital or atomic arsenal.

For an index of our loss of contact with the earth we need only look at the condition of the American farmer – who must enact our society's dependence on the land. In an age of unparalleled affluence and leisure, the American farmer is harder pressed and harder worked than ever before; his margin of profit is small, his hours are long; his outlays for land and equipment and the expenses of maintenance and operation are growing rapidly greater; he cannot compete with industry for labor; he is being forced more and more to depend on the use of destructive chemicals and on the wasteful methods of haste. As a class, farmers are one of the despised minorities. So far as I can see, farming is considered marginal or incidental to the economy of the country, and farmers, when they are thought of at all, are thought of as hicks and yokels, whose lives do not fit into the modern scene. The average American farmer is now an old man whose children have moved away to the cities. His knowledge, and his intimate connection with the land, are about to be lost. The small independent farmer is going the way of the small independent craftsmen and storekeepers. He is being forced off the land into the cities, his place taken by absentee owners, corporations, and machines. Some would justify all this in the name of efficiency. As I see it, it is an enormous social and economic and cultural blunder. For the small farmers who lived on their farms *cared* about their land. And given their established connection to their land – which was often hereditary and traditional as well as economic – they could have been encouraged to care for it more competently than they have so far. The corporations and machines that replace them will never be bound to the land by the sense of birthright and continuity, or by the love that enforces care. They will be bound by the rule of efficiency, which takes thought only of the volume of the year's produce, and takes no thought of the life of the land, not measurable in pounds or dollars, which will assure the livelihood and the health of the coming generations.

If we are to hope to correct our abuses of each other and of other races and of our land, and if our effort to correct these abuses is to be more than a political fad that will in the long run be only another form of abuse, then we are going to have to go far beyond public protest and political action. We are going to have to rebuild the substance and the integrity of private life in this country. We are going to have to gather up the fragments of knowledge and responsibility that we have parceled out to the bureaus and the corporations and the specialists, and put those fragments back together in our own minds and in our families and households and neighborhoods. We need better government, no doubt about it. But we also need better minds, better friendships, better marriages, better communities. We need persons and households that do not have to wait upon organizations, but can make necessary changes in themselves, on their own.

For most of the history of this country our motto, implied or spoken, has been Think Big. A better motto, and an essential one now, is Think Little. That implies the necessary change of thinking and feeling, and suggests the necessary work. Thinking Big has led us to the two biggest and cheapest political dodges of our time: plan-making and law-making. The lotus-eaters of this era are in Washington, D.C., Thinking Big. Somebody perceives a problem, and somebody in the government comes up with a plan or a law. The result, mostly, has been the persistence of the problem, and the enlargement and enrichment of the government.

But the discipline of thought is not generalization; it is detail, and it is personal behavior. While the government is 'studying' and funding and organizing its Big Thought, nothing is being done. But the citizen who is willing to Think Little, and, accepting the discipline of that, to go ahead on his own, is already solving the problem. A man who is trying to live as a neighbor to his neighbors will have a lively and practical understanding of the work of peace and brotherhood, and let there be no mistake about it – he is *doing* that work. A couple who make a good marriage, and raise healthy, morally competent children, are serving the world's future more directly and surely than any political leader, though they never utter a public word. A good farmer who is dealing with the problem of soil erosion on an acre of ground has a sounder grasp of that problem and *cares* more about it and is probably doing more to solve it than any bureaucrat who is talking about it in general. A man who is willing to undertake the discipline and the difficulty of mending his own ways is worth more to the conservation movement than a hundred who are insisting merely that the government and the industries mend *their* ways.

If you are concerned about the proliferation of trash, then by all means start an organization in your community to do something about it. But before – *and while* – you organize, pick up some cans and bottles yourself. That way, at least, you will assure yourself and others that you mean what you say. If you are concerned about air pollution, help push for government controls, but drive your car less, use less fuel in your home. If you are worried about the damming of wilderness rivers, join the Sierra Club, write to the government, but turn off the lights you're not using, don't install an air conditioner, don't be a sucker for electrical gadgets, don't waste water. In other words, if you are fearful of the destruction of the environment, then learn to quit being an environmental parasite. We all are, in one way or another, and the remedies are not always obvious, though they certainly will always be difficult. They require a new kind of life – harder, more laborious, poorer in luxuries and gadgets, but also, I am certain, richer in meaning and more abundant in real pleasure. To have a healthy environment we will all have to give up things we like; we may even have to give up things we have come to think of as necessities. But to be fearful of the disease and yet unwilling to pay for the cure is not just to be hypocritical; it is to be doomed. If you talk a good line without being changed by what you say, then you are not just hypocritical and doomed; you have become an agent of the disease. Consider, for an example, President Nixon, who advertises his grave concern about the destruction of the environment, and who turns up the air conditioner to make it cool enough to build a fire.

Odd as I am sure it will appear to some, I can think of no better form of personal involvement in the cure of the environment than that of gardening. A person who is growing a garden, if he is growing it organically, is improving a piece of the world. He is producing something to eat, which makes him somewhat independent of the grocery business, but he is also enlarging, for himself, the meaning of food and the pleasure of eating. The food he grows will be fresher, more nutritious, less contaminated by poisons and preservatives and dyes than what he can buy at a store. He is reducing the trash problem; a garden is not a disposable container, and it will digest and reuse its own wastes. If he enjoys working in his garden, then he is less dependent on an automobile or a merchant for his pleasure. He is involving himself directly in the work of feeding people.

If you think I'm wandering off the subject, let me remind you that most of the vegetables necessary for a family of four can be grown on a plot of forty by sixty feet. I think we might see in this an economic potential of considerable importance, since we now appear to be facing the possibility of widespread famine. How much food could be grown in the dooryards of cities and suburbs? How much could be grown along the extravagant right-of-ways of the interstate system? Or how much could be grown, by the intensive practices and economics of the garden or small farm, on so-called marginal lands? Louis Bromfield liked to point out that the people of France survived crisis after crisis because they were a nation of gardeners, who in times of want turned with great skill to their own small plots of ground. And F. H. King, an agriculture professor who traveled extensively in the Orient in 1907, talked to a Chinese farmer who supported a family of twelve, 'one donkey, one cow . . . and two pigs on 2.5 acres of cultivated land' – and who did this, moreover, by agricultural methods that were sound enough to have maintained his land in prime fertility through several thousand years of such use. These are possibilities that are readily apparent and attractive to minds that are prepared to Think Little. To Big Thinkers – the bureaucrats and businessmen of agriculture – they are invisible. But intensive, organic agriculture kept the farms of the Orient thriving for thousands of years, whereas extensive – which is to say, exploitive or extractive – agriculture has critically reduced the fertility of American farmlands in a few centuries or even a few decades.

A person who undertakes to grow a garden at home, by practices that will preserve rather than exploit the economy of the soil, has set his mind decisively against what is wrong with us. He is helping himself in a way that dignifies him and that is rich in meaning and pleasure. But he is doing something else that is more important: he is making vital contact with the soil and the weather on which his life depends. He will no longer look upon rain as a traffic impediment, or upon the sun as a holiday decoration. And his sense of humanity's dependence on the world will have grown precise enough, one would hope, to be politically clarifying and useful.

What I am saying is that if we apply our minds directly and competently to the needs of the earth, then we will have begun to make fundamental and necessary changes in our minds. We will begin to understand and to mistrust *and to change* our wasteful economy, which markets not just the produce of the earth, but also the earth's ability to produce. We will see that beauty and utility are alike dependent upon the health of the world. But we will also see through the fads and the fashions of protest. We will see that war and oppression and pollution are not separate issues, but are aspects of the same issue. Amid the outcries for the liberation of this group or that, we will know that no person is free except in the freedom of other persons, and that our only real freedom is to know and faithfully occupy our place – a much humbler place than we have been taught to think – in the order of creation.

But the change of mind I am talking about involves not just a change of knowledge, but also a change of attitude toward our essential ignorance, a change in our bearing in the face of mystery. The principles of ecology, if we will take them to heart, should keep us aware that our lives depend upon other lives and upon processes and energies in an interlocking system that, though we can destroy it, we can neither fully understand nor fully control. And our great dangerousness is that, locked in our selfish and myopic economy, we have been willing to change or destroy far beyond our power to understand. We are not humble enough or reverent enough.

Some time ago, I heard a representative of a paper company refer to conservation as a 'no-return investment.' This man's thinking was exclusively oriented to the annual profit of his industry. Circumscribed by the demand that the profit be great, he simply could not be answerable to any other demand – not even to the obvious needs of his own children.

Consider, in contrast, the profound ecological intelligence of Black Elk, 'a holy man of the Oglala Sioux,' who in telling his story said that it was not his own life that was important to him, but what he had shared with all life: 'It is the story of all life that is holy and it is good to tell, and of us two-leggeds sharing in it with the four-leggeds and the wings of the air and all green things . . .' And of the great vision that came to him when he was a child he said: 'I saw that the sacred hoop of my people was one of many hoops that made one circle, wide as daylight and as starlight, and in the center grew one mighty flowering tree to shelter all the children of one mother and father. And I saw that it was holy.'

(1970)

Nature as Measure

I live in a part of the country that at one time a good farmer could take some pleasure in looking at. When I first became aware of it, in the 1940s, the better land, at least, was generally well farmed. The farms were mostly small and were highly diversified, producing cattle, sheep, and hogs, tobacco, corn, and the small grains; nearly all the farmers milked a few cows for home use and to market milk or cream. Nearly every farm household maintained a garden, kept a flock of poultry, and fattened its own meat hogs. There was also an extensive 'support system' for agriculture: every community had its blacksmith shop, shops that repaired harness and machinery, and stores that dealt in farm equipment and supplies.

Now the country is not well farmed, and driving through it has become a depressing experience. Some good small farmers remain, and their farms stand out in the landscape like jewels. But they are few and far between, and they are getting fewer every year. The buildings and other improvements of the old farming are everywhere in decay or have vanished altogether. The produce of the country is increasingly specialized. The small dairies are gone. Most of the sheep flocks are gone, and so are most of the enterprises of the old household economy. There is less livestock and more cash-grain farming. When cash-grain farming comes in, the fences go, the livestock goes, erosion increases, and the fields become weedy.

Like the farmland, the farm communities are declining and eroding. The farmers who are still farming do not farm with as much skill as they did forty years ago, and there are not nearly so many farmers farming as there were forty years ago. As the old have died, they have not been replaced; as the young come of age, they leave farming or leave the community. And as the land and the people deteriorate, so necessarily must the support system. None of the small rural towns is thriving as it did forty years ago. The proprietors of small businesses give up or die and are not replaced. As the farm trade declines, farm equipment franchises are revoked. The remaining farmers must drive longer and longer distances for machines and parts and repairs.

Looking at the country now, one cannot escape the conclusion that there are no longer enough people on the land to farm it well and to take proper care of it. A further and more ominous conclusion is that there is no longer a considerable number of people knowledgeable enough to look at the country and see that it is not properly cared for – though the face of the country is now everywhere marked by the agony of our enterprise of self-destruction.

And suddenly in this wasting countryside there is talk of raising production quotas on Burley tobacco by 24 percent, and tobacco growers are coming under pressure from the manufacturers to decrease their use of chemicals. Everyone I have talked to is doubtful that we have enough people left in farming to meet the increased demand for either quantity or quality, and doubtful that we still have the barnroom to house the increased acreage. In other words, the demand going up has met the culture coming down. No one can be optimistic about the results.

Tobacco, I know, is not a food, but it comes from the same resources of land and people that food comes from, and this emerging dilemma in the production of tobacco can only foreshadow a similar dilemma in the production of food. At every point in our food economy, present conditions remaining, we must expect to come to a time when demand (for quantity or quality) going up will meet the culture coming down. The fact is that we have nearly destroyed American farming, and in the process have nearly destroyed our country.

How has this happened? It has happened because of the application to farming of far too simple a standard. For many years, as a nation, we have asked our land only to produce, and we have asked our farmers only to produce. We have believed that this single economic standard not only guaranteed good performance but also preserved the ultimate truth and rightness of our aims. We have bought unconditionally the economists' line that competition and innovation would solve all problems, and that we would finally accomplish a technological end-run around biological reality and the human condition.

Competition and innovation have indeed solved, for the time being, the problem of production. But the solution has been extravagant, thoughtless, and far too expensive. We have been winning, to our inestimable loss, a competition against our own land and our own people. At present, what we have to show for this 'victory' is a surplus of food. But this is a surplus achieved by the ruin of its sources, and it has been used, by apologists for our present economy, to disguise the damage by which it was produced. Food, clearly, is the most important economic

. product – except when there is a surplus. When there is a surplus, according to our present economic assumptions, food is the *least* important product. The surplus becomes famous as evidence to consumers that they have nothing to worry about, that there is no problem, that present economic assumptions are correct.

But our present economic assumptions are failing in agriculture, and to those having eyes to see the evidence is everywhere, in the cities as well as in the countryside. The singular demand for production has been unable to acknowledge the importance of the sources of production in nature and in human culture. Of course agriculture must be productive; that is a requirement as urgent as it is obvious. But urgent as it is, it is not the *first* requirement; there are two more requirements equally important and equally urgent. One is that if agriculture is to remain productive, it must preserve the land, and the fertility and ecological health of the land; the land, that is, must be used *well*. A further requirement, therefore, is that if the land is to be used well, the people who use it must know it well, must be highly motivated to use it well, must know how to use it well, must have time to use it well, and must be able to afford to use it well. Nothing that has happened in the agricultural revolution of the last fifty years has disproved or invalidated these requirements, though everything that has happened has ignored or defied them.

In light of the necessity that the farmland and the farm people should thrive while producing, we can see that the single standard of productivity has failed.

Now we must learn to replace that standard by one that is more comprehensive: the standard of nature. The effort to do this is not new. It was begun early in this century by Liberty Hyde Bailey of the Cornell University College of Agriculture, by F. H. King of the University of Wisconsin College of Agriculture and the United States Department of Agriculture, by J. Russell Smith, professor of economic geography at Columbia University, by the British agricultural scientist Sir Albert Howard, and by others; and it has continued into our own time in the work of such scientists as John Todd, Wes Jackson, and others. The standard of nature is not so simple or so easy a standard as the standard of productivity. The term 'nature' is not so definite or stable a concept as the weights and measures of productivity. But we know what we mean when we say that the first settlers in any American place recognized that place's agricultural potential 'by its nature' – that is, by the depth and quality of its soil, the kind and quality of its native vegetation, and so on. And we know what we mean when we say that all too often we have proceeded to ignore the nature of our places in farming them. By returning to 'the nature of the place' as standard, we acknowledge the necessary limits of our own intentions. Farming cannot take place except in nature; therefore, if nature does not thrive, farming cannot thrive. But we know too that nature includes us. It is not a place into which we reach from some safe standpoint outside it. We are in it and are a part of it while we use it. If it does not thrive, we cannot thrive. The appropriate measure of farming then is the world's health and our health, and this is inescapably *one* measure.

But the oneness of this measure is far different from the singularity of the standard of productivity that we have been using; it is far more complex. One of its concerns, one of the inevitable natural measures, is productivity; but it is also concerned for the health of all the creatures belonging to a given place, from the creatures of the soil and water to the humans and other creatures of the land surface to the birds of the air. The use of nature as measure proposes an atonement between ourselves and our world, between economy and ecology, between the domestic and the wild. Or it proposes a conscious and careful recognition of the interdependence between ourselves and nature that in fact has always existed and, if we are to live, must always exist.

Industrial agriculture, built according to the single standard of productivity, has dealt with nature, including human nature, in the manner of a monologist or an orator. It has not asked for anything, or waited to hear any response. It has told nature what it wanted, and in various clever ways has taken what it wanted. And since it proposed no limit on its wants, exhaustion has been its inevitable and foreseeable result. This, clearly, is a dictatorial or totalitarian form of behavior, and it is as totalitarian in its use of people as it is in its use of nature. Its connections to the world and to humans and the other creatures become more and more abstract, as its economy, its authority, and its power become more and more centralized.

On the other hand, an agriculture using nature, including human nature, as its measure would approach the world in the manner of a conversationalist. It would not impose its vision and its demands upon a world that it conceives of as a stockpile of raw material, inert and indifferent to any use that may be made of it. It would not proceed directly or soon to some supposedly ideal state of things. It *would* proceed directly and soon to serious thought about our condition and our predicament. On all farms, farmers would undertake to know responsibly where they are and to 'consult the genius of the place.' They would ask what nature would be doing there if no one were farming there. They would ask what nature would permit them to do there, and what they could do there with the least harm to the place and to their natural and human neighbors. And they would ask what nature would *help* them to do there. And after each asking, knowing that nature will respond, they would attend carefully to her response. The use of the place would necessarily change, and the response of the place to that use would necessarily change the user. The conversation itself would thus assume a kind of creaturely life, binding the place and its inhabitants together, changing and growing to no end, no final accomplishment, that can be conceived or foreseen.

Farming in this way, though it certainly would proceed by desire, is not visionary in the political or utopian sense. In a conversation, you always expect a reply. And if you honor the other party to the conversation, if you honor the *otherness* of the other party, you understand that you must not expect always to receive a reply that you foresee or a reply that you will like. A conversation is immitigably two-sided and always to some degree mysterious; it requires faith.

For a long time now we have understood ourselves as traveling toward some sort of industrial paradise, some new Eden conceived and constructed entirely by human ingenuity. And we have thought ourselves free to use and abuse nature in any way that might further this enterprise. Now we face overwhelming evidence that we are not smart enough to recover Eden by assault, and that nature does not tolerate or excuse our abuses. If, in spite of the evidence against us, we are finding it hard to relinquish our old ambition, we are also seeing more clearly every day how that ambition has reduced and enslaved us. We see how everything – the whole world – is belittled by the idea that all creation is moving or ought to move toward an end that some body, some human body, has thought up. To be free of that end and that ambition would be a delightful and precious thing. Once free of it, we might again go about our work and our lives with a seriousness and pleasure denied to us when we merely submit to a fate already determined by gigantic politics, economics, and technology.

Such freedom is implicit in the adoption of nature as the measure of economic life. The reunion of nature and economy proposes a necessary democracy, for neither economy nor nature can be abstract in practice. When we adopt nature as measure, we require practice that is locally knowledgeable. The particular farm, that is, must not be treated as any farm. And the particular knowledge of particular places is beyond the competence of any centralized power or authority. Farming by the measure of nature, which is to say the nature of the particular place, means that farmers must tend farms that they know and love, farms small enough to know and love, using tools and methods that they know and love, in the company of neighbors that they know and love.

In recent years, our society has been required to think again of the issues of use and abuse of human beings. We understand, for instance, that the inability to distinguish between a particular woman and any woman is a condition predisposing to abuse. It is time that we learn to apply the same understanding to our country. The inability to distinguish between a farm and any farm is a condition predisposing to abuse, and abuse has been the result. Rape, indeed, has been the result, and we have seen that we are not exempt from the damage we have inflicted. Now we must think of marriage.

(1989)

The Total Economy

Let us begin by assuming what appears to be true: that the so-called environmental crisis is now pretty well established as a fact of our age. The problems of pollution, species extinction, loss of wilderness, loss of farmland, and loss of topsoil may still be ignored or scoffed at, but they are not denied. Concern for these problems has acquired a certain standing, a measure of discussability, in the media and in some scientific, academic, and religious institutions.

This is good, of course; obviously, we can't hope to solve these problems without an increase of public awareness and concern. But in an age burdened with 'publicity,' we have to be aware also that as issues rise into popularity they rise also into the danger of oversimplification. To speak of this danger is especially necessary in confronting the destructiveness of our relationship to nature, which is the result, in the first place, of gross oversimplification.

The 'environmental crisis' has happened because the human household or economy is in conflict at almost every point with the household of nature. We have built our household on the assumption that the natural household is simple and can be simply used. We have assumed increasingly over the last five hundred years that nature is merely a supply of 'raw materials,' and that we may safely possess those materials merely by taking them. This taking, as our technical means have increased, has involved always less reverence or respect, less gratitude, less local knowledge, and less skill. Our methodologies of land use have strayed from our old sympathetic attempts to imitate natural processes, and have come more and more to resemble the methodology of mining, even as mining itself has become more powerful technologically and more brutal.

And so we will be wrong if we attempt to correct what we perceive as 'environmental' problems without correcting the economic oversimplification that caused them. This oversimplification is now

either a matter of corporate behavior or of behavior under the influence of corporate behavior. This is sufficiently clear to many of us.
What is not sufficiently clear, perhaps to any of us, is the extent of
our complicity, as individuals and especially as individual consumers, in the behavior of the corporations.

What has happened is that most people in our country, and apparently most people in the 'developed' world, have given proxies to the
corporations to produce and provide *all of* their food, clothing, and
shelter. Moreover, they are rapidly increasing their proxies to corporations or governments to provide entertainment, education, child
care, care of the sick and the elderly, and many other kinds of 'service' that once were carried on informally and inexpensively by
individuals or households or communities. Our major economic
practice, in short, is to delegate the practice to others.

The danger now is that those who are concerned will believe that
the solution to the 'environmental crisis' can be merely political –
that the problems, being large, can be solved by large solutions
generated by a few people to whom we will give our proxies to police
the economic proxies that we have already given. The danger, in
other words, is that people will think they have made a sufficient
change if they have altered their 'values,' or had a 'change of heart,'
or experienced a 'spiritual awakening,' and that such a change in passive consumers will necessarily cause appropriate changes in the
public experts, politicians, and corporate executives to whom they
have granted their political and economic proxies.

The trouble with this is that a proper concern for nature and our
use of nature must be practiced, not by our proxy-holders, but by
ourselves. A change of heart or of values without a practice is only
another pointless luxury of a passively consumptive way of life. The
'environmental crisis,' in fact, can be solved only if people, individually and in their communities, recover responsibility for their
thoughtlessly given proxies. If people begin the effort to take back
into their own power a significant portion of their economic responsibility, then their inevitable first discovery is that the 'environmental
crisis' is no such thing; it is not a crisis of our environs or surroundings; it is a crisis of our lives as individuals, as family members, as

community members, and as citizens. We have an 'environmental crisis' because *we* have consented to an economy in which by eating, drinking, working, resting, traveling, and enjoying ourselves we are destroying the natural, the God-given, world.

We live, as we must sooner or later recognize, in an era of sentimental economics and, consequently, of sentimental politics. Sentimental communism holds in effect that everybody and everything should suffer for the good of 'the many' who, though miserable in the present, will be happy in the future for exactly the same reasons that they are miserable in the present.

Sentimental capitalism is not so different from sentimental communism as the corporate and political powers claim to suppose. Sentimental capitalism holds in effect that everything small, local, private, personal, natural, good, and beautiful must be sacrificed in the interest of the 'free market' and the great corporations, which will bring unprecedented security and happiness to 'the many' – in, of course, the future.

These forms of political economy may be described as sentimental because they depend absolutely upon a political faith for which there is no justification. They seek to preserve the gullibility of the people by issuing a cold check on a fund of political virtue that does not exist. Communism and 'free-market' capitalism both are modern versions of oligarchy. In their propaganda, both justify violent means by good ends, which always are put beyond reach by the violence of the means. The trick is to define the end vaguely – 'the greatest good of the greatest number' or 'the benefit of the many' – and keep it at a distance. For example, the United States government's agricultural policy, or nonpolicy, since 1952 has merely consented to the farmers' predicament of high costs and low prices; it has never envisioned or advocated in particular the prosperity of farmers or of farmland, but has only promised 'cheap food' to consumers and 'survival' to the 'larger and more efficient' farmers who supposedly could adapt to and endure the attrition of high costs and low prices. And after each inevitable wave of farm failures and the inevitable enlargement of the destitution and degradation of the countryside, there have been the inevitable reassurances from government propagandists and university experts that American agriculture was now more efficient and that everybody would be better off in the future.

The fraudulence of these oligarchic forms of economy is in their principle of displacing whatever good they recognize (as well as their debts) from the present to the future. Their success depends upon persuading people, first, that whatever they have now is no good, and, second, that the promised good is certain to be achieved in the future. This obviously contradicts the principle – common, I believe, to all the religious traditions – that if ever we are going to do good to one another, then the time to do it is now; we are to receive no reward for promising to do it in the future. And both communism and capitalism have found such principles to be a great embarrassment. If you are presently occupied in destroying every good thing in sight in order to do good in the future, it is inconvenient to have people saying things like 'Love thy neighbor as thyself' or 'Sentient beings are numberless, I vow to save them.' Communists and capitalists alike, 'liberal' capitalists and 'conservative' capitalists alike, have needed to replace religion with some form of determinism, so that they can say to their victims, 'I'm doing this because I can't do otherwise. It is not my fault. It is inevitable.' This is a lie, obviously, and religious organizations have too often consented to it.

The idea of an economy based upon several kinds of ruin may seem a contradiction in terms, but in fact such an economy is possible, as we see. It is possible, however, on one implacable condition: the only future good that it assuredly leads to is that it will destroy itself. And how does it disguise this outcome from its subjects, its short-term beneficiaries, and its victims? It does so by false accounting. It substitutes for the real economy, by which we build and maintain (or do not maintain) our household, a symbolic economy of money, which in the long run, because of the self-interested manipulations of the 'controlling interests,' cannot symbolize or account for anything but itself. And so we have before us the spectacle of unprecedented 'prosperity' and 'economic growth' in a land of degraded farms, forests, ecosystems, and watersheds, polluted air, failing families, and perishing communities.

This moral and economic absurdity exists for the sake of the allegedly 'free' market, the single principle of which is this: commodities will be produced wherever they can be produced at the lowest cost and consumed wherever they will bring the highest price. To make too cheap and sell too high has always been the program of industrial capitalism. The global 'free market' is merely capitalism's so far successful attempt to enlarge the geographic scope of its greed, and moreover to give to its greed the status of a 'right' within its presumptive territory. The global 'free market' is free to the corporations precisely because it dissolves the boundaries of the old national colonialisms, and replaces them with a new colonialism without restraints or boundaries. It is pretty much as if all the rabbits have now been forbidden to have holes, thereby 'freeing' the hounds.

The 'right' of a corporation to exercise its economic power without restraint is construed, by the partisans of the 'free market,' as a form of freedom, a political liberty implied presumably by the right of individual citizens to own and use property.

But the 'free market' idea introduces into government a sanction of an inequality that is not implicit in any idea of democratic liberty: namely that the 'free market' is freest to those who have the most money, and is not free at all to those with little or no money. Wal-Mart, for example, as a large corporation 'freely' competing against local, privately owned businesses, has virtually all the freedom, and its small competitors virtually none.

To make too cheap and sell too high, there are two requirements. One is that you must have a lot of consumers with surplus money and unlimited wants. For the time being, there are plenty of these consumers in the 'developed' countries. The problem, for the time being easily solved, is simply to keep them relatively affluent and dependent on purchased supplies.

The other requirement is that the market for labor and raw materials should remain depressed relative to the market for retail commodities. This means that the supply of workers should exceed demand, and that the land-using economies should be allowed or encouraged to overproduce.

To keep the cost of labor low, it is necessary first to entice or force country people everywhere in the world to move into the cities – in the manner prescribed by the Committee for Economic Development after World War II – and, second, to continue to introduce labor-replacing technology. In this way it is possible to maintain a 'pool' of people who are in the threatful position of being mere consumers, landless and poor, and who therefore are eager to go to work for low wages – precisely the condition of migrant farm workers in the United States.

To cause the land-using economies to overproduce is even simpler. The farmers and other workers in the world's land-using economies, by and large, are not organized. They are therefore unable to control production in order to secure just prices. Individual producers must go individually to the market and take for their produce simply whatever they are paid. They have no power to bargain or to make demands. Increasingly, they must sell, not to neighbors or to neighboring towns and cities, but to large and remote corporations. There is no competition among the buyers (supposing there is more than one), who *are* organized and are 'free' to exploit the advantage of low prices. Low prices encourage overproduction, as producers attempt to make up their losses 'on volume,' and overproduction inevitably makes for low prices. The land-using economies thus spiral downward as the money economy of the exploiters spirals upward. If economic attrition in the land-using population becomes so severe as to threaten production, then governments can subsidize production without production controls, which necessarily will encourage overproduction, which will lower prices – and so the subsidy to rural producers becomes, in effect, a subsidy to the purchasing corporations. In the land-using economies, production is further cheapened by destroying, with low prices and low standards of quality, the cultural imperatives for good work and land stewardship.

This sort of exploitation, long familiar in the foreign and domestic colonialism of modern nations, has now become 'the global economy,' which is the property of a few supranational corporations. The economic theory used to justify the global economy in its 'free market' version is, again, perfectly groundless and sentimental. The idea is that what is good for the corporations will sooner or later – though not of course immediately – be good for everybody.

That sentimentality is based, in turn, upon a fantasy: the proposition that the great corporations, in 'freely' competing with one another for raw materials, labor, and market share, will drive each other indefinitely, not only toward greater 'efficiencies' of manufacture, but also toward higher bids for raw materials and labor and lower prices to consumers. As a result, all the world's people will be economically secure – in the future. It would be hard to object to such a proposition if only it were true.

But one knows, in the first place, that 'efficiency' in manufacture always means reducing labor costs by replacing workers with cheaper workers or with machines.

In the second place, the 'law of competition' does *not* imply that many competitors will compete indefinitely. The law of competition is a simple paradox: competition destroys competition. The law of competition implies that many competitors, competing on the 'free market' without restraint, will ultimately and inevitably reduce the number of competitors to one. The law of competition, in short, is the law of war.

In the third place, the global economy is based upon cheap long-distance transportation, without which it is not possible to move goods from the point of cheapest origin to the point of highest sale. And cheap long-distance transportation is the basis of the idea that regions and nations should abandon any measure of economic self-sufficiency in order to specialize in production for export of the few commodities, or the single commodity, that can be most cheaply produced. Whatever may be said for the 'efficiency' of such a system, its result (and, I assume, its purpose) is to destroy local production capacities, local diversity, and local economic independence. It destroys the economic security that it promises to make.

This idea of a global 'free market' economy, despite its obvious moral flaws and its dangerous practical weaknesses, is now the ruling orthodoxy of the age. Its propaganda is subscribed to and distributed by most political leaders, editorial writers, and other 'opinion makers.' The powers that be, while continuing to budget huge sums for 'national defense,' have apparently abandoned any idea of national or local self-sufficiency, even in food. They also have given up the idea that a national or local government might justly place restraints upon economic activity in order to protect its land and its people.

The global economy is now institutionalized in the World Trade Organization, which was set up, without election anywhere, to rule international trade on behalf of the 'free market' – which is to say on behalf of the supranational corporations – and to *over*rule, in secret sessions, any national or regional law that conflicts with the 'free market.' The corporate program of global 'free trade' and the presence of the World Trade Organization have legitimized extreme forms of expert thought. We are told confidently that if Kentucky loses its milk-producing capacity to Wisconsin (and if Wisconsin's is lost to California), that will be a 'success story.' Experts such as Stephen C. Blank, of the University of California, Davis, have recommended that 'developed' countries, such as the United States and the United Kingdom, where food can no longer be produced cheaply enough, should give up agriculture altogether.

The folly at the root of this foolish economy began with the idea that a corporation should be regarded, legally, as 'a person.' But the limitless destructiveness of this economy comes about precisely because a corporation is *not* a person. A corporation, essentially, is a pile of money to which a number of persons have sold their moral allegiance. Unlike a person, a corporation does not age. It does not arrive, as most persons finally do, at a realization of the shortness and smallness of human lives; it does not come to see the future as the lifetime of the children and grandchildren of anybody in particular. It can experience no personal hope or remorse, no change of heart. It cannot humble itself. It goes about its business as if it were immortal, with the single purpose of becoming a bigger pile of money. The stockholders essentially are usurers, people who 'let their money work for them,' expecting high pay in return for causing others to work for low pay. The World Trade Organization enlarges the old idea of the corporation-as-person by giving the global corporate economy the status of a super-government with the power to overrule nations.

I don't mean to say, of course, that all corporate executives and stockholders are bad people. I am only saying that all of them are very seriously implicated in a bad economy.

Unsurprisingly, among people who wish to preserve things other than money – for instance, every region's native capacity to produce essential goods – there is a growing perception that the global 'free market' economy is inherently an enemy to the natural world, to human health and freedom, to industrial workers, and to farmers and others in the land-use economies; and, furthermore, that it is inherently an enemy to good work and good economic practice.

I believe that this perception is correct and that it can be shown to be correct merely by listing the assumptions implicit in the idea that corporations should be 'free' to buy low and sell high in the world at large. These assumptions, so far as I can make them out, are as follows:

1. That there is no conflict between the 'free market' and political freedom, and no connection between political democracy and economic democracy.
2. That there can be no conflict between economic advantage and economic justice.
3. That there is no conflict between greed and ecological or bodily health.
4. That there is no conflict between self-interest and public service.
5. That it is all right for a nation's or a region's subsistence to be foreign-based, dependent on long-distance transport, and entirely controlled by corporations.
6. That the loss or destruction of the capacity anywhere to

produce necessary goods does not matter and involves no cost.

7. That, therefore, wars over commodities – our recent Gulf War, for example – are legitimate and permanent economic functions.

8. That this sort of sanctioned violence is justified also by the predominance of centralized systems of production, supply, communications, and transportation that are extremely vulnerable not only to acts of war between nations, but also to sabotage and terrorism.

9. That it is all right for poor people in poor countries to work at poor wages to produce goods for export to affluent people in rich countries.

10. That there is no danger and no cost in the proliferation of exotic pests, vermin, weeds, and diseases that accompany international trade, and that increase with the volume of trade.

11. That an economy is a machine, of which people are merely the interchangeable parts. One has no choice but to do the work (if any) that the economy prescribes, and to accept the prescribed wage.

12. That, therefore, vocation is a dead issue. One does not do the work that one chooses to do because one is called to it by Heaven or by one's natural abilities, but does instead the work that is determined and imposed by the economy. Any work is all right as long as one gets paid for it. (This assumption explains the prevailing 'liberal' and 'conservative' indifference toward displaced workers, farmers, and small-business people.)

13. That stable and preserving relationships among people, places, and things do not matter and are of no worth.

14. That cultures and religions have no legitimate practical or economic concerns.

These assumptions clearly prefigure a condition of total economy. A total economy is one in which everything – 'life forms,' for instance, or the 'right to pollute' – is 'private property' and has a price and is for sale. In a total economy, significant and sometimes critical choices that once belonged to individuals or communities become the property of corporations. A total economy, operating internationally, necessarily shrinks the powers of state and national governments, not only because those governments have signed over significant powers to an international bureaucracy or because political leaders become the paid hacks of the corporations, but also because political processes – and especially democratic processes – are too slow to react to unrestrained economic and technological development on a global scale. And when state and national governments begin to act in effect as agents of the global economy, selling their people for low wages and their people's products for low prices, then the rights and liberties of citizenship must necessarily shrink. A total economy is an unrestrained taking of profits from the disintegration of nations, communities, households, landscapes, and ecosystems. It licenses symbolic or artificial wealth to 'grow' by means of the destruction of the real wealth of all the world.

Among the many costs of the total economy, the loss of the principle of vocation is probably the most symptomatic and, from a cultural standpoint, the most critical. It is by the replacement of vocation with economic determinism that the exterior workings of a total economy destroy human character and culture also from the inside.

In an essay on the origin of civilization in traditional cultures, Ananda Coomaraswamy wrote that 'the principle of justice is the same throughout . . . [It is] that each member of the community should perform the task for which he is fitted by nature.' The two ideas, justice and vocation, are inseparable. That is why Coomaraswamy spoke of industrialism as 'the mammon of injustice,' incompatible with civilization. It is by way of the practice of vocation that sanctity and reverence enter into the human economy. It was thus possible for traditional cultures to conceive that 'to work is to pray.'

•

Aware of industrialism's potential for destruction, as well as the considerable political danger of great concentrations of wealth and power in industrial corporations, American leaders developed, and for a while used, certain means of limiting and restraining such concentrations, and of somewhat equitably distributing wealth and property. The means were: laws against trusts and monopolies, the principle of collective bargaining, the concept of 100 percent parity between the land-using and the manufacturing economies, and the progressive income tax. And to protect domestic producers and production capacities, it is possible for governments to impose tariffs on cheap imported goods. These means are justified by the government's obligation to protect the lives, livelihoods, and freedoms of its citizens. There is, then, no necessity that requires our government to sacrifice the livelihoods of our small farmers, small-business people, and workers, along with our domestic economic independence, to the global 'free market.' But now all of these means are either weakened or in disuse. The global economy is intended as a means of subverting them.

In default of government protections against the total economy of the supranational corporations, people are where they have been many times before: in danger of losing their economic security and their freedom, both at once. But at the same time the means of defending themselves belongs to them in the form of a venerable principle: powers not exercised by government return to the people. If the government does not propose to protect the lives, the livelihoods, and the freedoms of its people, then the people must think about protecting themselves.

How are they to protect themselves? There seems, really, to be only one way, and that is to develop and put into practice the idea of a local economy – something that growing numbers of people are now doing. For several good reasons, they are beginning with the idea of a local food economy. People are trying to find ways to shorten the distance between producers and consumers, to make the connections between the two more direct, and to make this local economic activity a benefit to the local community. They are trying to learn to use the consumer economies of local towns and cities to preserve the livelihoods of local farm families and farm communities. They want to use the local economy to give consumers an influence over the kind and quality of their food, and to preserve and enhance the local landscapes. They want to give everybody in the local community a direct, long-term interest in the prosperity, health, and beauty of their homeland. This is the only way presently available to make the total economy less total. It was once the only way to make a national or a colonial economy less total, but now the necessity is greater.

I am assuming that there is a valid line of thought leading from the idea of the total economy to the idea of a local economy. I assume that the first thought may be a recognition of one's ignorance and vulnerability as a consumer in the total economy. As such a consumer, one does not know the history of the products one uses. Where, exactly, did they come from? Who produced them? What toxins were used in their production? What were the human and ecological costs of producing and then of disposing of them? One sees that such questions cannot be answered easily, and perhaps not at all. Though one is shopping amid an astonishing variety of products, one is denied certain significant choices. In such a state of economic ignorance it is not possible to choose products that were produced locally or with reasonable kindness toward people and toward nature. Nor is it possible for such consumers to influence production for the better. Consumers who feel a prompting toward land stewardship find that in this economy they can have no stewardly practice. To be a consumer in the total economy, one must agree to be totally ignorant, totally passive, and totally dependent on distant supplies and self-interested suppliers.

And then, perhaps, one begins to *see* from a local point of view. One begins to ask, What is here, what is in my neighborhood, what is in me, that can lead to something better? From a local point of view, one can see that a global 'free market' economy is possible only if nations and localities accept or ignore the inherent weakness of a production economy based on exports and a consumer economy based on imports. An export economy is beyond local influence, and so is an import economy. And cheap long-distance transport is possible only if granted cheap fuel, international peace, control of terrorism, prevention of sabotage, and the solvency of the international economy.

Perhaps also one begins to see the difference between a small local business that must share the fate of the local community and a large absentee corporation that is set up to escape the fate of the local community by ruining the local community.

So far as I can see, the idea of a local economy rests upon only two principles: neighborhood and subsistence.

In a viable neighborhood, neighbors ask themselves what they can do or provide for one another, and they find answers that they and their place can afford. This, and nothing else, is the *practice* of neighborhood. This practice must be, in part, charitable, but it must also be economic, and the economic part must be equitable; there is a significant charity in just prices.

Of course, everything needed locally cannot be produced locally. But a viable neighborhood is a community, and a viable community is made up of neighbors who cherish and protect what they have in common. This is the principle of subsistence. A viable community, like a viable farm, protects its own production capacities. It does not import products that it can produce for itself. And it does not export local products until local needs have been met. The economic products of a viable community are understood either as belonging to the community's subsistence or as surplus, and only the surplus is considered to be marketable abroad. A community, if it is to be viable, cannot think of producing solely for export, and it cannot permit importers to use cheaper labor and goods from other places to destroy the local capacity to produce goods that are needed locally. In charity, moreover, it must refuse to import goods that are produced at the cost of human or ecological degradation elsewhere. This principle of subsistence applies not just to localities, but to regions and nations as well.

The principles of neighborhood and subsistence will be disparaged by the globalists as 'protectionism' – and that is exactly what it is. It is a protectionism that is just and sound, because it protects local producers and is the best assurance of adequate supplies to local consumers. And the idea that local needs should be met first and only surpluses exported does *not* imply any prejudice against charity toward people in other places or trade with them. The principle of neighborhood at home always implies the principle of charity abroad. And the principle of subsistence is in fact the best guarantee of giveable or marketable surpluses. This kind of protection is not 'isolationism.'

Albert Schweitzer, who knew well the economic situation in the colonies of Africa, wrote about seventy years ago: 'Whenever the timber trade is good, permanent famine reigns in the Ogowe region, because the villagers abandon their farms to fell as many trees as possible.' We should notice especially that the goal of production was 'as many . . . as possible.' And Schweitzer made my point exactly: 'These people could achieve true wealth if they could develop their agriculture and trade to meet their own needs.' Instead they produced timber for export to 'the world market,' which made them dependent upon imported goods that they bought with money earned from their exports. They gave up their local means of subsistence, and imposed the false standard of a foreign demand ('as many trees as possible') upon their forests. They thus became helplessly dependent on an economy over which they had no control.

Such was the fate of the native people under the African colonialism of Schweitzer's time. Such is, and can only be, the fate of everybody under the global colonialism of our time. Schweitzer's description of the colonial economy of the Ogowe region is in principle not different from the rural economy in Kentucky or Iowa or Wyoming now. A total economy, for all practical purposes, is a total government. The 'free trade,' which from the standpoint of the corporate economy brings 'unprecedented economic growth,' from the standpoint of the land and its local populations, and ultimately from the standpoint of the cities, is destruction and slavery. Without prosperous local economies, the people have no power and the land no voice.

(2000)

Writer and Region

I first read *Huckleberry Finn* when I was a young boy. My great-grandmother's copy was in the bookcase in my grandparents' living room in Port Royal, Kentucky. It was the Webster edition, with E. W. Kemble's illustrations. My mother may have told me that it was a classic, but I did not *know* that it was, for I had no understanding of that category, and I did not read books because they were classics. I don't remember starting to read *Huckleberry Finn*, or how many times I read it; I can only testify that it is a book that is, to me, literally familiar: involved in my family life.

I can say too that I 'got a lot out of it.' From early in my childhood I was not what was known as a good boy. My badness was that I was headstrong and did not respond positively to institutions. School and Sunday school and church were prisons to me. I loved being out of them, and I did not behave well in them. *Huckleberry Finn* gave me a comforting sense of precedent, and it refined my awareness of the open, outdoor world that my 'badness' tended toward.

That is to say that *Huckleberry Finn* made my boyhood imaginable to me in a way that it otherwise would not have been. And later, it helped to make my grandfather's boyhood in Port Royal imaginable to me. Still later, when I had come to some knowledge of literature and history, I saw that that old green book had, fairly early, made imaginable to me my family's life as inhabitants of the great river system to which we, like Mark Twain, belonged. The world my grandfather had grown up in, in the eighties and nineties, was not greatly changed from the world of Mark Twain's boyhood in the thirties and forties. And the vestiges of that world had not entirely passed away by the time of my own boyhood in the thirties and forties of the next century.

My point is that *Huckleberry Finn* is about a world I know, or knew, which it both taught me about and taught me to imagine. That it did this before I could have known that it was doing so, and certainly before anybody told me to expect it to do so, suggests its greatness to me more forcibly than any critical assessment I have ever read. It is called a great American book; I think of it, because I have so experienced it, as a transfiguring regional book.

As a boy resentful of enclosures, I think I felt immediately the great beauty, the great liberation, at first so fearful to him, of the passage in Chapter 1 when Huck, in a movement that happens over and over in his book, escapes the strictures of the evangelical Miss Watson and, before he even leaves the house, comes into the presence of the country:

> By-and-by they fetched the niggers in and had prayers, and then everybody was off to bed. I went up to my room with a piece of candle and put it on the table. Then I set down in a chair by the window and tried to think of something cheerful, but it warn't no use. I felt so lonesome I most wished I was dead. The stars was shining, and the leaves rustled in the woods ever so mournful; and I heard an owl, away off, who-whooing about somebody that was dead, and a whippoorwill and a dog crying about somebody that was going to die; and the wind was trying to whisper something to me and I couldn't make out what it was, and so it made the cold shivers run over me.

It is a fearful liberation because the country, so recently settled by white people, is already both haunted and threatened. But the liberation is nevertheless authentic, both for Huck and for the place and the people he speaks for. In the building and summoning rhythm of his catalog of the night sounds, in the sudden realization (his and ours) of the equality of his voice to his subject, we feel a young intelligence breaking the confines of convention and expectation to confront the world itself: the night, the woods, and eventually the river and all it would lead to.

By now we can see the kinship, in this respect, between Huck's voice and earlier ones to the east. We feel the same sort of outbreak as we read:

When I wrote the following pages, or rather the bulk of them, I lived alone, in the woods, a mile from any neighbor, in a house which I had built myself, on the shore of Walden Pond, in Concord, Massachusetts, and earned my living by the work of my hands only.

That was thirty years before *Huckleberry Finn*. The voice is certainly more cultivated, more adult, more reticent, but the compulsion to get *out* is the same.

And a year after that we hear:

I loaf and invite my soul,
I lean and loaf at ease . . . observing a spear of summer grass.

And we literally *see* the outbreak here as Whitman's line grows long and prehensile to include the objects and acts of a country's life that had not been included in verse before.

But Huck's voice is both fresher and historically more improbable than those. There is something miraculous about it. It is not Mark Twain's voice. It is the voice, we can only say, of a great genius named Huckleberry Finn, who inhabited a somewhat lesser genius named Mark Twain, who inhabited a frustrated businessman named Samuel Clemens. And Huck speaks of and for and as his place, the gathering place of the continent's inland waters. His is a voice governed always by the need to flow, to move outward.

It seems miraculous also that this voice should have risen suddenly out of the practice of 'comic journalism,' a genre amusing enough sometimes, but extremely limited, now hard to read and impossible to need. It was this way of writing that gave us what I understand as regional*ism*: work that is ostentatiously provincial, condescending, and exploitive. That *Huckleberry Finn* starts from there is evident from its first paragraph. The wonder is that within three pages the genius of the book is fully revealed, and it is a regional genius that for 220 pages (in the Library of America edition) remains untainted by regionalism. The voice is sublimely confident of its own adequacy to its own necessities, its eloquence. Throughout those pages the book never condescends to its characters or its subject; it never glances over its shoulder at literary opinion; it never fears for its reputation in any 'center of culture.' It reposes, like Eliot's Chinese jar, moving and still, at the center of its own occasion.

I should add too that the outbreak or upwelling of this voice, impulsive and freedom-bent as it is, is not disorderly. The freeing of Huck's voice is not a feat of power. The voice is enabled by an economy and a sense of pace that are infallible, and innately formal.

That the book fails toward the end (in the sixty-seven pages, to be exact, that follow the reappearance of Tom Sawyer) is pretty generally acknowledged. It does not fail exactly into the vice that is called regionalism, though its failure may have influenced or licensed the regionalism that followed; rather, it fails into a curious frivolity. It has been all along a story of escape. A runaway slave is an escaper, and Huck is deeply implicated, finally by his deliberate choice, in Jim's escape; but he is making his own escape as well, from Miss Watson's indoor piety. After Tom reenters the story, these authentic escapes culminate in a bogus one: the freeing of a slave who, as Tom knows, has already been freed. It is as though Mark Twain has recovered authorship of the book from Huck Finn at this point – only to discover that he does not know how to write it.

Then occurs the wounding and recovery of Tom and the surprising entrance of his Aunt Polly who, true to her character, clears things up in no time – a delightful scene; there is wonderful writing in the book right through to the end. But Mark Twain is not yet done with his theme of escape. The book ends with Huck's determination to 'light out for the Territory' to escape being adopted and 'sivilized' by Tom's Aunt Sally. And here, I think, we are left face-to-face with a flaw in Mark Twain's character that is also a flaw in our national character, a flaw in our history, and a flaw in much of our literature.

As I have said, Huck's point about Miss Watson is well taken and well made. There is an extremity, an enclosure, of conventional piety and propriety that needs to be escaped, and a part of the business of young people is to escape it. But this point, having been made once, does not need to be made again. In the last sentence, Huck is made to suggest a virtual identity between Miss Watson and Aunt Sally. But the two women are not at all alike. Aunt Sally is a sweet, motherly, entirely affectionate woman, from whom there is little need to escape because she has no aptitude for confinement. The only time she succeeds in confining Huck, she does so by *trusting* him. And so when the book says, 'Aunt Sally she's going to adopt me and sivilize me and I can't stand it. I been there before,' one can only conclude that it is not Huck talking about Aunt Sally, but Mark Twain talking, still, about the oppressive female piety of Miss Watson.

Something is badly awry here. At the end of this great book we are asked to believe – or to believe that Huck believes – that there are no choices between the 'civilization' represented by pious slave owners like Miss Watson or lethal 'gentlemen' like Colonel Sherburn and lighting out for the Territory. This hopeless polarity marks the exit of Mark Twain's highest imagination from his work. Afterwards we get *Pudd'nhead Wilson*, a fine book, but inferior to *Huckleberry Finn*, and then the inconsolable grief, bitterness, and despair of the last years.

It is arguable, I think, that our country's culture is still suspended as if at the end of *Huckleberry Finn*, assuming that its only choices are either a deadly 'civilization' of piety and violence or an escape into some 'Territory' where we may remain free of adulthood and community obligation. We want to be free; we want to have rights; we want to have power; we do not yet want much to do with responsibility. We have imagined the great and estimable freedom of boyhood, of which Huck Finn remains the finest spokesman. We have imagined the bachelorhoods of nature and genius and power: the contemplative, the artist, the hunter, the cowboy, the general, the president – lives dedicated and solitary in the Territory of individuality. But boyhood and bachelorhood have remained our norms of 'liberation,' for women as well as men. We have hardly begun to imagine the coming to responsibility that is the meaning, and the liberation, of growing up. We have hardly begun to imagine community life, and the tragedy that is at the heart of community life.

Mark Twain's avowed preference for boyhood, as the time of truthfulness, is well known. Beyond boyhood, he glimpsed the possibility of bachelorhood, an escape to 'the Territory,' where individual freedom and integrity might be maintained – and so, perhaps, he imagined Pudd'nhead Wilson, a solitary genius devoted to truth and justice, standing apart in the preserve of cynical honesty.

He also imagined Aunt Polly and Aunt Sally. They, I think, are the true grown-ups of the Mississippi novels. They have their faults, of course, which are the faults of their time and place, but mainly they are decent people, responsible members of the community, faithful to duties, capable of love, trust, and long-suffering, willing to care for orphan children. The characters of both women are affectionately drawn; Mark Twain evidently was moved by them. And yet he made no acknowledgment of their worth. He insists on regarding them as dampeners of youthful high spirits, and in the end he refuses to distinguish them at all from the objectionable Miss Watson.

There is, then, something stunted in *Huckleberry Finn*. I have hated to think so – for a long time I tried consciously *not* to think so – but it is so. What is stunted is the growth of Huck's character. When Mark Twain replaces Huck as author, he does so apparently to make sure that Huck remains a boy. Huck's growing up, which through the crisis of his fidelity to Jim ('All right, then, I'll *go* to hell') has been central to the drama of the book, is suddenly thwarted first by the Tom-foolery of Jim's 'evasion' and then by Huck's planned escape to the 'Territory.' The real 'evasion' of the last chapters is Huck's, or Mark Twain's, evasion of the community responsibility that would have been a natural and expectable next step after his declaration of loyalty to his friend. Mark Twain's failure or inability to imagine this possibility was a disaster for his finest character, Huck, whom we next see not as a grown man, but as partner in another boyish evasion, a fantastical balloon excursion to the Pyramids.

•

I am supposing, then, that *Huckleberry Finn* fails in failing to imagine a responsible, adult community life. And I am supposing further that this is the failure of Mark Twain's life, and of our life, so far, as a society.

Community life, as I suggested earlier, is tragic, and it is so because it involves unremittingly the need to survive mortality, partiality, and evil. Because Huck Finn and Mark Twain so clung to boyhood, and to the boy's vision of free bachelorhood, neither could enter community life as I am attempting to understand it. A boy can experience grief and horror, but he cannot experience that fulfillment and catharsis of grief, fear, and pity that we call tragedy and still remain a boy. Nor can he experience tragedy in solitude or as a stranger, for tragedy is experienceable only in the context of a beloved community. The fulfillment and catharsis that Aristotle described as the communal result of tragic drama is an artificial enactment of the way a mature community survives tragedy in fact. The community wisdom of tragic drama is in the implicit understanding that no community can survive that cannot survive the worst. Tragic drama attests to the community's need to survive the worst that it knows, or imagines, can happen.

In his own life, Mark Twain experienced deep grief over the deaths of loved ones, and also severe financial losses. But these experiences seem to have had the effect of isolating him, rather than binding him to a community. Great personal loss, moreover, is not much dealt with in those Mississippi books that are most native to his imagination: *Tom Sawyer*, *Huckleberry Finn*, and *Life on the Mississippi*. The only such event that I remember in those books is the story, in *Life on the Mississippi*, of his brother Henry's death after an explosion on the steamboat *Pennsylvania*. Twain's account of this is extremely moving, but it is peculiar in that he represents himself – though his mother, a brother, and a sister still lived – as Henry's *only* mourner. No other family member is mentioned.

What is wanting, apparently, is the tragic imagination that, through communal form or ceremony, permits great loss to be recognized, suffered, and borne, and that makes possible some sort of consolation and renewal. What is wanting is the return to the beloved community, or to the possibility of one. That would return us to a renewed and corrected awareness of our partiality and mortality, but also to healing and to joy in a renewed awareness of our love and hope for one another. Without that return we may know innocence and horror and grief, but not tragedy and joy, not consolation or forgiveness or redemption. There is grief and horror in Mark Twain's life and work, but not the tragic imagination or the imagined tragedy that finally delivers from grief and horror.

He seems instead to have gone deeper and deeper into grief and horror as his losses accumulated, and deeper into outrage as he continued to meditate on the injustices and cruelties of history. At the same time he withdrew further and further from community and the imagining of community, until at last his Hadleyburg – such a village as he had earlier written about critically enough, but with sympathy and good humor too – is used merely as a target. It receives an anonymous and indiscriminate retribution for its greed and self-righteousness – evils that community life has always had to oppose, correct, ignore, indulge, or forgive in order to survive. All observers of communities have been aware of such evils, Huck Finn having been one of the acutest of them, but now it is as if Huck has been replaced by Colonel Sherburn. 'The Man that Corrupted Hadleyburg' is based on the devastating assumption that people are no better than their faults. In old age, Mark Twain had become obsessed with 'the damned human race' and the malevolence of God – ideas that were severely isolating and, ultimately, self-indulgent. He was finally incapable of that magnanimity that is the most difficult and the most necessary: forgiveness of human nature and human circumstance. Given human nature and human circumstance, our only relief is in this forgiveness, which then restores us to community and its ancient cycle of loss and grief, hope and joy.

And so it seems to me that Mark Twain's example remains crucial for us, for both its virtues and its faults. He taught American writers to be writers by teaching them to be *regional* writers. The great gift of *Huckleberry Finn*, in itself and to us, is its ability to be regional without being provincial. The provincial is always self-conscious. It is the conscious sentimentalization of or condescension to or apology for a province, what I earlier called regionalism. At its most acute, it is the fear of provinciality. There is, as I said, none of that in the first thirty-two chapters of *Huckleberry Finn*. (In the final eleven chapters it is there in the person of Tom Sawyer, who is a self-made provincial.) Mark Twain apparently knew, or he had the grace to trust Huck to know, that *every* writer is a regional writer, even those who write about a fashionable region such as New York City. The value of this insight, embodied as it is in a great voice and a great tale, is simply unreckonable. If he had done nothing else, that would have made him indispensable to us.

But his faults are our own, just as much as his virtues. There are two chief faults and they are related: the yen to escape to the Territory, and retribution against the life that one has escaped or wishes to escape. Mark Twain was new, for his place, in his virtue. In his faults he was old, a spokesman for tendencies already long established in our history.

That these tendencies remain well established among us ought to be clear enough. Wallace Stegner had them in mind when he wrote in *The Sound of Mountain Water*:

> For many, the whole process of intellectual and literary growth is
> a movement, not through or beyond, but away from the people
> and society they know best, the faiths they still at bottom accept,
> the little raw provincial world for which they keep an apologetic
> affection.

Mr. Stegner's 'away from' indicates, of course, an escape to the Territory – and there are many kinds of Territory to escape to. The Territory that hinterland writers have escaped to has almost always been first of all that of some metropolis or 'center of culture.' This is not inevitably dangerous; great cities are probably necessary to the life of the arts, and all of us who have gone to them have benefited. But once one has reached the city, other Territories open up, and some of these *are* dangerous. There is, first, the Territory of retribution against one's origins. In our country, this is not just a Territory, but virtually a literary genre. From the sophisticated, cosmopolitan city, one's old home begins to look like a 'little raw provincial world.' One begins to deplore 'small town gossip' and 'the suffocating proprieties of small town life' – forgetting that gossip occurs only among people who know one another and that propriety is a dead issue only among strangers. The danger is not just in the falsification, the false generalization, that necessarily attends a *distant* scorn or anger, but also in the loss of the subject or the vision of community life and in the very questionable exemption that scorners and avengers customarily issue to themselves.

And so there is the Territory of self-righteousness. It is easy to assume that we do not participate in what we are not in the presence of. But if we are members of a society, we participate, willy-nilly, in its evils. Not to know this is obviously to be in error, but it is also to neglect some of the most necessary and the most interesting work. How do we reduce our dependency on what is wrong? The answer to that question will necessarily be practical; the wrong will be correctable by practice and by practical standards. Another name for self-righteousness is economic and political unconsciousness.

There is also the Territory of historical self-righteousness: if *we* had lived south of the Ohio in 1830, *we* would not have owned slaves; if *we* had lived on the frontier, *we* would have killed no Indians, violated no treaties, stolen no land. The probability is overwhelming that if we had belonged to the generations we deplore, we too would have behaved deplorably. The probability is overwhelming that we *belong* to a generation that will be found by its successors to have behaved deplorably. Not to know that is, again, to be in error and to neglect essential work, and some of this work, as before, is work of the imagination. How can we imagine our situation or our history if we think we are superior to it?

Then there is the Territory of despair, where it is assumed that what is objectionable is 'inevitable,' and so again the essential work is neglected. How can we have something better if we do not imagine it? How can we imagine it if we do not hope for it? How can we hope for it if we do not attempt to realize it?

There is the Territory of the national or the global point of view, in which one does not pay attention to anything in particular.

Akin to that is the Territory of abstraction, a regionalism of the mind. This Territory originally belonged to philosophers, mathematicians, economists, tank thinkers, and the like, but now some claims are being staked out in it for literature. At a meeting in honor of *The Southern Review*, held in the fall of 1985 at Baton Rouge, one of the needs identified, according to an article in the *New York Times Book Review*,* was 'to redefine Southernness without resort to geography.' If the participants all agreed on any one thing, the article concluded,

> it is perhaps that accepted definitions of regionalism have been unnecessarily self-limiting up to now. The gradual disappearance of the traditional, material South does not mean that Southernness is disappearing, any more than blackness is threatened by integration, or sacredness by secularization. If anything, these metaregions . . . , based as they are upon values, achieve distinction in direct proportion to the homogenization of the physical world. By coming to terms with a concept of regionalism that is no longer based on geographical or material considerations, *The Southern Review* is sidestepping those forces that would organize the world around an unnatural consensus.

Parts of that statement are not comprehensible. Blackness, I would think, *would* be threatened by integration, and sacredness by secularization. Dilution, at least, is certainly implied in both instances. We might as well say that fire is a state of mind and thus is not threatened by water. And how might blackness and sacredness, which have never been regions, be 'metaregions'? And is the natural world subject to limitless homogenization? There are, after all, southern species of plants and animals that will not thrive in the north, and vice versa.

---

* Mark K. Stengel, 'Modernism on the Mississippi: *The Southern Review* 1935–85,' *New York Times Book Review*, November 24, 1985, pp. 3, 35.

This 'metaregion,' this region 'without resort to geography,' is a map without a territory, which is to say a map impossible to correct, a map subject to become fantastical and silly like that Southern chivalry-of-the-mind that Mark Twain so properly condemned. How this 'metaregion' could resist homogenization and 'unnatural consensus' is not clear. At any rate, it abandons the real region to the homogenizers: You just homogenize all you want to, and we will sit here being Southern in our minds.

Similar to the Territory of abstraction is the Territory of artistic primacy or autonomy, in which it is assumed that no value is inherent in subjects but that value is conferred upon subjects by the art and the attention of the artist. The subjects of the world are only 'raw material.' As William Matthews writes in a recent article,* 'A poet beginning to make something needs raw material, something to transform.' For Marianne Moore, he says,

> subject matter is not in itself important, except that it gives her the opportunity to speak about something that engages her passions. What is important instead is what she can discover to say.

And he concludes:

> It is not, of course, the subject that is or isn't dull, but the quality of attention we do or do not pay to it, and the strength of our will to transform. Dull subjects are those we have failed.

This assumes that for the animals and humans who are not fine artists, who have discovered nothing to say, the world is dull, which is not true. It assumes also that attention is of interest in itself, which is not true either. In fact, attention is of value only insofar as it is paid in the proper discharge of an obligation. To pay attention is to come into the presence of a subject. In one of its root senses, it is to 'stretch toward' a subject, in a kind of aspiration. We speak of 'paying

---

* 'Dull Subjects,' *New England Review and Bread Loaf Quarterly*, Winter 1985, pp. 142–52.

attention' because of a correct perception that attention is *owed* – that without our attention and our attending, our subjects, including ourselves, are endangered.

Mr. Matthews's trivializing of subjects in the interest of poetry industrializes the art. He is talking about an art oriented exclusively to production, like coal mining. Like an industrial entrepreneur, he regards the places and creatures and experiences of the world as 'raw material,' valueless until exploited.

The test of imagination, ultimately, is not the territory of art or the territory of the mind, but the territory underfoot. That is not to say that there is no territory of art or of the mind, only that it is not a separate territory. It is not exempt either from the principles above it or from the country below it. It is a territory, then, that is subject to correction – by, among other things, paying attention. To remove it from the possibility of correction is finally to destroy art and thought, and the territory underfoot as well.

Memory, for instance, must be a pattern upon the actual country, not a cluster of relics in a museum or a written history. What Barry Lopez speaks of as a sort of invisible landscape of communal association and usage must serve the visible as a guide and as a protector; the visible landscape must verify and correct the invisible. Alone, the invisible landscape becomes false, sentimental, and useless, just as the visible landscape, alone, becomes a strange land, threatening to humans and vulnerable to human abuse.

To assume that the context of literature is 'the literary world' is, I believe, simply wrong. That its real habitat is the household and the community – that it can and does affect, even in practical ways, the life of a place – may not be recognized by most theorists and critics for a while yet. But they will finally come to it, because finally they will have to. And when they do, they will renew the study of literature and restore it to importance.

Emerson in 'The American Scholar,' worrying about the increasing specialization of human enterprises, thought that the individual, to be whole, 'must sometimes return from his own labor to embrace all the other laborers' – a solution that he acknowledged to be impossible. The result, he saw, was that 'man is thus metamorphosed into a thing, into many things.' The solution that he apparently did think possible was a return out of specialization and separateness to the human definition, so that a thinker or scholar would not be a 'mere thinker,' a thinking specialist, but 'Man Thinking.' But this return is not meant to be a retreat into abstraction, for Emerson understood 'Man Thinking' as a thinker committed to action: 'Action is with the scholar subordinate, but it is essential. Without it, he is not yet man.'

And action, of course, implies place and community. There can be disembodied thought, but not disembodied action. Action – embodied thought – requires local and communal reference. To act, in short, is to live. Living 'is a total act. Thinking is a partial act.' And one does not live alone. Living is a communal act, whether or not its communality is acknowledged. And so Emerson writes:

> I grasp the hands of those next me, and take my place in the ring
> to suffer and to work, taught by an instinct, that so shall the dumb
> abyss be vocal with speech.

Emerson's spiritual heroism can sometimes be questionable or tiresome, but he can also write splendidly accurate, exacting sentences, and that is one of them. We see how it legislates against what we now call 'groupiness.' Neighborhood is a given condition, not a contrived one; he is not talking about a 'planned community' or a 'network', but about the necessary interdependence of those who are 'next' each other. We see how it invokes dance, acting in concert, as a metaphor of almost limitless reference. We see how the phrase 'to suffer and to work' refuses sentimentalization. We see how common work, common suffering, and a common willingness to join and belong are understood as the conditions that make speech possible in 'the dumb abyss' in which we are divided.

This leads us, probably, to as good a definition of the beloved community as we can hope for: common experience and common effort on a common ground to which one willingly belongs. The life of such a community has been very little regarded in American literature. Our writers have been much more concerned with the individual who is misunderstood or mistreated by a community that is in no sense beloved, as in *The Scarlet Letter*. From Thoreau to Hemingway and his successors, a great deal of sympathy and interest has been given to the individual as pariah or gadfly or exile. In Faulkner, a community is the subject, but it is a community disintegrating, as it was doomed to do by the original sins of land greed, violent honor, and slavery. There are in Faulkner some characters who keep alive the hope of community, or at least the fundamental decencies on which community depends, and in Faulkner, as in Mark Twain, these are chiefly women: Dilsey, Lena Grove, the properly outraged Mrs. Littlejohn.

The one American book I know that is about a beloved community – a settled, established white American community with a sustaining common culture, and mostly beneficent toward both its members and its place – is Sarah Orne Jewett's *The Country of the Pointed Firs*. The community that the book describes, the coastal village of Dunnet, Maine, and the neighboring islands and back country, is an endangered species on the book's own evidence: many of its characters are old and childless, without heirs or successors – and with the Twentieth Century ahead of it, it could not last. But though we see it in its last days, we see it whole.

We see it whole, I think, because we see it both in its time and in its timelessness. The centerpiece of the book, the Bowden family reunion, is described in the particularity of a present act, but it is perceived also – as such an event must be – as a reenactment; to see is to remember:

There was a wide path mowed for us across the field, and, as we moved along, the birds flew up out of the thick second crop of clover, and the bees hummed as if it still were June. There was a flashing of white gulls over the water where the fleet of boats rode the low waves together in the cove, swaying their small masts as if they kept time to our steps. The plash of the water could be heard faintly, yet still be heard; we might have been a company of ancient Greeks.

Thus, though it precisely renders its place and time, the book never subsides into the flimsy contemporaneity of 'local color.' The narrator of the book is one who departs and returns, and her returns are homecomings – to herself as well as to the place:

> The first salt wind from the east, the first sight of a lighthouse set boldly on its outer rock, the flash of a gull, the waiting procession of seaward-bound firs on an island, made me feel solid and definite again, instead of a poor incoherent being. Life was resumed, and anxious living blew away as if it had not been. I could not breathe deep enough or long enough. It was a return to happiness.

Anyone acquainted with the sentimentalities of American regionalism will look on that word 'happiness' with suspicion. But here it is not sentimental, for the work and suffering of the community are fully faced and acknowledged. The narrator's return is not to an idyll of the boondocks; it is a reentrance into Emerson's 'ring.' The community is happy in that it has survived its remembered tragedies, has re-shaped itself coherently around its known losses, has included kindly its eccentrics, invalids, oddities, and even its one would-be exile. The wonderful heroine of the book, and its emblem, Mrs. Elmira Todd, a childless widow, who in her youth 'had loved one who was far above her,' is a healer – a grower, gatherer, and dispenser of medicinal herbs.

She is also a dispenser of intelligent talk about her kinfolk and neighbors. More than any book I know, this one makes its way by conversation, engrossing exchanges of talk in which Mrs. Todd and many others reveal to the narrator their life and history and geography. And perhaps the great cultural insight of the book is stated by Mrs. Todd:

Conversation's got to have some root in the past, or else you've got to explain every remark you make, an' it wears a person out.

The conversation wells up out of memory, and in a sense *is* the community, the presence of its past and its hope, speaking in the dumb abyss.

(1987)

Damage

1

I have a steep wooded hillside that I wanted to be able to pasture occasionally, but it had no permanent water supply.

About halfway to the top of the slope there is a narrow bench, on which I thought I could make a small pond. I hired a man with a bulldozer to dig one. He cleared away the trees and then formed the pond, cutting into the hill on the upper side, piling the loosened dirt in a curving earthwork on the lower.

The pond appeared to be a success. Before the bulldozer quit work, water had already begun to seep in. Soon there was enough to support a few head of stock. To heal the exposed ground, I fertilized it and sowed it with grass and clover.

We had an extremely wet fall and winter, with the usual freezing and thawing. The ground grew heavy with water, and soft. The earthwork slumped; a large slice of the woods floor on the upper side slipped down into the pond.

The trouble was the familiar one: too much power, too little knowledge. The fault was mine.

I *was* careful to get expert advice. But this only exemplifies what I already knew. No expert knows everything about every place, not even everything about any place. If one's knowledge of one's whereabouts is insufficient, if one's judgment is unsound, then expert advice is of little use.

2

In general, I have used my farm carefully. It could be said, I think, that I have improved it more than I have damaged it.

My aim has been to go against its history and to repair the damage of other people. But now a part of its damage is my own.

The pond was a modest piece of work, and so the damage is not extensive. In the course of time and nature it will heal.

And yet there *is* damage – to my place, and to me. I have carried out, before my own eyes and against my intention, a part of the modern tragedy: I have made a lasting flaw in the face of the earth, for no lasting good.

Until that wound in the hillside, my place, is healed, there will be something impaired in my mind. My peace is damaged. I will not be able to forget it.

3

It used to be that I could think of art as a refuge from such troubles. From the imperfections of life, one could take refuge in the perfections of art. One could read a good poem – or better, write one.

Art was what was truly permanent, therefore what truly mattered. The rest was 'but a spume that plays / Upon a ghostly paradigm of things.'

I am no longer able to think that way. That is because I now live in my subject. My subject is my place in the world, and I live in my place.

There is a sense in which I no longer 'go to work.' If I live in my place, which is my subject, then I am 'at' my work even when I am not working. It is 'my' work because I cannot escape it.

If I live in my subject, then writing about it cannot 'free' me of it or 'get it out of my system.' When I am finished writing, I can only return to what I have been writing about.

While I have been writing about it, time will have changed it. Over longer stretches of time, *I* will change it. Ultimately, it will be changed by what I write, inasmuch as I, who change my subject, am changed by what I write about it.

If I have damaged my subject, then I have damaged my art. What aspired to be whole has met damage face to face, and has come away wounded. And so it loses interest both in the anesthetic and in the purely aesthetic.

It accepts the clarification of pain, and concerns itself with healing. It cultivates the scar that is the course of time and nature over damage: the landmark and mindmark that is the notation of a limit.

To lose the scar of knowledge is to renew the wound.

An art that heals and protects its subject is a geography of scars.

4

'You never know what is enough unless you know what is more than enough.'

I used to think of Blake's sentence as a justification of youthful excess. By now I know that it describes the peculiar condemnation of our species. When the road of excess has reached the palace of wisdom it is a healed wound, a long scar.

Culture preserves the map and the records of past journeys so that no generation will permanently destroy the route.

The more local and settled the culture, the better it stays put, the less the damage. It is the foreigner whose road of excess leads to a desert.

Blake gives the just proportion or control in another proverb: 'No bird soars too high, if he soars with his own wings.' Only when our acts are empowered with more than bodily strength do we need to think of limits.

It was no thought or word that called culture into being, but a tool or a weapon. After the stone axe we needed song and story to remember innocence, to record effect – and so to describe the limits, to say what can be done without damage.

The use only of our bodies for work or love or pleasure, or even for combat, sets us free again in the wilderness, and we exult.

But a man with a machine and inadequate culture – such as I was when I made my pond – is a pestilence. He shakes more than he can hold.

(1974)

The Work of Local Culture

For many years, my walks have taken me down an old fencerow in a wooded hollow on what was once my grandfather's farm. A battered galvanized bucket is hanging on a fence post near the head of the hollow, and I never go by it without stopping to look inside. For what is going on in that bucket is the most momentous thing I know, the greatest miracle that I have ever heard of: it is making earth. The old bucket has hung there through many autumns, and the leaves have fallen around it and some have fallen into it. Rain and snow have fallen into it, and the fallen leaves have held the moisture and so have rotted. Nuts have fallen into it, or been carried into it by squirrels; mice and squirrels have eaten the meat of the nuts and left the shells; they and other animals have left their droppings; insects have flown into the bucket and died and decayed; birds have scratched in it and left their droppings or perhaps a feather or two. This slow work of growth and death, gravity and decay, which is the chief work of the world, has by now produced in the bottom of the bucket several inches of black humus. I look into that bucket with fascination because I am a farmer of sorts and an artist of sorts, and I recognize there an artistry and a farming far superior to mine, or to that of any human. I have seen the same process at work on the tops of boulders in a forest, and it has been at work immemorially over most of the land surface of the world. All creatures die into it, and they live by it.

The old bucket started out a far better one than you can buy now. I think it has been hanging on that post for something like fifty years. I think so because I remember hearing, when I was just a small boy, a story about a bucket that must have been this one. Several of my grandfather's black hired hands went out on an early spring day to burn a tobacco plant bed, and they took along some eggs to boil to eat with their dinner. When dinner time came and they looked around for something to boil the eggs in, they could find only an old bucket that at one time had been filled with tar. The boiling water softened the residue of tar, and one of the eggs came out of the water black. The hands made much sport of seeing who would have to eat the black egg, welcoming their laughter in the midst of their day's work. The man who had to eat the black egg was Floyd Scott, whom I remember well. Dry scales of tar still adhere to the inside of the bucket.

However small a landmark the old bucket is, it is not trivial. It is one of the signs by which I know my country and myself. And to me it is irresistibly suggestive in the way it collects leaves and other woodland sheddings as they fall through time. It collects stories, too, as they fall through time. It is irresistibly metaphorical. It is doing in a passive way what a human community must do actively and thoughtfully. A human community, too, must collect leaves and stories, and turn them to account. It must build soil, and build that memory of itself – in lore and story and song – that will be its culture. These two kinds of accumulation, of local soil and local culture, are intimately related.

In the woods, the bucket is no metaphor; it simply reveals what is always happening in the woods, if the woods is let alone. Of course, in most places in my part of the country, the human community did not leave the woods alone. It felled the trees and replaced them with pastures and crops. But this did not revoke the law of the woods, which is that the ground must be protected by a cover of vegetation and that the growth of the years must return – or be returned – to the ground to rot and build soil. A good local culture, in one of its most important functions, is a collection of the memories, ways, and skills necessary for the observance, within the bounds of domesticity, of this natural law. If the local culture cannot preserve and improve the local soil, then, as both reason and history inform us, the local community will decay and perish, and the work of soil building will be resumed by nature.

A human community, then, if it is to last long, must exert a sort of centripetal force, holding local soil and local memory in place.

Practically speaking, human society has no work more important than this. Once we have acknowledged this principle, we can only be alarmed at the extent to which it has been ignored. For although our present society does generate a centripetal force of great power, this is not a local force, but one centered almost exclusively in our great commercial and industrial cities, which have drawn irresistibly into themselves both the products of the countryside and the people and talents of the country communities.

There is, as one assumes there must be, a countervailing or centrifugal force that also operates in our society, but this returns to the countryside not the residue of the land's growth to refertilize the fields, not the learning and experience of the greater world ready to go to work locally, and not – or not often – even a just monetary compensation. What are returned, instead, are overpriced manufactured goods, pollution in various forms, and garbage. A landfill on the edge of my own rural county in Kentucky, for example, daily receives about eighty truckloads of garbage. Fifty to sixty of these loads come from cities in New York, New Jersey, and Pennsylvania. Thus, the end result of the phenomenal modern productivity of the countryside is a debased countryside, which becomes daily less pleasant, and which will inevitably become less productive.

The cities, which have imposed this inversion of forces on the country, have been unable to preserve themselves from it. The typical modern city is surrounded by a circle of affluent suburbs, eating its way outward, like ringworm, leaving the so-called inner city desolate, filthy, ugly, and dangerous.

My walks in the hills and hollows around my home have inevitably produced in my mind the awareness that I live in a diminished country. The country has been and is being reduced by the great centralizing process that is our national economy. As I walk, I am always reminded of the slow, patient building of soil in the woods. And I am reminded of the events and companions of my life – for my walks, after so long, are cultural events. But under the trees and in the fields I see also the gullies and scars, healed or healing or fresh, left by careless logging and bad farming. I see the crumbling stone walls and the wire fences that have been rusting out ever since the 1930s. In the returning woods growth of the hollows, I see the sagging and the fallen barns, the empty and ruining houses, the houseless chimneys and foundations. As I look at this evidence of human life poorly founded, played out, and gone, I try to recover some understanding, some vision, of what this country was at the beginning: the great oaks and beeches and hickories, walnuts and maples, lindens and ashes, tulip poplars, standing in beauty and dignity now unimaginable, the black soil of their making, also no longer imaginable, lying deep at their feet – an incalculable birthright sold for money, most of which we did not receive. Most of the money made on the products of this place has gone to fill the pockets of people in distant cities who did not produce the products.

If my walks take me along the roads and streams, I see also the trash and the junk, carelessly manufactured and carelessly thrown away, the glass and the broken glass and the plastic and the aluminum that will lie here longer than the lifetime of trees – longer than the lifetime of our species, perhaps. And I know that this also is what we have to show for our participation in the American economy, for most of the money made on these things too has been made elsewhere.

It would be somewhat more pleasant for country people if they could blame all this on city people. But the old opposition of country versus city – though still true, and truer than ever economically, for the country is more than ever the colony of the city – is far too simple to explain our problem. For country people more and more live like city people, and so connive in their own ruin. More and more country people, like city people, allow their economic and social standards to be set by television and salesmen and outside experts. Our garbage mingles with New Jersey garbage in our local landfill, and it would be hard to tell which is which.

As local community decays along with local economy, a vast amnesia settles over the countryside. As the exposed and disregarded soil departs with the rains, so local knowledge and local memory move away to the cities or are forgotten under the influence of homogenized sales talk, entertainment, and education. This loss of local knowledge and local memory – that is, of local culture – has been ignored, or written off as one of the cheaper 'prices of progress,' or made the business of folklorists. Nevertheless, local culture has a value, and part of its value is economic. This can be demonstrated readily enough.

For example, when a community loses its memory, its members no longer know one another. How can they know one another if they have forgotten or have never learned one another's stories? If they do not know one another's stories, how can they know whether or not to trust one another? People who do not trust one another do not help one another, and moreover they fear one another. And this is our predicament now. Because of a general distrust and suspicion, we not only lose one another's help and companionship, but we are all now living in jeopardy of being sued.

We don't trust our 'public servants' because we know that they don't respect us. They don't respect us, as we understand, because they don't know us; they don't know our stories. They expect us to sue them if they make mistakes, and so they must insure themselves, at great expense to them and to us. Doctors in a country community must send their patients to specialists in the city, not necessarily because they believe that they are wrong in their diagnoses, but because they know that they are not infallible and they must protect themselves against lawsuits, at great expense to us.

The government of my home county, which has a population of about ten thousand people, pays an annual liability insurance premium of about $34,000. Add to this the liability premiums that are paid by every professional person who is 'at risk' in the county, and you get some idea of the load we are carrying. Several decent family livelihoods are annually paid out of the county to insurance companies for a service that is only negative and provisional.

All of this money is lost to us by the failure of community. A good community, as we know, insures itself by trust, by good faith and good will, by mutual help. A good community, in other words, is a good local economy. It depends on itself for many of its essential needs and is thus shaped, so to speak, from the inside – unlike most modern populations that depend on distant purchases for almost everything and are thus shaped from the outside by the purposes and the influence of salesmen.

I was walking one Sunday afternoon several years ago with an older friend. We went by the ruining log house that had belonged to his grandparents and great-grandparents. The house stirred my friend's memory, and he told how the oldtime people used to visit each other in the evenings, especially in the long evenings of winter. There used to be a sort of institution in our part of the country known as 'sitting till bedtime.' After supper, when they weren't too tired, neighbors would walk across the fields to visit each other. They popped corn, my friend said, and ate apples and talked. They told each other stories. They told each other stories, as I knew myself, that they all had heard before. Sometimes they told stories about each other, about themselves, living again in their own memories and thus keeping their memories alive. Among the hearers of these stories were always the children. When bedtime came, the visitors lit their lanterns and went home. My friend talked about this, and thought about it, and then he said, 'They had everything but money.'

They were poor, as country people have often been, but they had each other, they had their local economy in which they helped each other, they had each other's comfort when they needed it, and they had their stories, their history together in that place. To have everything but money is to have much. And most people of the present can only marvel to think of neighbors entertaining themselves for a whole evening without a single imported pleasure and without listening to a single minute of sales talk.

Most of the descendants of those people have now moved away, partly because of the cultural and economic failures that I mentioned earlier, and most of them no longer sit in the evenings and talk to anyone. Most of them now sit until bedtime watching TV, submitting every few minutes to a sales talk. The message of both the TV programs and the sales talks is that the watchers should spend whatever is necessary to be like everybody else.

By television and other public means, we are encouraged to believe that we are far advanced beyond sitting till bedtime with the neighbors on a Kentucky ridgetop, and indeed beyond anything we ever were before. But if, for example, there should occur a forty-eight-hour power failure, we would find ourselves in much more backward circumstances than our ancestors. What, for starters, would we do for entertainment? Tell each other stories? But most of us no longer talk with each other, much less tell each other stories. We tell our stories now mostly to doctors or lawyers or psychiatrists or insurance adjusters or the police, not to our neighbors for their (and our) entertainment. The stories that now entertain us are made up for us in New York or Los Angeles or other centers of such commerce.

But a forty-eight-hour power failure would involve almost unimaginable deprivations. It would be difficult to travel, especially in cities. Most of the essential work could not be done. Our windowless modern schools and other such buildings that depend on air conditioning could not be used. Refrigeration would be impossible; food would spoil. It would be difficult or impossible to prepare meals. If it was winter, heating systems would fail. At the end of forty-eight hours many of us would be hungry.

Such a calamity (and it is a modest one among those that our time has made possible) would thus reveal how far most of us are now living from our cultural and economic sources, and how extensively we have destroyed the foundations of local life. It would show us how far we have strayed from the locally centered life of such neighborhoods as the one my friend described – a life based to a considerable extent on what we now call solar energy, which is decentralized, democratic, clean, and free. If we note that much of the difference we are talking about can be accounted for as an increasing dependence on energy sources that are centralized, undemocratic, filthy, and expensive, we will have completed a sort of historical parable.

How has this happened? There are many reasons for it. One of the chief reasons is that everywhere in our country the local succession of the generations has been broken. We can trace this change through a series of stories that we may think of as cultural landmarks.

Throughout most of our literature, the normal thing was for the generations to succeed one another in place. The memorable stories occurred when this succession failed or became difficult or was somehow threatened. The norm is given in Psalm 128, in which this succession is seen as one of the rewards of righteousness: 'Thou shalt see thy children's children, and peace upon Israel.'

The longing for this result seems to have been universal. It presides also over *The Odyssey*, in which Odysseus' desire to return home is certainly regarded as normal. And this story is also much concerned with the psychology of family succession. Telemachus, Odysseus' son, comes of age in preparing for the return of his long-absent father; and it seems almost that Odysseus is enabled to return home by his son's achievement of enough manhood to go in search of him. Long after the return of both father and son, Odysseus' life will complete itself, as we know from Teiresias' prophecy in Book XI, much in the spirit of Psalm 128:

> A seaborne death
> soft as this hand of mist will come upon you
> when you are wearied out with sick old age,
> your country folk in blessed peace around you.

The Bible makes much of what it sees as the normal succession, in such stories as those of Abraham, Isaac, and Jacob, or of David and Solomon, in which the son completes the work or the destiny of the father. The parable of the prodigal son is prepared for by such Old Testament stories as that of Jacob, who errs, wanders, returns, is forgiven, and takes his place in the family lineage.

Shakespeare was concerned throughout his working life with the theme of the separation and rejoining of parents and children. It is there at the beginning in *The Comedy of Errors*, and he is still thinking about it when he gets to *King Lear* and *Pericles* and *The Tempest*. When Lear walks onstage with Cordelia dead in his arms, the theme of return is fulfilled, only this time in the way of tragedy.

Wordsworth's poem 'Michael,' written in 1800, is in the same line of descent. It is the story of a prodigal son, and return is still understood as the norm; before the boy's departure, he and his father make a 'covenant' that he will return home and carry on his father's life as a shepherd on their ancestral pastures. But the ancient theme here has two significant differences: the son leaves home for an economic reason, and he does not return. Old Michael, the father, was long ago 'bound / In surety for his brother's son.' This nephew has failed in his business, and Michael is 'summoned to discharge the forfeiture.' Rather than do this by selling a portion of their patrimony, the aged parents decide that they must send their son to work for another kinsman in the city in order to earn the necessary money. The country people all are poor; there is no money to be earned at home. When the son has cleared the debt from the land, he will return to it to 'possess it, free as the wind / That passes over it.' But the son goes to the city, is corrupted by it, eventually commits a crime, and is forced 'to seek a hiding place beyond the seas.'

'Michael' is a sort of cultural watershed. It carries on the theme of return that goes back to the beginnings of Western culture, but that return now is only a desire and a memory; in the poem it fails to happen. Because of that failure, we see in 'Michael' not just a local story of the Lake District of England, which it is, but the story of rural families in the industrial nations from Wordsworth's time until today. The children go to the cities, for reasons imposed by the external economy, and they do not return; eventually the parents die and the family land, like Michael's, is sold to a stranger. By now it has happened millions of times.

And by now the transformation of the ancient story is nearly complete. Our society, on the whole, has forgotten or repudiated the theme of return. Young people still grow up in rural families and go off to the cities, not to return. But now it is felt that this is what they *should* do. Now the norm is to leave and not return. And this applies as much to urban families as to rural ones. In the present urban economy the parent-child succession is possible only among the economically privileged. The children of industrial underlings are not likely to succeed their parents at work, and there is no reason for them to wish to do so. We are not going to have an industrial 'Michael' in which it is perceived as tragic that a son fails to succeed his father on an assembly line.

According to the new norm, the child's destiny is not to succeed the parents, but to outmode them; succession has given way to supersession. And this norm is institutionalized not in great communal stories, but in the education system. The schools are no longer oriented to a cultural inheritance that it is their duty to pass on unimpaired, but to the career, which is to say the future, of the child. The orientation is thus necessarily theoretical, speculative, and mercenary. The child is not educated to return home and be of use to the place and community; he or she is educated to *leave* home and earn money in a provisional future that has nothing to do with place or community. And parents with children in school are likely to find themselves immediately separated from their children, and made useless to them, by the intervention of new educational techniques, technologies, methods, and languages. School systems innovate as compulsively and as eagerly as factories. It is no wonder that, under these circumstances, 'educators' tend to look upon the parents as a bad influence and wish to take the children away from home as early as possible. And many parents, in truth, are now finding their children an encumbrance at home, where there is no useful work for them to do, and are glad enough to turn them over to the state for the use of the future. The extent to which this order of things is now dominant is suggested by a recent magazine article on the discovery of what purports to be a new idea:

> The idea that a parent can be a teacher at home has caught the attention of educators . . . Parents don't have to be graduates of Harvard or Yale to help their kids learn and achieve.*

Thus the home as a place where a child can learn becomes an *idea* of the professional 'educator,' who retains control of the idea. The

---

* Marianne Merrill Moates, 'Learning . . . Every Day,' *Creative Ideas for Living*, July/August 1988, p. 89.

home, as the article makes clear, is not to be a place where children may learn on their own, but a place where they are taught by parents according to the instructions of professional 'educators.' In fact, the Home and School Institute, Inc., of Washington, D.C. (known, of course, as 'the HSI'), has been 'founded to show . . . how to involve families in their kids' educations.'

In such ways as this, the nuclei of home and community have been invaded by the organizations, just as have the nuclei of cells and atoms. And we must be careful to see that the old cultural centers of home and community were made vulnerable to this invasion by their failure as economies. If there is no household or community economy, then family members and neighbors are no longer useful to one another. When people are no longer useful to one another, then the centripetal force of family and community fails, and people fall into dependence on exterior economies and organizations. The hegemony of professionals and professionalism erects itself on local failure, and from then on the locality exists merely as a market for consumer goods and as a source of 'raw material,' human and natural. The local schools no longer serve the local community; they serve the government's economy and the economy's government. Unlike the local community, the government and the economy cannot be served with affection, but only with professional zeal or professional boredom. Professionalism means more interest in salaries and less interest in what used to be known as disciplines. And so we arrive at the idea, endlessly reiterated in the news media, that education can be improved by bigger salaries for teachers – which may be true, but education cannot be improved, as the proponents too often imply, by bigger salaries alone. There must also be love of learning and of the cultural tradition and of excellence – and this love cannot exist, because it makes no sense, apart from the love of a place and a community. Without this love, education is only the importation into a local community of centrally prescribed 'career preparation' designed to facilitate the export of young careerists.

Our children are educated, then, to leave home, not to stay home, and the costs of this education have been far too little acknowledged.

One of the costs is psychological, and the other is at once cultural and ecological.

The natural or normal course of human growing up must begin with some sort of rebellion against one's parents, for it is clearly impossible to grow up if one remains a child. But the child, in the process of rebellion and of achieving the emotional and economic independence that rebellion ought to lead to, finally comes to understand the parents as fellow humans and fellow sufferers, and in some manner returns to them as their friend, forgiven and forgiving the inevitable wrongs of family life. That is the old norm.

The new norm, according to which the child leaves home as a student and never lives at home again, interrupts the old course of coming of age at the point of rebellion, so that the child is apt to remain stalled in adolescence, never achieving any kind of reconciliation or friendship with the parents. Of course, such a return and reconciliation cannot be achieved without the recognition of mutual practical need. In the present economy, however, where individual dependences are so much exterior to both household and community, family members often have no practical need or use for one another. Hence the frequent futility of attempts at a purely psychological or emotional reconciliation.

And this interposition of rebellion and then of geographical and occupational distance between parents and children may account for the peculiar emotional intensity that our society attaches to innovation. We appear to hate whatever went before, very much as an adolescent hates parental rule, and to look on its obsolescence as a kind of vengeance. Thus we may explain industry's obsessive emphasis on 'this year's model,' or the preoccupation of the professional 'educators' with theoretical and methodological innovation. Similarly, in modern literature we have had for many years an emphasis on 'originality' and 'the anxiety of influence' (an adolescent critical theory), as opposed, say, to Spenser's filial admiration for Chaucer, or Dante's for Virgil.

But if the new norm interrupts the development of the relation between children and parents, that same interruption, ramifying through a community, destroys the continuity and so the integrity of local life. As the children depart, generation after generation, the place loses its memory of itself, which is its history and its culture. And the local history, if it survives at all, loses its place. It does no good for historians, folklorists, and anthropologists to collect the songs and the stories and the lore that make up local culture and store them in books and archives. They cannot collect and store – because they cannot know – the pattern of reminding that can survive only in the living human community in its place. It is this pattern that is the life of local culture and that brings it usefully or pleasurably to mind. Apart from its local landmarks and occasions, the local culture may be the subject of curiosity or of study, but it is also dead.

The loss of local culture is, in part, a practical loss and an economic one. For one thing, such a culture contains, and conveys to succeeding generations, the history of the use of the place and the knowledge of how the place may be lived in and used. For another, the pattern of reminding implies affection for the place and respect for it, and so, finally, the local culture will carry the knowledge of how the place may be well and lovingly used, and also the implicit command to use it *only* well and lovingly. The only true and effective 'operator's manual for spaceship earth' is not a book that any human will ever write; it is hundreds of thousands of local cultures.

Lacking an authentic local culture, a place is open to exploitation, and ultimately destruction, from the center. Recently, for example, I heard the dean of a prominent college of agriculture interviewed on the radio. What have we learned, he was asked, from last summer's drouth? And he replied that 'we' need to breed more drouth resistance into plants, and that 'we' need a government 'safety net' for farmers. He might have said that farmers need to reexamine their farms and their circumstances in light of the drouth, and to think again on such subjects as diversification, scale, and the mutual helpfulness of neighbors. But he did not say that. To him, the drouth was merely an opportunity for agribusiness corporations and the government, by which the farmers and rural communities could only become more dependent on the economy that is destroying them. This is as good an example as any of the centralized thinking of a centralized economy – to which the only effective answer that I know is a strong local community with a strong local economy and a strong local culture.

For a long time now, the prevailing assumption has been that if the nation is all right, then all the localities within it will be all right also. I see little reason to believe that this is true. At present, in fact, both the nation and the national economy are living at the expense of localities and local communities – as all small-town and country people have reason to know. In rural America, which is in many ways a colony of what the government and the corporations think of as the nation, most of us have experienced the losses that I have been talking about: the departure of young people, of soil and other so-called natural resources, and of local memory. We feel ourselves crowded more and more into a dimensionless present, in which the past is forgotten and the future, even in our most optimistic 'projections,' is forbidding and fearful. Who can desire a future that is determined entirely by the purposes of the most wealthy and the most powerful, and by the capacities of machines?

Two questions, then, remain: Is a change for the better possible? And who has the power to make such a change? I still believe that a change for the better is possible, but I confess that my belief is partly hope and partly faith. No one who hopes for improvement should fail to see and respect the signs that we may be approaching some sort of historical waterfall, past which we will not, by changing our minds, be able to change anything else. We know that at any time an ecological or a technological or a political event that we will have allowed may remove from us the power to make change and leave us with the mere necessity to submit to it. Beyond that, the two questions are one: the possibility of change depends on the existence of people who have the power to change.

Does this power reside at present in the national government? That seems to me extremely doubtful. To anyone who has read the papers during the recent presidential campaign, it must be clear that at the highest level of government there is, properly speaking, no political discussion. Are the corporations likely to help us? We know, from long experience, that the corporations will assume no responsibility that is not forcibly imposed upon them by government. The record of the corporations is written too plainly in verifiable damage to permit us to expect much from them. May we look for help to the universities? Well, the universities are more and more the servants of government and the corporations.

Most urban people evidently assume that all is well. They live too far from the exploited and endangered sources of their economy to need to assume otherwise. Some urban people are becoming disturbed about the contamination of air, water, and food, and that is promising, but there are not enough of them yet to make much difference. There is enough trouble in the 'inner cities' to make them likely places of change, and evidently change is in them, but it is desperate and destructive change. As if to perfect their exploitation by other people, the people of the 'inner cities' are destroying both themselves and their places.

My feeling is that if improvement is going to begin anywhere, it will have to begin out in the country and in the country towns. This is not because of any intrinsic virtue that can be ascribed to rural people, but because of their circumstances. Rural people are living, and have lived for a long time, at the site of the trouble. They see all around them, every day, the marks and scars of an exploitive national economy. They have much reason, by now, to know how little real help is to be expected from somewhere else. They still have, moreover, the remnants of local memory and local community. And in rural communities there are still farms and small businesses that can be changed according to the will and the desire of individual people.

In this difficult time of failed public expectations, when thoughtful people wonder where to look for hope, I keep returning in my own mind to the thought of the renewal of the rural communities. I know that one revived rural community would be more convincing and more encouraging than all the government and university programs of the last fifty years, and I think that it could be the beginning of the renewal of our country, for the renewal of rural communities ultimately implies the renewal of urban ones. But to be authentic, a true encouragement and a true beginning, this would have to be a revival accomplished mainly by the community itself. It would have to be done not from the outside by the instruction of visiting experts, but from the inside by the ancient rule of neighborliness, by the love of precious things, and by the wish to be at home.

(1988)

The Unsettling of America

One of the peculiarities of the white race's presence in America is how little intention has been applied to it. As a people, wherever we have been, we have never really intended to be. The continent is said to have been discovered by an Italian who was on his way to India. The earliest explorers were looking for gold, which was, after an early streak of luck in Mexico, always somewhere farther on. Conquests and foundings were incidental to this search – which did not, and could not, end until the continent was finally laid open in an orgy of goldseeking in the middle of the last century. Once the unknown of geography was mapped, the industrial marketplace became the new frontier, and we continued, with largely the same motives and with increasing haste and anxiety, to displace ourselves – no longer with unity of direction, like a migrant flock, but like the refugees from a broken anthill. In our own time we have invaded foreign lands and the moon with the high-toned patriotism of the conquistadors, and with the same mixture of fantasy and avarice.

That is too simply put. It is substantially true, however, as a description of the dominant tendency in American history. The temptation, once that has been said, is to ascend altogether into rhetoric and inveigh equally against all our forebears and all present holders of office. To be just, however, it is necessary to remember that there has been another tendency: the tendency to stay put, to say, 'No farther. This is the place.' So far, this has been the weaker tendency, less glamorous, certainly less successful. It is also the older of these tendencies, having been the dominant one among the Indians.

The Indians did, of course, experience movements of population, but in general their relation to place was based upon old usage and association, upon inherited memory, tradition, veneration. The land was their homeland. The first and greatest American revolution, which has never been superseded, was the coming of people who did not look upon the land as a homeland. But there were always those among the newcomers who saw that they had come to a good place and who saw its domestic possibilities. Very early, for instance, there were men who wished to establish agricultural settlements rather than quest for gold or exploit the Indian trade. Later, we know that every advance of the frontier left behind families and communities who intended to remain and prosper where they were.

But we know also that these intentions have been almost systematically overthrown. Generation after generation, those who intended to remain and prosper where they were have been dispossessed and driven out, or subverted and exploited where they were, by those who were carrying out some version of the search for El Dorado. Time after time, in place after place, these conquerors have fragmented and demolished traditional communities, the beginnings of domestic cultures. They have always said that what they destroyed was outdated, provincial, and contemptible. And with alarming frequency they have been believed and trusted by their victims, especially when their victims were other white people.

If there is any law that has been consistently operative in American history, it is that the members of any *established* people or group or community sooner or later become 'redskins' – that is, they become the designated victims of an utterly ruthless, officially sanctioned and subsidized exploitation. The colonists who drove off the Indians came to be intolerably exploited by their imperial governments. And that alien imperialism was thrown off only to be succeeded by a domestic version of the same thing; the class of independent small farmers who fought the war of independence has been exploited by, and recruited into, the industrial society until by now it is almost extinct. Today, the most numerous heirs of the farmers of Lexington and Concord are the little groups scattered all over the country whose names begin with 'Save': Save Our Land, Save the Valley, Save Our Mountains, Save Our Streams, Save Our Farmland. As so often before, these are *designated* victims – people without official sanction, often without official friends, who are struggling to preserve their places, their values, and their lives as they know them and prefer to live them against the agencies of their own government, which are using their own tax moneys against them.

The only escape from this destiny of victimization has been to 'succeed' – that is, to 'make it' into the class of exploiters, and then to remain so specialized and so 'mobile' as to be unconscious of the effects of one's life or livelihood. This escape is, of course, illusory, for one man's producer is another's consumer, and even the richest and most mobile will soon find it hard to escape the noxious effluents and fumes of their various public services.

Let me emphasize that I am not talking about an evil that is merely contemporary or 'modern,' but one that is as old in America as the white man's presence here. It is an intention that was *organized* here almost from the start. 'The New World,' Bernard DeVoto wrote in *The Course of Empire*, 'was a constantly expanding market . . . Its value in gold was enormous but it had still greater value in that it expanded and integrated the industrial systems of Europe.'

And he continues: 'The first belt-knife given by a European to an Indian was a portent as great as the cloud that mushroomed over Hiroshima . . . Instantly the man of 6000 B.C. was bound fast to a way of life that had developed seven and a half millennia beyond his own. He began to live better and he began to die.'

The principal European trade goods were tools, cloth, weapons, ornaments, novelties, and alcohol. The sudden availability of these things produced a revolution that 'affected every aspect of Indian life. The struggle for existence . . . became easier. Immemorial handicrafts grew obsolescent, then obsolete. Methods of hunting were transformed. So were methods – and the purposes – of war. As war became deadlier in purpose and armament a surplus of women developed, so that marriage customs changed and polygamy became common. The increased usefulness of women in the preparation of pelts worked to the same end . . . Standards of wealth, prestige, and honor changed. The Indians acquired commercial values and developed business cults. They became more mobile . . .

'In the sum it was cataclysmic. A culture was forced to change much faster than change could be adjusted to. All corruptions of culture produce breakdowns of morale, of communal integrity, and of personality, and this force was as strong as any other in the white man's subjugation of the red man.'

I have quoted these sentences from DeVoto because, the obvious differences aside, he is so clearly describing a revolution that did not stop with the subjugation of the Indians, but went on to impose substantially the same catastrophe upon the small farms and the farm communities, upon the shops of small local tradesmen of all sorts, upon the workshops of independent craftsmen, and upon the households of citizens. It is a revolution that is still going on. The economy is still substantially that of the fur trade, still based on the same general kinds of commercial items: technology, weapons, ornaments, novelties, and drugs. The one great difference is that by now the revolution has deprived the mass of consumers of any independent access to the staples of life: clothing, shelter, food, even water. Air remains the only necessity that the average user can still get for himself, and the revolution has imposed a heavy tax on that by way of pollution. Commercial conquest is far more thorough and final than military defeat. The Indian became a redskin, not by loss in battle, but by accepting a dependence on traders that made *necessities* of industrial goods. This is not merely history. It is a parable.

DeVoto makes it clear that the imperial powers, having made themselves willing to impose this exploitive industrial economy upon the Indians, could not then keep it from contaminating their own best intentions: 'More than four-fifths of the wealth of New France was furs, the rest was fish, and it had no agricultural wealth. One trouble was that whereas the crown's imperial policy required it to develop the country's agriculture, the crown's economy required the colony's furs, an adverse interest.' And La Salle's dream of developing Louisiana (agriculturally and otherwise) was frustrated because 'The interest of the court in Louisiana colonization was to secure a bridgehead for an attack on the silver mines of northern Mexico . . .'

One cannot help but see the similarity between this foreign colonialism and the domestic colonialism that, by policy, converts productive farm, forest, and grazing lands into strip mines. Now, as then, we see the abstract values of an industrial economy preying upon the native productivity of land and people. The fur trade was only the first establishment on this continent of a mentality whose triumph is its catastrophe.

My purposes in beginning with this survey of history are (1) to show how deeply rooted in our past is the mentality of exploitation; (2) to show how fundamentally revolutionary it is; and (3) to show how crucial to our history – hence, to our own minds – is the question of how we will relate to our land. This question, now that the corporate revolution has so determinedly invaded the farmland, returns us to our oldest crisis.

We can understand a great deal of our history – from Cortés's destruction of Tenochtitlán in 1521 to the bulldozer attack on the coalfields four-and-a-half centuries later – by thinking of ourselves as divided into conquerors and victims. In order to understand our own time and predicament and the work that is to be done, we would do well to shift the terms and say that we are divided between exploitation and nurture. The first set of terms is too simple for the purpose because, in any given situation, it proposes to divide people into two mutually exclusive groups; it becomes complicated only when we are dealing with situations in succession – as when a colonist who persecuted the Indians then resisted persecution by the crown. The terms *exploitation* and *nurture*, on the other hand, describe a division not only between persons but also within persons. We are all to some extent the products of an exploitive society, and it would be foolish and self-defeating to pretend that we do not bear its stamp.

Let me outline as briefly as I can what seem to me the characteristics of these opposite kinds of mind. I conceive a strip miner to be a model exploiter, and as a model nurturer I take the old-fashioned idea or ideal of a farmer. The exploiter is a specialist, an expert; the nurturer is not. The standard of the exploiter is efficiency; the standard of the nurturer is care. The exploiter's goal is money, profit; the nurturer's goal is health – his land's health, his own, his family's, his community's, his country's. Whereas the exploiter asks of a piece of land only how much and how quickly it can be made to produce, the nurturer asks a question that is much more complex and difficult: What is its carrying capacity? (That is: How much can be taken from it without diminishing it? What can it produce *dependably* for an indefinite time?) The exploiter wishes to earn as much as possible by as little work as possible; the nurturer expects, certainly, to have a decent living from his work, but his characteristic wish is to work *as well* as possible. The competence of the exploiter is in organization; that of the nurturer is in order – a human order, that is, that accommodates itself both to other order and to mystery. The exploiter typically serves an institution or organization; the nurturer serves land, household, community, place. The exploiter thinks in terms of numbers, quantities, 'hard facts'; the nurturer in terms of character, condition, quality, kind.

It seems likely that all the 'movements' of recent years have been representing various claims that nurture has to make against exploitation. The women's movement, for example, when its energies are most accurately placed, is arguing the cause of nurture; other times it is arguing the right of women to be exploiters – which men have no *right* to be. The exploiter is clearly the prototype of the 'masculine' man – the wheeler-dealer whose 'practical' goals require the sacrifice of flesh, feeling, and principle. The nurture, on the other hand, has always passed with ease across the boundaries of the so-called sexual roles. Of necessity and without apology, the preserver of seed, the planter, becomes midwife and nurse. Breeder is always metamorphosing into brooder and back again. Over and over again, spring after spring, the questing mind, idealist and visionary, must pass through the planting to become nurturer of the real. The farmer, sometimes known as husbandman, is by definition half mother; the only question is how good a mother he or she is. And the land itself is not mother or father only, but both. Depending on crop and season, it is at one time receiver of seed, bearer and nurturer of young; at another, raiser of seed-stalk, bearer and shedder of seed. And in response to these changes, the farmer crosses back and forth from one zone of spousehood to another, first as planter and then as gatherer. Farmer and land are thus involved in a sort of dance in which the partners are always at opposite sexual poles, and the lead keeps changing: the farmer, as seed-bearer, causes growth; the land, as seed-bearer, causes the harvest.

The exploitive always involves the abuse or the perversion of nurture and ultimately its destruction. Thus, we saw how far the exploitive revolution had penetrated the official character when our recent secretary of agriculture remarked that 'food is a weapon.' This was given a fearful symmetry indeed when, in discussing the possible use of nuclear weapons, a secretary of defense spoke of 'palatable' levels of devastation. Consider the associations that have since ancient times clustered around the idea of food – associations of mutual care, generosity, neighborliness, festivity, communal joy, religious ceremony – and you will see that these two secretaries represent a cultural catastrophe. The concerns of farming and those of war, once thought to be diametrically opposed, have become identical. Here we have an example of men who have been made vicious, not presumably by nature or circumstance, but by their *values*.

Food is *not* a weapon. To use it as such – to foster a mentality willing to use it as such – is to prepare, in the human character and community, the destruction of the sources of food. The first casualties of the exploitive revolution are character and community. When those fundamental integrities are devalued and broken, then perhaps it is inevitable that food will be looked upon as a weapon, just as it is inevitable that the earth will be looked upon as fuel and people as numbers or machines. But character and community – that is, culture in the broadest, richest sense – constitute, just as much as nature, the source of food. Neither nature nor people alone can produce human sustenance, but only the two together, culturally wedded. The poet Edwin Muir said it unforgettably:

> Men are made of what is made,
> The meat, the drink, the life, the corn,
> Laid up by them, in them reborn.
> And self-begotten cycles close
> About our way; indigenous art
> And simple spells make unafraid
> The haunted labyrinths of the heart
> And with our wild succession braid
> The resurrection of the rose.

•

To think of food as a weapon, or of a weapon as food, may give an illusory security and wealth to a few, but it strikes directly at the life of all.

The concept of food-as-weapon is not surprisingly the doctrine of a Department of Agriculture that is being used as an instrument of foreign political and economic speculation. This militarizing of food is the greatest threat so far raised against the farmland and the farm communities of this country. If present attitudes continue, we may expect government policies that will encourage the destruction, by overuse, of farmland. This, of course, has already begun. To answer the official call for more production – evidently to be used to bait or bribe foreign countries – farmers are plowing their waterways and permanent pastures; lands that ought to remain in grass are being planted in row crops. Contour plowing, crop rotation, and other conservation measures seem to have gone out of favor or fashion in official circles and are practiced less and less on the farm. This exclusive emphasis on production will accelerate the mechanization and chemicalization of farming, increase the price of land, increase overhead and operating costs, and thereby further diminish the farm population. Thus the tendency, if not the intention, of Mr. Butz's confusion of farming and war is to complete the deliverance of American agriculture into the hands of corporations.

The cost of this corporate totalitarianism in energy, land, and social disruption will be enormous. It will lead to the exhaustion of farmland and farm culture. Husbandry will become an extractive industry; because maintenance will entirely give way to production, the fertility of the soil will become a limited, unrenewable resource like coal or oil.

This may not happen. It *need* not happen. But it is necessary to recognize that it *can* happen. That it can happen is made evident not only by the words of such men as Mr. Butz, but more clearly by the large-scale industrial destruction of farmland already in progress. If it does happen, we are familiar enough with the nature of American salesmanship to know that it will be done in the name of the starving millions, in the name of liberty, justice, democracy, and brotherhood, and to free the world from communism. We must, I think, be prepared to see, and to stand by, the truth: that the land should not be destroyed for *any* reason, not even for any apparently good reason. We must be prepared to say that enough food, year after year, is possible only for a limited number of people, and that this possibility can be preserved only by the steadfast, knowledgeable *care* of those people. Such 'crash programs' as apparently have been contemplated by the Department of Agriculture in recent years will, in the long run, cause more starvation than they can remedy.

Meanwhile, the dust clouds rise again over Texas and Oklahoma. 'Snirt' is falling in Kansas. Snowdrifts in Iowa and the Dakotas are black with blown soil. The fields lose their humus and porosity, become less retentive of water, depend more on pesticides, herbicides, chemical fertilizers. Bigger tractors become necessary because the compacted soils are harder to work – and their greater weight further compacts the soil. More and bigger machines, more chemical and methodological shortcuts are needed because of the shortage of manpower on the farm – and the problems of overcrowding and unemployment increase in the cities. It is estimated that it now costs (by erosion) two bushels of Iowa topsoil to grow one bushel of corn. It is variously estimated that from five to twelve calories of fossil fuel energy are required to produce one calorie of hybrid corn energy. An official of the National Farmers Union says that 'a farmer who earns $10,000 to $12,000 a year typically leaves an estate valued at about $320,000' – which means that when that farm is financed again, either by a purchaser or by an heir (to pay the inheritance taxes), it simply cannot support its new owner and pay for itself. And the *Progressive Farmer* predicts the disappearance of 200,000 to 400,000 farms each year during the next twenty years if the present trend continues.

The first principle of the exploitive mind is to divide and conquer. And surely there has never been a people more ominously and painfully divided than we are – both against each other and within

ourselves. Once the revolution of exploitation is under way, states-
manship and craftsmanship are gradually replaced by salesmanship.*
Its stock in trade in politics is to sell despotism and avarice as freedom and democracy. In business it sells sham and frustration as
luxury and satisfaction. The 'constantly expanding market' first
opened in the New World by the fur traders is still expanding – no
longer so much by expansions of territory or population, but by the
calculated outdating, outmoding, and degradation of goods and by
the hysterical self-dissatisfaction of consumers that is indigenous to
an exploitive economy.

This gluttonous enterprise of ugliness, waste, and fraud thrives in
the disastrous breach it has helped to make between our bodies
and our souls. As a people, we have lost sight of the profound
communion – even the union – of the inner with the outer life.
Confucius said: 'If a man have not order within him / He can not
spread order about him . . .' Surrounded as we are by evidence of the
disorders of our souls and our world, we feel the strong truth in
those words as well as the possibility of healing that is in them.
We see the likelihood that our surroundings, from our clothes to our
countryside, are the products of our inward life – our spirit, our
vision – as much as they are products of nature and work. If this is
true, then we cannot live as we do and be as we would like to be.
There is nothing more absurd, to give an example that is only apparently trivial, than the millions who wish to live in luxury and idleness
and yet be slender and good-looking. We have millions, too, whose
livelihoods, amusements, and comforts are all destructive, who
nevertheless wish to live in a healthy environment; they want to run
their recreational engines in clean, fresh air. There is now, in fact, no
'benefit' that is not associated with disaster. That is because power
can be disposed morally or harmlessly only by thoroughly unified
characters and communities.

What caused these divisions? There are no doubt many causes,
complex both in themselves and in their interaction. But pertinent to

---

* The craft of persuading people to buy what they do not need, and do not
want, for more than it is worth.

all of them, I think, is our attitude toward work. The growth of the exploiters' revolution on this continent has been accompanied by the growth of the idea that work is beneath human dignity, particularly any form of hand work. We have made it our overriding ambition to escape work, and as a consequence have debased work until it is only fit to escape from. We have debased the products of work and have been, in turn, debased by them. Out of this contempt for work arose the idea of a nigger: at first some person, and later some thing, to be used to relieve us of the burden of work. If we began by making niggers of people, we have ended by making a nigger of the world. We have taken the irreplaceable energies and materials of the world and turned them into jimcrack 'labor-saving devices.' We have made of the rivers and oceans and winds niggers to carry away our refuse, which we think we are too good to dispose of decently ourselves. And in doing this to the world that is our common heritage and bond, we have returned to making niggers of people: we have become each other's niggers.

But is work something that we have a right to escape? And can we escape it with impunity? We are probably the first entire people ever to think so. All the ancient wisdom that has come down to us counsels otherwise. It tells us that work is necessary to us, as much a part of our condition as mortality; that good work is our salvation and our joy, that shoddy or dishonest or self-serving work is our curse and our doom. We have tried to escape the sweat and sorrow promised in Genesis – only to find that, in order to do so, we must forswear love and excellence, health and joy.

Thus we can see growing out of our history a condition that is physically dangerous, morally repugnant, ugly. Contrary to the blandishments of the salesmen, it is not particularly comfortable or happy. It is not even affluent in any meaningful sense, because its abundance is dependent on sources that are being rapidly exhausted by its methods. To see these things is to come up against the question: Then what *is* desirable?

One possibility is just to tag along with the fantasists in government and industry who would have us believe that we can pursue our ideals of affluence, comfort, mobility, and leisure indefinitely. This curious faith is predicated on the notion that we will soon develop unlimited new sources of energy: domestic oil fields, shale oil, gasified coal, nuclear power, solar energy, and so on. This is fantastical because the basic cause of the energy crisis is not scarcity; it is moral ignorance and weakness of character. We don't know *how* to use energy, or what to use it *for*. And we cannot restrain ourselves. Our time is characterized as much by the abuse and waste of human energy as it is by the abuse and waste of fossil fuel energy. Nuclear power, if we are to believe its advocates, is presumably going to be well used by the same mentality that has egregiously devalued and misapplied man- and womanpower. If we had an unlimited supply of solar or wind power, we would use that destructively, too, for the same reasons.

Perhaps all of those sources of energy are going to be developed. Perhaps all of them can sooner or later be developed without threatening our survival. But not all of them together can guarantee our survival, and they cannot define what is desirable. We will not find those answers in Washington, D.C., or in the laboratories of oil companies. In order to find them, we will have to look closer to ourselves.

I believe that the answers are to be found in our history: in its until now subordinate tendency of settlement, of domestic permanence. This was the ambition of thousands of immigrants; it is formulated eloquently in some of the letters of Thomas Jefferson; it was the dream of the freed slaves; it was written into law in the Homestead Act of 1862. There are few of us whose families have not at some time been moved to see its vision and to attempt to enact its possibility. I am talking about the idea that as many as possible should share in the ownership of the land and thus be bound to it by economic interest, by the investment of love and work, by family loyalty, by memory and tradition. How much land this should be is a question, and the answer will vary with geography. The Homestead Act said 160 acres. The freedmen of the 1860s hoped for forty. We know that, particularly in other countries, families have lived decently on far fewer acres than that.

The old idea is still full of promise. It is potent with healing and with health. It has the power to turn each person away from the big-time promising and planning of the government, to confront in himself, in the immediacy of his own circumstances and where-abouts, the question of what methods and ways are best. It proposes an economy of necessities rather than an economy based upon anxiety, fantasy, luxury, and idle wishing. It proposes the independent, free-standing citizenry that Jefferson thought to be the surest safeguard of democratic liberty. And perhaps most important of all, it proposes an agriculture based upon intensive work, local energies, care, and long-living communities – that is, to state the matter from a consumer's point of view: a dependable, long-term food supply.

This is a possibility that is obviously imperiled – by antipathy in high places, by adverse public fashions and attitudes, by the deteri-oration of our present farm communities and traditions, by the flawed education and the inexperience of our young people. Yet it alone can promise us the continuity of attention and devotion without which the human life of the earth is impossible.

Sixty years ago, in another time of crisis, Thomas Hardy wrote these stanzas:

> Only a man harrowing clods
> In a slow silent walk
> With an old horse that stumbles and nods
> Half asleep as they stalk.

> Only thin smoke without flame
> From the heaps of couch-grass;
> Yet this will go onward the same
> Though Dynasties pass.

Today most of our people are so conditioned that they do not wish to harrow clods either with an old horse or with a new tractor. Yet

Hardy's vision has come to be more urgently true than ever. The great difference these sixty years have made is that, though we feel that this work *must* go onward, we are not so certain that it will. But the care of the earth is our most ancient and most worthy and, after all, our most pleasing responsibility. To cherish what remains of it, and to foster its renewal, is our only legitimate hope.

(1977)

The Agrarian Standard

The Unsettling of America was published twenty-five years ago; it is still in print and is still being read. As its author, I am tempted to be glad of this, and yet, if I believe what I said in that book, and I still do, then I should be anything but glad. The book would have had a far happier fate if it could have been disproved or made obsolete years ago.

It remains true because the conditions it describes and opposes, the abuses of farmland and farming people, have persisted and become worse over the last twenty-five years. In 2002 we have less than half the number of farmers in the United States that we had in 1977. Our farm communities are far worse off now than they were then. Our soil erosion rates continue to be unsustainably high. We continue to pollute our soils and streams with agricultural poisons. We continue to lose farmland to urban development of the most wasteful sort. The large agribusiness corporations that were mainly national in 1977 are now global, and are replacing the world's agricultural diversity, useful primarily to farmers and local consumers, with bioengineered and patented monocultures that are merely profitable to corporations. The purpose of this new global economy, as Vandana Shiva has rightly said, is to replace 'food democracy' with a worldwide 'food dictatorship.'

To be an agrarian writer in such a time is an odd experience. One keeps writing essays and speeches that one would prefer not to write, that one wishes would prove unnecessary, that one hopes nobody will have any need for in twenty-five years. My life as an agrarian writer has certainly involved me in such confusions, but I have never doubted for a minute the importance of the hope I have tried to serve: the hope that we might become a healthy people in a healthy land.

We agrarians are involved in a hard, long, momentous contest, in which we are so far, and by a considerable margin, the losers. What we have undertaken to defend is the complex accomplishment of knowledge, cultural memory, skill, self-mastery, good sense, and fundamental decency – the high and indispensable art – for which we probably can find no better name than 'good farming.' I mean farming as defined by agrarianism as opposed to farming as defined by industrialism: farming as the proper use and care of an immeasurable gift.

I believe that this contest between industrialism and agrarianism now defines the most fundamental human difference, for it divides not just two nearly opposite concepts of agriculture and land use, but also two nearly opposite ways of understanding ourselves, our fellow creatures, and our world.

The way of industrialism is the way of the machine. To the industrial mind, a machine is not merely an instrument for doing work or amusing ourselves or making war; it is an explanation of the world and of life. The machine's entirely comprehensible articulation of parts defines the acceptable meanings of our experience, and it prescribes the kinds of meanings the industrial scientists and scholars expect to discover. These meanings have to do with nomenclature, classification, and rather short lineages of causation. Because industrialism cannot understand living things except as machines, and can grant them no value that is not utilitarian, it conceives of farming and forestry as forms of mining; it cannot use the land without abusing it.

Industrialism prescribes an economy that is placeless and displacing. It does not distinguish one place from another. It applies its methods and technologies indiscriminately in the American East and the American West, in the United States and in India. It thus continues the economy of colonialism. The shift of colonial power from European monarchy to global corporation is perhaps the dominant theme of modern history. All along – from the European colonization of Africa, Asia, and the New World, to the domestic colonialism of American industries, to the colonization of the entire rural world by the global corporations – it has been the same story of the gathering of an exploitive economic power into the hands of a few people who are alien to the places and the people they exploit. Such an economy is bound to destroy locally adapted agrarian economies everywhere it goes, simply because it is too ignorant not to do so. And it has succeeded precisely to the extent that it has been able to inculcate the same ignorance in workers and consumers. A part of the function of industrial education is to preserve and protect this ignorance.

To the corporate and political and academic servants of global industrialism, the small family farm and the small farming community are not known, are not imaginable, and are therefore unthinkable, except as damaging stereotypes. The people of 'the cutting edge' in science, business, education, and politics have no patience with the local love, local loyalty, and local knowledge that make people truly native to their places and therefore good caretakers of their places. This is why one of the primary principles in industrialism has always been to get the worker away from home. From the beginning it has been destructive of home employment and home economies. The office or the factory or the institution is the place for work. The economic function of the household has been increasingly the consumption of purchased goods. Under industrialism, the farm too has become increasingly consumptive, and farms fail as the costs of consumption overpower the income from production.

The idea of people working at home, as family members, as neighbors, as natives and citizens of their places, is as repugnant to the industrial mind as the idea of self-employment. The industrial mind is an organizational mind, and I think this mind is deeply disturbed and threatened by the existence of people who have no boss. This may be why people with such minds, as they approach the top of the political hierarchy, so readily sell themselves to 'special interests.' They cannot bear to be unbossed. They cannot stand the lonely work of making up their own minds.

The industrial contempt for anything small, rural, or natural translates into contempt for uncentralized economic systems, any sort of local self-sufficiency in food or other necessities. The industrial 'solution' for such systems is to increase the scale of work and trade. It is to bring Big Ideas, Big Money, and Big Technology into small rural communities, economies, and ecosystems – the brought-in industry and the experts being invariably alien to and contemptuous of the places to which they are brought in. There is never any question of propriety, of adapting the thought or the purpose or the technology to the place.

The result is that problems correctable on a small scale are replaced by large-scale problems for which there are no large-scale corrections. Meanwhile, the large-scale enterprise has reduced or destroyed the possibility of small-scale corrections. This exactly describes our present agriculture. Forcing all agricultural localities to conform to economic conditions imposed from afar by a few large corporations has caused problems of the largest possible scale, such as soil loss, genetic impoverishment, and ground-water pollution, which are correctable only by an agriculture of locally adapted, solar-powered, diversified small farms – a correction that, after a half century of industrial agriculture, will be difficult to achieve.

The industrial economy thus is inherently violent. It impoverishes one place in order to be extravagant in another, true to its colonialist ambition. A part of the 'externalized' cost of this is war after war.

Industrialism begins with technological invention. But agrarianism begins with givens: land, plants, animals, weather, hunger, and the birthright knowledge of agriculture. Industrialists are always ready to ignore, sell, or destroy the past in order to gain the entirely unprecedented wealth, comfort, and happiness supposedly to be found in the future. Agrarian farmers know that their very identity depends on their willingness to receive gratefully, use responsibly, and hand down intact an inheritance, both natural and cultural, from the past. Agrarians understand themselves as the users and caretakers of some things they did not make, and of some things that they cannot make.

I said a while ago that to agrarianism farming is the proper use and care of an immeasurable gift. The shortest way to understand this, I suppose, is the religious way. Among the commonplaces of the Bible, for example, are the admonitions that the world was made and approved by God, that it belongs to Him, and that its good things come to us from Him as gifts. Beyond those ideas is the idea that the whole Creation exists only by participating in the life of God, sharing in His being, breathing His breath. 'The world,' Gerard Manley Hopkins said, 'is charged with the grandeur of God.' Such thoughts seem strange to us now, and what has estranged us from them is our economy. The industrial economy could not have been derived from such thoughts any more than it could have been derived from the golden rule.

If we believed that the existence of the world is rooted in mystery and in sanctity, then we would have a different economy. It would still be an economy of use, necessarily, but it would be an economy also of return. The economy would have to accommodate the need to be worthy of the gifts we receive and use, and this would involve a return of propitiation, praise, gratitude, responsibility, good use, good care, and a proper regard for future generations. What is most conspicuously absent from the industrial economy and industrial culture is this idea of return. Industrial humans relate themselves to the world and its creatures by fairly direct acts of violence. Mostly we take without asking, use without respect or gratitude, and give nothing in return. Our economy's most voluminous product is waste – valuable materials irrecoverably misplaced, or randomly discharged as poisons.

To perceive the world and our life in it as gifts originating in sanctity is to see our human economy as a continuing moral crisis. Our life of need and work forces us inescapably to use in time things belonging to eternity, and to assign finite values to things already recognized as infinitely valuable. This is a fearful predicament. It calls for prudence, humility, good work, propriety of scale. It calls for the complex responsibilities of caretaking and giving-back that we mean by 'stewardship.' To all of this the idea of the immeasurable value of the resource is central.

•

We can get to the same idea by a way a little more economic and practical, and this is by following through our literature the ancient theme of the small farmer or husbandman who leads an abundant life on a scrap of land often described as cast-off or poor. This figure makes his first literary appearance, so far as I know, in Virgil's Fourth Georgic:

> I saw a man,
> An old Cilician, who occupied
> An acre or two of land that no one wanted,
> A patch not worth the ploughing, unrewarding
> For flocks, unfit for vineyards; he however
> By planting here and there among the scrub
> Cabbages or white lilies and verbena
> And flimsy poppies, fancied himself a king
> In wealth, and coming home late in the evening
> Loaded his board with unbought delicacies.

Virgil's old squatter, I am sure, is a literary outcropping of an agrarian theme that has been carried from earliest times until now mostly in family or folk tradition, not in writing, though other such people can be found in books. Wherever found, they don't vary by much from Virgil's prototype. They don't have or require a lot of land, and the land they have is often marginal. They practice subsistence agriculture, which has been much derided by agricultural economists and other learned people of the industrial age, and they always associate frugality with abundance.

In my various travels, I have seen a number of small homesteads like that of Virgil's old farmer, situated on 'land that no one wanted' and yet abundantly productive of food, pleasure, and other goods. And especially in my younger days, I was used to hearing farmers of a certain kind say, 'They may run me out, but they won't starve me out' or 'I may get shot, but I'm not going to starve.' Even now, if they cared, I think agricultural economists could find small farmers who have prospered, not by 'getting big,' but by practicing the ancient rules of thrift and subsistence, by accepting the limits of their small farms, and by knowing well the value of having a little land.

How do we come at the value of a little land? We do so, following this strand of agrarian thought, by reference to the value of *no* land. Agrarians value land because somewhere back in the history of their consciousness is the memory of being landless. This memory is implicit, in Virgil's poem, in the old farmer's happy acceptance of 'an acre or two of land that no one wanted.' If you have no land you have nothing: no food, no shelter, no warmth, no freedom, no life. If we remember this, we know that all economies begin to lie as soon as they assign a fixed value to land. People who have been landless know that the land is invaluable; it is worth everything. Preagricultural humans, of course, knew this too. And so, evidently, do the animals. It is a fearful thing to be without a 'territory.' Whatever the market may say, the worth of the land is what it always was: it is worth what food, clothing, shelter, and freedom are worth; it is worth what life is worth. This perception moved the settlers from the Old World into the New. Most of our American ancestors came here because they knew what it was to be landless; to be landless was to be threatened by want and also by enslavement. Coming here, they bore the ancestral memory of serfdom. Under feudalism, the few who owned the land owned also, by an inescapable political logic, the people who worked the land.

Thomas Jefferson, who knew all these things, obviously was thinking of them when he wrote in 1785 that 'it is not too soon to provide by every possible means that as few as possible shall be without a little portion of land. The small landholders are the most precious part of a state . . .' He was saying, two years before the adoption of our Constitution, that a democratic state and democratic liberties depend upon democratic ownership of the land. He was already anticipating and fearing the division of our people into settlers, the people who wanted 'a little portion of land' as a home, and, virtually opposite to those, the consolidators and exploiters of the land and the land's wealth, who would not be restrained by what Jefferson called 'the natural affection of the human mind.' He wrote as he did in 1785 because he feared exactly the political theory that we now have: the idea that government exists to guarantee the right of the most wealthy to own or control the land without limit.

In any consideration of agrarianism, this issue of limitation is critical. Agrarian farmers see, accept, and live within their limits. They understand and agree to the proposition that there is 'this much and no more.' Everything that happens on an agrarian farm is determined or conditioned by the understanding that there is only so much land, so much water in the cistern, so much hay in the barn, so much corn in the crib, so much firewood in the shed, so much food in the cellar or freezer, so much strength in the back and arms – and no more. This is the understanding that induces thrift, family coherence, neighborliness, local economies. Within accepted limits, these virtues become necessities. The agrarian sense of abundance comes from the experienced possibility of frugality and renewal within limits.

This is exactly opposite to the industrial idea that abundance comes from the violation of limits by personal mobility, extractive machinery, long-distance transport, and scientific or technological breakthroughs. If we use up the good possibilities in this place, we will import goods from some other place, or we will go to some other place. If nature releases her wealth too slowly, we will take it by force. If we make the world too toxic for honeybees, some compound brain, Monsanto perhaps, will invent tiny robots that will fly about, pollinating flowers and making honey.

To be landless in an industrial society obviously is not at all times to be jobless and homeless. But the ability of the industrial economy to provide jobs and homes depends on prosperity, and on a very shaky kind of prosperity too. It depends on 'growth' of the wrong things such as roads and dumps and poisons – on what Edward Abbey called 'the ideology of the cancer cell' – and on greed with purchasing power. In the absence of growth, greed, and affluence, the dependants of an industrial economy too easily suffer the consequences of having no land: joblessness, homelessness, and want. This is not a theory. We have seen it happen.

I don't think that being landed necessarily means owning land. It does mean being connected to a home landscape from which one may live by the interactions of a local economy and without the routine intervention of governments, corporations, or charities.

In our time it is useless and probably wrong to suppose that a great many urban people ought to go out into the countryside and become homesteaders or farmers. But it is not useless or wrong to suppose that urban people have agricultural responsibilities that they should try to meet. And in fact this is happening. The agrarian population among us is growing, and by no means is it made up merely of some farmers and some country people. It includes urban gardeners, urban consumers who are buying food from local farmers, organizers of local food economies, consumers who have grown doubtful of the healthfulness, the trustworthiness, and the dependability of the corporate food system – people, in other words, who understand what it means to be landless.

Apologists for industrial agriculture rely on two arguments. In one of them, they say that the industrialization of agriculture, and its dominance by corporations, has been 'inevitable.' It has come about and it continues by the agency of economic and technological determinism. There has been simply nothing that anybody could do about it.

The other argument is that industrial agriculture has come about by choice, inspired by compassion and generosity. Seeing the shadow of mass starvation looming over the world, the food conglomerates, the machinery companies, the chemical companies, the seed companies, and the other suppliers of 'purchased inputs' have done all that they have done in order to solve 'the problem of hunger' and to 'feed the world.'

We need to notice, first, that these two arguments, often used and perhaps believed by the same people, exactly contradict each other. Second, though supposedly it has been imposed upon the world by economic and technological forces beyond human control, industrial agriculture has been pretty consistently devastating to nature, to farmers, and to rural communities, at the same time that it has been highly profitable to the agribusiness corporations, which have submitted not quite reluctantly to its 'inevitability.' And, third, tearful over human suffering as they always have been, the agribusiness corporations have maintained a religious faith in the profitability of their charity. They have instructed the world that it is better for people to buy food from the corporate global economy than to raise it for themselves. What is the proper solution to hunger? Not food from the local landscape, but industrial development. After decades of such innovative thought, hunger is still a worldwide calamity.

The primary question for the corporations, and so necessarily for us, is not how the world will be fed, but who will control the land, and therefore the wealth, of the world. If the world's people accept the industrial premises that favor bigness, centralization, and (for a few people) high profitability, then the corporations will control all of the world's land and all of its wealth. If, on the contrary, the world's people might again see the advantages of local economies, in which people live, so far as they are able to do so, from their home landscapes, and work patiently toward that end, eliminating waste and the cruelties of landlessness and homelessness, then I think they might reasonably hope to solve 'the problem of hunger,' and several other problems as well.

But do the people of the world, allured by TV, supermarkets, and big cars, or by dreams thereof, *want* to live from their home landscapes? *Could* they do so, if they wanted to? Those are hard questions, not readily answerable by anybody. Throughout the industrial decades, people have become increasingly and more numerously ignorant of the issues of land use, of food, clothing, and shelter. What would they do, and what *could* they do, if they were forced by war or some other calamity to live from their home landscapes?

It is a fact, well attested but little noticed, that our extensive, mobile, highly centralized system of industrial agriculture is extremely vulnerable to acts of terrorism. It will be hard to protect an agriculture of genetically impoverished monocultures that is entirely dependent on cheap petroleum and long-distance transportation. We know too that the great corporations, which grow and act so far beyond the restraint of 'the natural affections of the human mind,' are vulnerable to the natural depravities of the human mind, such as greed, arrogance, and fraud.

The agricultural industrialists like to say that their agrarian opponents are merely sentimental defenders of ways of farming that are hopelessly old-fashioned, justly dying out. Or they say that their opponents are the victims, as Richard Lewontin put it, of 'a false nostalgia for a way of life that never existed.' But these are not criticisms. They are insults.

For agrarians, the correct response is to stand confidently on our fundamental premise, which is both democratic and ecological: the land is a gift of immeasurable value. If it is a gift, then it is a gift to all the living in all time. To withhold it from some is finally to destroy it for all. For a few powerful people to own or control it all, or decide its fate, is wrong.

From that premise we go directly to the question that begins the agrarian agenda and is the discipline of all agrarian practice: What is the best way to use land? Agrarians know that this question necessarily has many answers, not just one. We are not asking what is the best way to farm everywhere in the world, or everywhere in the United States, or everywhere in Kentucky or Iowa. We are asking what is the best way to farm in each one of the world's numberless places, as defined by topography, soil type, climate, ecology, history, culture, and local need. And we know that the standard cannot be determined only by market demand or productivity or profitability or technological capability, or by any other single measure, however important it may be. The agrarian standard, inescapably, is local adaptation, which requires bringing local nature, local people, local economy, and local culture into a practical and enduring harmony.

(2002)

The Pleasures of Eating

Many times, after I have finished a lecture on the decline of American farming and rural life, someone in the audience has asked, 'What can city people do?'

'Eat responsibly,' I have usually answered. Of course, I have tried to explain what I meant by that, but afterwards I have invariably felt that there was more to be said than I had been able to say. Now I would like to attempt a better explanation.

I begin with the proposition that eating is an agricultural act. Eating ends the annual drama of the food economy that begins with planting and birth. Most eaters, however, are no longer aware that this is true. They think of food as an agricultural product, perhaps, but they do not think of themselves as participants in agriculture. They think of themselves as 'consumers.' If they think beyond that, they recognize that they are passive consumers. They buy what they want – or what they have been persuaded to want – within the limits of what they can get. They pay, mostly without protest, what they are charged. And they mostly ignore certain critical questions about the quality and the cost of what they are sold: How fresh is it? How pure or clean is it, how free of dangerous chemicals? How far was it transported, and what did transportation add to the cost? How much did manufacturing or packaging or advertising add to the cost? When the food product has been manufactured or 'processed' or 'precooked,' how has that affected its quality or price or nutritional value?

Most urban shoppers would tell you that food is produced on farms. But most of them do not know what farms, or what kinds of farms, or where the farms are, or what knowledge or skills are involved in farming. They apparently have little doubt that farms will continue to produce, but they do not know how or over what obstacles. For them, then, food is pretty much an abstract idea – something they do not know or imagine – until it appears on the grocery shelf or on the table.

The specialization of production induces specialization of consumption. Patrons of the entertainment industry, for example, entertain themselves less and less and have become more and more passively dependent on commercial suppliers. This is certainly true also of patrons of the food industry, who have tended more and more to be *mere* consumers – passive, uncritical, and dependent. Indeed, this sort of consumption may be said to be one of the chief goals of industrial production. The food industrialists have by now persuaded millions of consumers to prefer food that is already prepared. They will grow, deliver, and cook your food for you and (just like your mother) beg you to eat it. That they do not yet offer to insert it, prechewed, into your mouth is only because they have found no profitable way to do so. We may rest assured that they would be glad to find such a way. The ideal industrial food consumer would be strapped to a table with a tube running from the food factory directly into his or her stomach.

Perhaps I exaggerate, but not by much. The industrial eater is, in fact, one who does not know that eating is an agricultural act, who no longer knows or imagines the connections between eating and the land, and who is therefore necessarily passive and uncritical – in short, a victim. When food, in the minds of eaters, is no longer associated with farming and with the land, then the eaters are suffering a kind of cultural amnesia that is misleading and dangerous. The current version of the 'dream home' of the future involves 'effortless' shopping from a list of available goods on a television monitor and heating precooked food by remote control. Of course, this implies and depends on a perfect ignorance of the history of the food that is consumed. It requires that the citizenry should give up their hereditary and sensible aversion to buying a pig in a poke. It wishes to make the selling of pigs in pokes an honorable and glamorous activity. The dreamer in this dream home will perforce know nothing about the kind or quality of this food, or where it came from, or how it was produced and prepared, or what ingredients, additives, and residues it contains – unless, that is, the dreamer undertakes a close and constant study of the food industry, in which case he or she might as well wake up and play an active and responsible part in the economy of food.

There is, then, a politics of food that, like any politics, involves our freedom. We still (sometimes) remember that we cannot be free if our minds and voices are controlled by someone else. But we have neglected to understand that we cannot be free if our food and its sources are controlled by someone else. The condition of the passive consumer of food is not a democratic condition. One reason to eat responsibly is to live free.

But if there is a food politics, there are also a food aesthetics and a food ethics, neither of which is dissociated from politics. Like industrial sex, industrial eating has become a degraded, poor, and paltry thing. Our kitchens and other eating places more and more resemble filling stations, as our homes more and more resemble motels. 'Life is not very interesting,' we seem to have decided. 'Let its satisfactions be minimal, perfunctory, and fast.' We hurry through our meals to go to work and hurry through our work in order to 'recreate' ourselves in the evenings and on weekends and vacations. And then we hurry, with the greatest possible speed and noise and violence, through our recreation for what? To eat the billionth hamburger at some fast-food joint hell-bent on increasing the 'quality' of our life? And all this is carried out in a remarkable obliviousness to the causes and effects, the possibilities and the purposes, of the life of the body in this world.

One will find this obliviousness represented in virgin purity in the advertisements of the food industry, in which food wears as much makeup as the actors. If one gained one's whole knowledge of food from these advertisements (as some presumably do), one would not know that the various edibles were ever living creatures, or that they all come from the soil, or that they were produced by work. The passive American consumer, sitting down to a meal of pre-prepared or fast food, confronts a platter covered with inert, anonymous substances that have been processed, dyed, breaded, sauced, gravied, ground, pulped, strained, blended, prettified, and sanitized beyond resemblance to any part of any creature that ever lived. The products of nature and agriculture have been made, to all appearances, the products of industry. Both eater and eaten are thus in exile from biological reality. And the result is a kind of solitude, unprecedented in human experience, in which the eater may think of eating as, first, a purely commercial transaction between him and a supplier and then as a purely appetitive transaction between him and his food.

And this peculiar specialization of the act of eating is, again, of obvious benefit to the food industry, which has good reasons to obscure the connection between food and farming. It would not do for the consumer to know that the hamburger she is eating came from a steer who spent much of his life standing deep in his own excrement in a feedlot, helping to pollute the local streams, or that the calf that yielded the veal cutlet on her plate spent its life in a box in which it did not have room to turn around. And, though her sympathy for the slaw might be less tender, she should not be encouraged to meditate on the hygienic and biological implications of mile-square fields of cabbage, for vegetables grown in huge monocultures are dependent on toxic chemicals – just as animals in close confinement are dependent on antibiotics and other drugs.

The consumer, that is to say, must be kept from discovering that, in the food industry – as in any other industry – the overriding concerns are not quality and health, but volume and price. For decades now the entire industrial food economy, from the large farms and feedlots to the chains of supermarkets and fast-food restaurants, has been obsessed with volume. It has relentlessly increased scale in order to increase volume in order (presumably) to reduce costs. But as scale increases, diversity declines; as diversity declines, so does health; as health declines, the dependence on drugs and chemicals necessarily increases. As capital replaces labor, it does so by substituting machines, drugs, and chemicals for human workers and for the natural health and fertility of the soil. The food is produced by any means or any shortcut that will increase profits. And the business of the cosmeticians of advertising is to persuade the consumer that food so produced is good, tasty, healthful, and a guarantee of marital fidelity and long life.

It is possible, then, to be liberated from the husbandry and wifery of the old household food economy. But one can be thus liberated only by entering a trap (unless one sees ignorance and helplessness as the signs of privilege, as many people apparently do). The trap is the ideal of industrialism: a walled city surrounded by valves that let merchandise in but no consciousness out. How does one escape this trap? Only voluntarily, the same way that one went in: by restoring one's consciousness of what is involved in eating; by reclaiming responsibility for one's own part in the food economy. One might begin with the illuminating principle of Sir Albert Howard's *The Soil and Health*, that we should understand 'the whole problem of health in soil, plant, animal, and man as one great subject.' Eaters, that is, must understand that eating takes place inescapably in the world, that it is inescapably an agricultural act, and that how we eat determines, to a considerable extent, how the world is used. This is a simple way of describing a relationship that is inexpressibly complex. To eat responsibly is to understand and enact, so far as one can, this complex relationship. What can one do? Here is a list, probably not definitive:

1. Participate in food production to the extent that you can. If you have a yard or even just a porch box or a pot in a sunny window, grow something to eat in it. Make a little compost of your kitchen scraps and use it for fertilizer. Only by growing some food for yourself can you become acquainted with the beautiful energy cycle that revolves from soil to seed to flower to fruit to food to offal to decay, and around again. You will be fully responsible for any food that you grow for yourself, and you will know all about it. You will appreciate it fully, having known it all its life.

2. Prepare your own food. This means reviving in your own mind and life the arts of kitchen and household. This should enable you to eat more cheaply, and it will give you a measure of 'quality control': you will have some reliable knowledge of what has been added to the food you eat.

3. Learn the origins of the food you buy, and buy the food

that is produced closest to your home. The idea that every locality should be, as much as possible, the source of its own food makes several kinds of sense. The locally produced food supply is the most secure, the freshest, and the easiest for local consumers to know about and to influence.

4. Whenever possible, deal directly with a local farmer, gardener, or orchardist. All the reasons listed for the previous suggestion apply here. In addition, by such dealing you eliminate the whole pack of merchants, transporters, processors, packagers, and advertisers who thrive at the expense of both producers and consumers.

5. Learn, in self-defense, as much as you can of the economy and technology of industrial food production. What is added to food that is not food, and what do'you pay for these additions?

6. Learn what is involved in the *best* farming and gardening.

7. Learn as much as you can, by direct observation and experience if possible, of the life histories of the food species.

The last suggestion seems particularly important to me. Many people are now as much estranged from the lives of domestic plants and animals (except for flowers and dogs and cats) as they are from the lives of the wild ones. This is regrettable, for these domestic creatures are in diverse ways attractive; there is much pleasure in knowing them. And farming, animal husbandry, horticulture, and gardening, at their best, are complex and comely arts; there is much pleasure in knowing them, too.

It follows that there is great *dis*pleasure in knowing about a food economy that degrades and abuses those arts and those plants and animals and the soil from which they come. For anyone who does know something of the modern history of food, eating away from home can be a chore. My own inclination is to eat seafood instead of red meat or poultry when I am traveling. Though I am by no means a vegetarian, I dislike the thought that some animal has been made miserable in order to feed me. If I am going to eat meat, I want it to be from an animal that has lived a pleasant, uncrowded life out-doors, on bountiful pasture, with good water nearby and trees for shade. And I am getting almost as fussy about food plants. I like to eat vegetables and fruits that I know have lived happily and health-ily in good soil, not the products of the huge, bechemicaled factory-fields that I have seen, for example, in the Central Valley of California. The industrial farm is said to have been patterned on the factory production line. In practice, it looks more like a concentra-tion camp.

The pleasure of eating should be an *extensive* pleasure, not that of the mere gourmet. People who know the garden in which their vegetables have grown and know that the garden is healthy will remember the beauty of the growing plants, perhaps in the dewy first light of morning when gardens are at their best. Such a mem-ory involves itself with the food and is one of the pleasures of eating. The knowledge of the good health of the garden relieves and frees and comforts the eater. The same goes for eating meat. The thought of the good pasture and of the calf contentedly graz-ing flavors the steak. Some, I know, will think it bloodthirsty or worse to eat a fellow creature you have known all its life. On the contrary, I think it means that you eat with understanding and with gratitude. A significant part of the pleasure of eating is in one's accurate consciousness of the lives and the world from which food comes. The pleasure of eating, then, may be the best availa-ble standard of our health. And this pleasure, I think, is pretty fully available to the urban consumer who will make the neces-sary effort.

I mentioned earlier the politics, aesthetics, and ethics of food. But to speak of the pleasure of eating is to go beyond those categories. Eating with the fullest pleasure – pleasure, that is, that does not depend on ignorance – is perhaps the profoundest enactment of our connection with the world. In this pleasure we experience and celebrate our dependence and our gratitude, for we are living from mystery, from creatures we did not make and powers we cannot comprehend. When I think of the meaning of food, I always

remember these lines by the poet William Carlos Williams, which
seem to me merely honest:

> There is nothing to eat,
> seek it where you will,
> but of the body of the Lord.
> The blessed plants
> and the sea, yield it
> to the imagination
> intact.

(1989)

Horse-Drawn Tools and the Doctrine of Labor Saving

Five years ago, when we enlarged our farm from about twelve acres to about fifty, we saw that we had come to the limits of the equipment we had on hand: mainly a rotary tiller and a Gravely walking tractor; we had been borrowing a tractor and mower to clip our few acres of pasture. Now we would have perhaps twenty-five acres of pasture, three acres of hay, and the garden; and we would also be clearing some land and dragging the cut trees out for firewood. I thought for a while of buying a second-hand 8N Ford tractor, but decided finally to buy a team of horses instead.

I have several reasons for being glad that I did. One reason is that it started me thinking more particularly and carefully than before about the development of agricultural technology. I had learned to use a team when I was a boy, and then had learned to use the tractor equipment that replaced virtually all the horse and mule teams in this part of the country after World War II. Now I was turning around, as if in the middle of my own history, and taking up the old way again.

Buying and borrowing, I gathered up the equipment I needed to get started: wagon, manure spreader, mowing machine, disk, a one-row cultivating plow for the garden. Most of these machines had been sitting idle for years. I put them back into working shape, and started using them. That was 1973. In the years since, I have bought a number of other horse-drawn tools, for myself and other people. My own outfit now includes a breaking plow, a two-horse riding cultivator, and a grain drill.

As I have repaired these old machines and used them, I have seen how well designed and durable they are, and what good work they do. When the manufacturers modified them for use with tractors, they did not much improve either the machines or the quality of their work. (It is necessary, of course, to note some exceptions. Some horsemen, for instance, would argue that alfalfa sod is best plowed with a tractor. And one must also except such tools as hay conditioners and chisel plows that came after the development of horse-drawn tools had ceased. We do not know what innovations, refinements, and improvements would have come if it had continued.) At the peak of their development, the old horse tools were excellent. The coming of the tractor made it possible for a farmer to do more work, but not better. And there comes a point, as we know, when *more* begins to imply *worse*. The mechanization of farming passed that point long ago – probably, or so I will argue, when it passed from horse power to tractor power.

The increase of power has made it possible for one worker to crop an enormous acreage, but for this 'efficiency' the country has paid a high price. From 1946 to 1976, because fewer people were needed, the farm population declined from thirty million to nine million; the rapid movement of these millions into the cities greatly aggravated that complex of problems which we now call the 'urbancrisis,' and the land is suffering for want of the care of those absent families. The coming of a tool, then, can be a cultural event of great influence and power. Once that is understood, it is no longer possible to be simpleminded about technological progress. It is no longer possible to ask, What is a good tool? without asking at the same time, How *well* does it work? and, What is its influence?

One could say, as a rule of thumb, that a good tool is one that makes it possible to work faster *and* better than before. When companies quit making them, the horse-drawn tools fulfilled both requirements. Consider, for example, the International High Gear No. 9 mowing machine. This is a horse-drawn mower that certainly improved on everything that came before it, from the scythe to previous machines in the International line. Up to that point, to cut fast and to cut well were two aspects of the same problem. Past that point the speed of the work could be increased, but not the quality.

I own one of these mowers. I have used it in my hayfield at the same time that a neighbor mowed there with a tractor mower; I have gone from my own freshly cut hayfield into others just mowed by tractors; and I can say unhesitatingly that, though the tractors do faster work, they do not do it better. The same is substantially true, I think, of other tools: plows, cultivators, harrows, grain drills, seeders, spreaders, etc. Through the development of the standard horse-drawn equipment, quality and speed increased together; after that, the principal increase has been in speed.

Moreover, as the speed has increased, care has tended to decline. For this, one's eyes can furnish ample evidence. But we have it also by the testimony of the equipment manufacturers themselves. Here, for example, is a quote from the public relations paper of one of the largest companies: 'Today we have multi-row planters that slap in a crop in a hurry, putting down seed, fertilizer, insecticide and herbicide in one quick swipe across the field.'

But good work and good workmanship cannot be accomplished by 'slaps' and 'swipes.' Such language seems to be derived from the he-man vocabulary of TV westerns, not from any known principles of good agriculture. What does the language of good agricultural workmanship sound like? Here is the voice of an old-time English farmworker and horseman, Harry Groom, as quoted in George Ewart Evans's *The Horse in the Furrow*: 'It's all rush today. You hear a young chap say in the pub: "I done thirty acres today." But it ain't messed over, let alone done. You take the rolling, for instance. Two mile an hour is fast enough for a roll or a harrow. With a roll, the slower the better. If you roll fast, the clods are not broken up, they're just pressed in further. Speed is everything now; just jump on the tractor and way across the field as if it's a dirt-track. You see it when a farmer takes over a new farm: he goes in and plants straightway, right out of the book. But if one of the old farmers took a new farm, and you walked round the land with him and asked him: "What are you going to plant here and here?" he'd look at you some queer; because he wouldn't plant nothing much at first. He'd wait a bit and see what the land was like: he'd *prove* the land first. A good practical man would hold on for a few weeks, and get the feel of the land under his feet. He'd walk on it and feel it through his boots and see if it was in good heart, before he planted anything: he'd sow only when he knew what the land was fit for.'

Granted that there is always plenty of room to disagree about farming methods, there is still no way to deny that in the first quotation we have a description of careless farming, and in the second a description of a way of farming as careful – as knowing, skillful, and loving – as any other kind of high workmanship. The difference between the two is simply that the second considers where and how the machine is used, whereas the first considers only the machine. The first is the point of view of a man high up in the air-conditioned cab of a tractor described as 'a beast that eats acres.' The second is that of a man who has worked close to the ground in the open air of the field, who has studied the condition of the ground as he drove over it, and who has cared and thought about it.

If we had tools thirty-five years ago that made it possible to do farm work both faster and better than before, then why did we choose to go ahead and make them no longer better, but just bigger and bigger and faster and faster? It was, I think, because we were already allowing the wrong people to give the wrong answers to questions raised by the improved horse-drawn machines. Those machines, like the ones that followed them, were *labor savers*. They may seem old-timey in comparison to today's 'acre eaters,' but when they came on the market they greatly increased the amount of work that one worker could do in a day. And so they confronted us with a critical question: How would we define labor saving?

We defined it, or allowed it to be defined for us by the corporations and the specialists, as if it involved no human considerations at all, as if the labor to be 'saved' were not human labor. We decided, in the language of some experts, to look on technology as a 'substitute for labor.' Which means that we did not intend to 'save' labor at all, but to *replace* it, and to *displace* the people who once supplied it. We never asked what should be done with the 'saved' labor; we let the 'labor market' take care of that. Nor did we ask the larger questions of what values we should place on people and their work and on the land. It appears that we abandoned ourselves unquestioningly to a course of technological evolution, which would value the development of machines far above the development of people.

And so it becomes clear that, by itself, my rule-of-thumb definition of a good tool (one that permits a worker to work both better and faster) does not go far enough. Even such a tool can cause bad results if its use is not directed by a benign and healthy social purpose. The coming of a tool, then, is not just a cultural event; it is also an historical crossroad – a point at which people must choose between two possibilities: to become more intensive or more extensive; to use the tool for quality or for quantity, for care or for speed.

In speaking of this as a choice, I am obviously assuming that the evolution of technology is *not* unquestionable or uncontrollable; that 'progress' and the 'labor market' do *not* represent anything so unyielding as natural law, but are aspects of an economy; and that any economy is in some sense a 'managed' economy, managed by an intention to distribute the benefits of work, land, and materials in a certain way. (The present agricultural economy, for instance, is slanted to give the greater portion of these benefits to the 'agribusiness' corporations. If this were not so, the recent farmers' strike would have been an 'agribusiness' strike as well.) If those assumptions are correct, we are at liberty to do a little historical supposing, not meant, of course, to 'change history' or 'rewrite it,' but to clarify somewhat this question of technological choice.

Suppose, then, that in 1945 we had valued the human life of farms and farm communities 1 percent more than we valued 'economic growth' and technological progress. And suppose we had espoused the health of homes, farms, towns, and cities with anything like the resolve and energy with which we built the 'military-industrial complex.' Suppose, in other words, that we had really meant what, all that time, most of us and most of our leaders were saying, and that we had really tried to live by the traditional values to which we gave lip service.

Then, it seems to me, we might have accepted certain mechanical and economic limits. We might have used the improved horse-drawn tools, or even the small tractor equipment that followed, not to displace workers and decrease care and skill, but to intensify production, improve maintenance, increase care and skill, and widen the margins of leisure, pleasure, and community life. We might, in other words, by limiting technology to a human or a democratic scale, have been able to use the saved labor *in the same places where we saved it.*

It is important to remember that 'labor' is a very crude, industrial term, fitted to the huge economic structures, the dehumanized technology, and the abstract social organization of urban-industrial society. In such circumstances, 'labor' means little more than the sum of two human quantities, human energy plus human time, which we identify as 'man-hours.' But the nearer home we put 'labor' to work, and the smaller and more familiar we make its circumstances, the more we enlarge and complicate and enhance its meaning. At work in a factory, workers are only workers, 'units of production' expending 'man-hours' at a task set for them by strangers. At work in their own communities, on their own farms or in their own households or shops, workers are *never* only workers, but rather persons, relatives, and neighbors. They work *for* those they work *among* and *with*. Moreover, workers tend to be independent in inverse proportion to the size of the circumstance in which they work. That is, the work of factory workers is ruled by the factory, whereas the work of housewives, small craftsmen, or small farmers is ruled by their own morality, skill, and intelligence. And so, when workers work independently and at home, the society as a whole may lose something in the way of organizational efficiency and economies of scale. But it begins to *gain* values not so readily quantifiable in the fulfilled humanity of the workers, who then bring to their work not just contracted quantities of 'man-hours,' but qualities such as independence, skill, intelligence, judgment, pride, respect, loyalty, love, reverence.

To put the matter in concrete terms, if the farm communities had been able to use the best horse-drawn tools to save labor in the true sense, then they might have used the saved time and energy, first of all, for leisure – something that technological progress has given to farmers. Second, they might have used it to improve their farms: to enrich the soil, prevent erosion, conserve water, put up better and more permanent fences and buildings; to practice forestry and its dependent crafts and economies; to plant orchards, vineyards, gardens of bush fruits; to plant market gardens; to improve pasture, breeding, husbandry, and the subsidiary enterprises of a local, small-herd livestock economy; to enlarge, diversify, and deepen the economies of households and homesteads. Third, they might have used it to expand and improve the specialized crafts necessary to the health and beauty of communities: carpentry, masonry, leatherwork, cabinetwork, metalwork, pottery, etc. Fourth, they might have used it to improve the homelife and the home instruction of children, thereby preventing the hardships and expenses now placed on schools, courts, and jails.

It is probable also that, if we *had* followed such a course, we would have averted or greatly ameliorated the present shortages of energy and employment. The cities would be much less crowded; the rates of crime and welfare dependency would be much lower; the standards of industrial production would probably be higher. And farmers might have avoided their present crippling dependence on money lenders.

I am aware that all this is exactly the sort of thinking that the technological determinists will dismiss as nostalgic or wishful. I mean it, however, not as a recommendation that we 'return to the past,' but as a criticism of the past; and my criticism is based on the assumption that we had in the past, and that we have now, a *choice* about how we should use technology and what we should use it for. As I understand it, this choice depends absolutely on our willingness to limit our desires as well as the scale and kind of technology we use to satisfy them. Without that willingness, there is no choice; we must simply abandon ourselves to whatever the technologists may discover to be possible.

The technological determinists, of course, do not accept that such a choice exists – undoubtedly because they resent the moral limits on their work that such a choice implies. They speak romantically of 'man's destiny' to go on to bigger and more sophisticated machines. Or they take the opposite course and speak the tooth-and-claw language of Darwinism. Ex-secretary of agriculture Earl Butz speaks, for instance, of 'Butz's Law of Economics' which is 'Adapt or Die.'

I am, I think, as enthusiastic about the principle of adaptation as Mr. Butz. We differ only on the question of what should be adapted. He believes that we should adapt to the machines, that humans should be forced to conform to technological conditions or standards. I believe that the machines should be adapted to us – to serve our *human* needs as our history, our heritage, and our most generous hopes have defined them.

(1978)

Getting Along with Nature

The defenders of nature and wilderness – like their enemies the defenders of the industrial economy – sometimes sound as if the natural and the human were two separate estates, radically different and radically divided. The defenders of nature and wilderness sometimes seem to feel that they must oppose any human encroachment whatsoever, just as the industrialists often apparently feel that they must make the human encroachment absolute or, as they say, 'complete the conquest of nature.' But there is danger in this opposition, and it can be best dealt with by realizing that these pure and separate categories are pure ideas and do not otherwise exist.

Pure nature, anyhow, is not good for humans to live in, and humans do not want to live in it – or not for very long. Any exposure to the elements that lasts more than a few hours will remind us of the desirability of the basic human amenities: clothing, shelter, cooked food, the company of kinfolk and friends – perhaps even of hot baths and music and books.

It is equally true that a condition that is *purely* human is not good for people to live in, and people do not want to live for very long in it. Obviously, the more artificial a human environment becomes, the more the word 'natural' becomes a term of value. It can be argued, indeed, that the conservation movement, as we know it today, is largely a product of the industrial revolution. The people who want clean air, clear streams, and wild forests, prairies, and deserts are the people who no longer have them.

People cannot live apart from nature; that is the first principle of the conservationists. And yet, people cannot live in nature without changing it. But this is true of *all* creatures; they depend upon nature, and they change it. What we call nature is, in a sense, the sum of the changes made by all the various creatures and natural forces in their intricate actions and influences upon each other and upon their places. Because of the woodpeckers, nature is different from what it would be without them. It is different also because of the borers and ants that live in tree trunks, and because of the bacteria that live in the soil under the trees. The making of these differences is the making of the world.

Some of the changes made by wild creatures we would call beneficent: beavers are famous for making ponds that turn into fertile meadows; trees and prairie grasses build soil. But sometimes, too, we would call natural changes destructive. According to early witnesses, for instance, large areas around Kentucky salt licks were severely trampled and eroded by the great herds of hoofed animals that gathered there. The buffalo 'streets' through hilly country were so hollowed out by hoof-wear and erosion that they remain visible almost two centuries after the disappearance of the buffalo. And so it can hardly be expected that humans would not change nature. Humans, like all other creatures, must make a difference; otherwise, they cannot live. But inlike other creatures, humans must make a choice as to the kind and scale of the difference they make. If they choose to make too small a difference, they diminish their humanity. If they choose to make too great a difference, they diminish nature, and narrow their subsequent choices; ultimately, they diminish or destroy themselves. Nature, then, is not only our source but also our limit and measure. Or, as the poet Edmund Spenser put it almost four hundred years ago, Nature, who is the 'greatest goddesse,' acts as a sort of earthly lieutenant of God, and Spenser represents her as both a mother and judge. Her jurisdiction is over the relations between the creatures; she deals 'Right to all . . . indifferently,' for she is 'the equall mother' of all 'And knittest each to each, as brother unto brother.' Thus, in Spenser, the natural principles of fecundity and order are pointedly linked with the principle of justice, which we may be a little surprised to see that he attributes also to nature. And yet in his insistence on an 'indifferent' natural justice, resting on the 'brotherhood' of *all* creatures, not just of humans, Spenser would now be said to be on sound ecological footing.

In nature we know that wild creatures sometimes exhaust their vital sources and suffer the natural remedy: drastic population reductions. If lynxes eat too many snowshoe rabbits – which they are said to do repeatedly – then the lynxes starve down to the carrying capacity of their habitat. It is the carrying capacity of the lynx's habitat, not the carrying capacity of the lynx's stomach, that determines the prosperity of lynxes. Similarly, if humans use up too much soil – which they have often done and are doing – then they will starve down to the carrying capacity of *their* habitat. This is nature's 'indifferent' justice. As Spenser saw in the sixteenth century, and as we must learn to see now, there is no appeal from this justice. In the hereafter, the Lord may forgive our wrongs against nature, but on earth, so far as we know, He does not overturn her decisions.

One of the differences between humans and lynxes is that humans can see that the principle of balance operates between lynxes and snowshoe rabbits, as between humans and topsoil; another difference, we hope, is that humans have the sense to act on their understanding. We can see, too, that a stable balance is preferable to a balance that tilts back and forth like a seesaw, dumping a surplus of creatures alternately from either end. To say this is to renew the question of whether or not the human relationship with nature is necessarily an adversary relationship, and it is to suggest that the answer is not simple.

But in dealing with this question and in trying to do justice to the presumed complexity of the answer, we are up against an American convention of simple opposition to nature that is deeply established both in our minds and in our ways. We have opposed the primeval forests of the East and the primeval prairies and deserts of the West, we have opposed man-eating beasts and crop-eating insects, sheep-eating coyotes and chicken-eating hawks. In our lawns and gardens and fields, we oppose what we call weeds. And yet more and more of us are beginning to see that this opposition is ultimately destructive even of ourselves, that it does not explain many things that need explaining – in short, that it is untrue.

If our proper relation to nature is not opposition, then what is it? This question becomes complicated and difficult for us because none of us, as I have said, wants to live in a 'pure' primeval forest or in a 'pure' primeval prairie; we do not want to be eaten by grizzly bears;

if we are gardeners, we have a legitimate quarrel with weeds; if, in Kentucky, we are trying to improve our pastures, we are likely to be enemies of the nodding thistle. But, do what we will, we remain under the spell of the primeval forests and prairies that we have cut down and broken; we turn repeatedly and with love to the thought of them and to their surviving remnants. We find ourselves attracted to the grizzly bears, too, and know that they and other great, dangerous animals remain alive in our imaginations as they have been all through human time. Though we cut down the nodding thistles, we acknowledge their beauty and are glad to think that there must be some place where they belong. (They may, in fact, not always be out of place in pastures; if, as seems evident, overgrazing makes an ideal seedbed for these plants, then we must understand them as a part of nature's strategy to protect the ground against abuse by animals.) Even the ugliest garden weeds earn affection from us when we consider how faithfully they perform an indispensable duty in covering the bare ground and in building humus. The weeds, too, are involved in the business of fertility.

We know, then, that the conflict between the human and the natural estates really exists and that it is to some extent necessary. But we are learning, or relearning, something else, too, that frightens us: namely, that this conflict often occurs at the expense of *both* estates. It is not only possible but altogether probable that by diminishing nature we diminish ourselves, and vice versa.

The conflict comes to light most suggestively, perhaps, when advocates for the two sides throw themselves into absolute conflict where no absolute difference can exist. An example of this is the battle between defenders of coyotes and defenders of sheep, in which the coyote-defenders may find it easy to forget that the sheep ranchers are human beings with some authentic complaints against coyotes, and the sheep-defenders find it easy to sound as if they advocate the total eradication of both coyotes and conservationists. Such conflicts – like the old one between hawk-defenders and chicken-defenders – tend to occur between people who use nature indirectly and people who use it directly. It is a dangerous mistake, I think, for either side to pursue such a quarrel on the assumption that victory would be a desirable result.

The fact is that people need both coyotes and sheep, need a world in which both kinds of life are possible. Outside the heat of conflict, conservationists probably know that a sheep is one of the best devices for making coarse foliage humanly edible and that wool is ecologically better than the synthetic fibers, just as most shepherds will be aware that wild nature is of value to them and not lacking in interest and pleasure.

The usefulness of coyotes is, of course, much harder to define than the usefulness of sheep. Coyote fur is not a likely substitute for wool, and, except as a last resort, most people don't want to eat coyotes. The difficulty lies in the difference between what is ours and what is nature's: what is ours is ours because it is directly useful. Coyotes are useful *indirectly*, as part of the health of nature, from which we and our sheep alike must live and take our health. The fact, moreover, may be that sheep and coyotes need each other, at least in the sense that neither would prosper in a place totally unfit for the other.

This sort of conflict, then, does not suggest the possibility of victory so much as it suggests the possibility of a compromise – some kind of peace, even an alliance, between the domestic and the wild. We know that such an alliance is necessary. Most conservationists now take for granted that humans thrive best in ecological health and that the test or sign of this health is the survival of a diversity of wild creatures. We know, too, that we cannot imagine ourselves apart from those necessary survivals of our own wildness that we call our instincts. And we know that we cannot have a healthy agriculture apart from the teeming wilderness in the topsoil, in which worms, bacteria, and other wild creatures are carrying on the fundamental work of decomposition, humus making, water storage, and drainage. 'In wildness is the preservation of the world,' as Thoreau said, may be a spiritual truth, but it is also a practical fact.

On the other hand, we must not fail to consider the opposite proposition – that, so long at least as humans are in the world, in human culture is the preservation of wildness – which is equally, and more demandingly, true. If wildness is to survive, then *we* must preserve it. We must preserve it by public act, by law, by institutionalizing wildernesses in some places. But such preservation is probably not enough. I have heard Wes Jackson of the Land Institute say, rightly I think, that if we cannot preserve our farmland, we cannot preserve the wilderness. That said, it becomes obvious that if we cannot preserve our cities, we cannot preserve the wilderness. This can be demonstrated practically by saying that the same attitudes that destroy wildness in the topsoil will finally destroy it everywhere; or by saying that if *everyone* has to go to a designated public wilderness for the necessary contact with wildness, then our parks will be no more natural than our cities.

But I am trying to say something more fundamental than that. What I am aiming at – because a lot of evidence seems to point this way – is the probability that nature and human culture, wildness and domesticity, are not opposed but are interdependent. Authentic experience of either will reveal the need of one for the other. In fact, examples from both past and present prove that a human economy and wildness can exist together not only in compatibility but to their mutual benefit.

One of the best examples I have come upon recently is the story of two Sonora Desert oases in Gary Nabhan's book, *The Desert Smells Like Rain*. The first of these oases, A'al Waipia, in Arizona, is dying because the park service, intending to preserve the natural integrity of the place as a bird sanctuary for tourists, removed the Papago Indians who had lived and farmed there. The place was naturally purer after the Indians were gone, but the oasis also began to shrink as the irrigation ditches silted up. As Mr. Nabhan puts it, 'an odd thing is happening to their "natural" bird sanctuary. They are losing the heterogeneity of the habitat, and with it, the birds. The old trees are dying . . . These riparian trees are essential for the breeding habitat of certain birds. Summer annual seed plants are conspicuously absent . . . Without the soil disturbance associated with plowing and flood irrigation, these natural foods for birds and rodents no longer germinate.'

The other oasis, Ki:towak, in old Mexico, still thrives because a Papago village is still there, still farming. The village's oldest man, Luis Nolia, is the caretaker of the oasis, cleaning the springs and ditches, farming, planting trees: 'Luis...blesses the oasis,' Mr. Nabhan says, 'for his work keeps it healthy.' An ornithologist who accompanied Mr. Nabhan found twice as many species of birds at the farmed oasis as he found at the bird sanctuary, a fact that Mr. Nabhan's Papago friend, Remedio, explained in this way: 'That's because those birds, they come where the people are. When the people live and work in a place, and plant their seeds and water their trees, the birds go live with them. They like those places, there's plenty to eat and that's when we are friends to them.'

Another example, from my own experience, is suggestive in a somewhat different way. At the end of July 1981, while I was using a team of horses to mow a small triangular hillside pasture that is bordered on two sides by trees, I was suddenly aware of wings close below me. It was a young red-tailed hawk, who flew up into a walnut tree. I mowed on to the turn and stopped the team. The hawk then glided to the ground not twenty feet away. I got off the mower, stood and watched, even spoke, and the hawk showed no fear. I could see every feather distinctly, claw and beak and eye, the creamy down of the breast. Only when I took a step toward him, separating myself from the team and mower, did he fly. While I mowed three or four rounds, he stayed near, perched in trees or standing erect and watchful on the ground. Once, when I stopped to watch him, he was clearly watching me, stooping to see under the leaves that screened me from him. Again, when I could not find him, I stooped, saying to myself, 'This is what he did to look at me,' and as I did so I saw him looking at me.

Why had he come? To catch mice? Had he seen me scare one out of the grass? Or was it curiosity?

A human, of course, cannot speak with authority of the motives of hawks. I am aware of the possibility of explaining the episode merely by the hawk's youth and inexperience. And yet it does not happen often or dependably that one is approached so closely by a hawk of any age. I feel safe in making a couple of assumptions. The first is that the hawk came because of the conjunction of the small pasture and its wooded borders, of open hunting ground and the security of trees. This is the phenomenon of edge or margin that we know to be one of the powerful attractions of a diversified landscape, both to wildlife and to humans. The human eye itself seems drawn to such margins, hungering for the difference made in the countryside by a hedgy fencerow, a stream, or a grove of trees. And we know that these margins are biologically rich, the meeting of two kinds of habitat. But another difference also is important here: the difference between a large pasture and a small one, or, to use Wes Jackson's terms, the difference between a field and a patch. The pasture I was mowing was a patch – small, intimate, nowhere distant from its edges.

My second assumption is that the hawk was emboldened to come so near because, though he obviously recognized me as a man, I was there with the team of horses, with whom he familiarly and confidently shared the world.

I am saying, in other words, that this little visit between the hawk and me happened because the kind and scale of my farm, my way of farming, and my technology *allowed* it to happen. If I had been driving a tractor in a hundred-acre cornfield, it would not have happened.

In some circles I would certainly be asked if one can or should be serious about such an encounter, if it has any value. And though I cannot produce any hard evidence, I would unhesitatingly answer yes. Such encounters involve another margin – the one between domesticity and wildness – that attracts us irresistibly; they are among the best rewards of outdoor work and among the reasons for loving to farm. When the scale of farming grows so great and obtrusive as to forbid them, the *life* of farming is impoverished.

But perhaps we do find hard evidence of a sort when we consider that *all* of us – the hawk, the horses, and I – were there for our benefit and, to some extent, for our *mutual* benefit: the horses live from the pasture and maintain it with their work, grazing, and manure; the team and I together furnish hunting ground to the hawk; the hawk serves us by controlling the field-mouse population.

These meetings of the human and the natural estates, the domestic and the wild, occur invisibly, of course, in any well-farmed field. The wilderness of a healthy soil, too complex for human comprehension, can yet be husbanded, can benefit from human care, and can deliver incalculable benefits in return. Mutuality of interest and reward is a possibility that can reach to any city backyard, garden, and park, but in any place under human dominance – which is, now, virtually everyplace – it is a possibility that is *both* natural and cultural. If humans want wildness to be possible, then they have to make it possible. If balance is the ruling principle and a stable balance the goal, then, for humans, attaining this goal requires a consciously chosen and deliberately made patnership with nature.

In other words, we can be true to nature only by being true to human nature – to our animal nature as well as to cultural patterns and restraints that keep us from acting like animals. When humans act like animals, they become the most dangerous of animals to themselves and other humans, and this is because of another critical difference between humans and animals: whereas animals are usually restrained by the limits of physical appetites, humans have mental appetites that can be far more gross and capacious than physical ones. Only humans squander and hoard, murder and pillage because of notions.

The work by which good human and natural possibilities are preserved is complex and difficult, and it probably cannot be accomplished by raw intelligence and information. It requires knowledge, skills, and restraints, some of which must come from our past. In the hurry of technological progress, we have replaced some tools and methods that worked with some that do not work. But we also need culture-borne instructions about who or what humans are and how and on what assumptions they should act. The Chain of Being, for instance – which gave humans a place between animals and angels in the order of Creation – is an old idea that has not been replaced by any adequate new one. It was simply rejected, and the lack of it leaves us without a definition.

Lacking that ancient definition, or any such definition, we do not know at what point to restrain or deny ourselves. We do not know how ambitious to be, what or how much we may safely desire, when or where to stop. I knew a barber once who refused to give a discount to a bald client, explaining that his artistry consisted, not in the cutting off, but in the knowing when to stop. He spoke, I think, as a true artist and a true human. The lack of such knowledge is extremely dangerous in and to an individual. But ignorance of when to stop is a modern epidemic; it is the basis of 'industrial progress' and 'economic growth.' The most obvious practical result of this ignorance is a critical disproportion of scale between the scale of human enterprises and their sources in nature.

The scale of the energy industry, for example, is too big, as is the scale of the transportation industry. The scale of agriculture, from a technological or economic point of view, is too big, but from a demographic point of view, the scale is too small. When there are enough people on the land to use it but not enough to husband it, then the wildness of the soil that we call fertility begins to diminish, and the soil itself begins to flee from us in water and wind.

If the human economy is to be fitted into the natural economy in such a way that both may thrive, the human economy must be built to proper scale. It is possible to talk at great length about the difference between proper and improper scale. It may be enough to say here that that difference is *suggested* by the difference between amplified and unamplified music in the countryside, or the difference between the sound of a motorboat and the sound of oarlocks. A proper human sound, we may say, is one that allows other sounds to be heard. A properly scaled human economy or technology allows a diversity of other creatures to thrive.

'The proper scale,' a friend wrote to me, 'confers freedom and simplicity . . . and doubtless leads to long life and health.' I think that it also confers joy. The renewal of our partnership with nature, the rejoining of our works to their proper places in the natural order, reshaped to their proper scale, implies the reenjoyment both of nature and of human domesticity. Though our task will be difficult, we will greatly mistake its nature if we see it as grim, or if we suppose that it must always be necessary to suffer at work in order to enjoy ourselves in places specializing in 'recreation.'

Once we grant the possibility of a proper human scale, we see that we have made a radical change of assumptions and values. We realize that we are less interested in technological 'breakthroughs' than in technological elegance. Of a new tool or method we will no longer ask: Is it fast? Is it powerful? Is it a labor saver? How many workers will it replace? We will ask instead: Can we (and our children) afford it? Is it fitting to our real needs? Is it becoming to us? Is it unhealthy or ugly? And though we may keep a certain interest in innovation and in what we may become, we will renew our interest in what we have been, realizing that conservationists must necessarily conserve *both* inheritances, the natural and the cultural.

To argue the necessity of wildness to, and in, the human economy is by no means to argue against the necessity of wilderness. The survival of wilderness – of places that we do not change, where we allow the existence even of creatures we perceive as dangerous – is necessary. Our sanity probably requires it. Whether we go to those places or not, we need to know that they exist. And I would argue that we do not need just the great public wildernesses, but millions of small private or semiprivate ones. Every farm should have one; wildernesses can occupy corners of factory grounds and city lots – places where nature is given a free hand, where no human work is done, where people go only as guests. These places function, I think, whether we intend them to or not, as sacred groves – places we respect and leave alone, not because we understand well what goes on there, but because we do not.

We go to wilderness places to be restored, to be instructed in the natural economies of fertility and healing, to admire what we cannot make. Sometimes, as we find to our surprise, we go to be chastened or corrected. And we go in order to return with renewed knowledge by which to judge the health of our human economy and our dwelling places. As we return from our visits to the wilderness, it is sometimes possible to imagine a series of fitting and decent transitions from wild nature to the human community and its supports: from forest to woodlot to the 'two-story agriculture' of tree crops and pasture to orchard to meadow to grainfield to garden to household to neighborhood to village to city – so that even when we reached the city we would not be entirely beyond the influence of the nature of that place.

What I have been implying is that I think there is a bad reason to go to the wilderness. We must not go there to escape the ugliness and the dangers of the present human economy. We must not let ourselves feel that to go there is to escape. In the first place, such an escape is now illusory. In the second place, if, even as conservationists, we see the human and the natural economies as necessarily opposite or opposed, we subscribe to the very opposition that threatens to destroy them both. The wild and the domestic now often seem isolated values, estranged from one another. And yet these are not exclusive polarities like good and evil. There can be continuity between them, and there must be.

What we find, if we weight the balance too much in favor of the domestic, is that we involve ourselves in dangers both personal and public. Not the least of these dangers is dependence on distant sources of money and materials. Farmers are in deep trouble now because they have become too dependent on corporations and banks. They have been using methods and species that enforce this dependence. But such a dependence is not safe, either for farmers or for agriculture. It is not safe for urban consumers. Ultimately, as we are beginning to see, it is not safe for banks and corporations – which, though they have evidently not thought so, are dependent upon farmers. Our farms are endangered because – like the interstate highways or modern hospitals or modern universities – they cannot be inexpensively used. To be usable at all they require great expense.

When the human estate becomes so precarious, our only recourse is to move it back toward the estate of nature. We undoubtedly need better plant and animal species than nature provided us. But we are beginning to see that they can be too much better – too dependent on us and on 'the economy,' too expensive. In farm animals, for instance, we want good commercial quality, but we can see that the ability to produce meat or milk can actually be a threat to the farmer and to the animal if not accompanied by qualities we would call natural: thriftiness, hardiness, physical vigor, resistance to disease and parasites, ability to breed and give birth without assistance, strong mothering instincts. These natural qualities decrease care, work, and worry; they also decrease the costs of production. They save feed and time; they make diseases and cures exceptional rather than routine.

We need crop and forage species of high productive ability also, but we do not need species that will not produce at all without expensive fertilizers and chemicals. Contrary to the premise of agribusiness advertisements and of most expert advice, farmers do not thrive by production or by 'skimming' a large 'cash flow.' They cannot solve their problems merely by increasing production or income. They thrive, like all other creatures, according to the difference between their income and their expenses.

One of the strangest characteristics of the industrial economy is the ability to increase production again and again without ever noticing – or without acknowledging – the *costs* of production. That one Holstein cow should produce 50,000 pounds of milk in a year may appear to be marvelous – a miracle of modern science. But what if her productivity is dependent upon the consumption of a huge amount of grain (about a bushel a day), and therefore upon the availability of cheap petroleum? What if she is too valuable (and too delicate) to be allowed outdoors in the rain? What if the proliferation of her kind will again drastically reduce the number of dairy farms and farmers? Or, to use a more obvious example, can we afford a bushel of grain at a cost of five to twenty bushels of topsoil lost to erosion?

'It is good to have Nature working for you,' said Henry Besuden, the dean of American Southdown breeders. 'She works for a minimum wage.' That is true. She works at times for almost nothing, requiring only that we respect her work and give her a chance, as when she maintains – indeed, improves – the fertility and productivity of a pasture by the natural succession of clover and grass or when she improves a clay soil for us by means of the roots of a grass sod. She works for us by preserving health or wholeness, which for all our ingenuity we cannot make. If we fail to respect her health, she deals out her justice by withdrawing her protection against disease – which we *can* make, and do.

To make this continuity between the natural and the human, we have only two sources of instruction: nature herself and our cultural tradition. If we listen only to the apologists for the industrial economy, who respect neither nature nor culture, we get the idea that it is somehow our goodness that makes us so destructive: the air is unfit to breathe, the water is unfit to drink, the soil is washing away, the cities are violent and the countryside neglected, all because we are intelligent, enterprising, industrious, and generous, concerned only to feed the hungry and to 'make a better future for our children.' Respect for nature causes us to doubt this, and our cultural tradition confirms and illuminates our doubt: no good thing is destroyed by goodness; good things are destroyed by wickedness. We may identify that insight as Biblical, but it is taken for granted by both the Greek and the Biblical lineages of our culture, from Homer and Moses to William Blake. Since the start of the industrial revolution, there have been voices urging that this inheritance may be safely replaced by intelligence, information, energy, and money. No idea, I believe, could be more dangerous.

(1982)

A Few Words for Motherhood

It is the season of motherhood again, and we are preoccupied with the pregnant and the unborn. When birth is imminent, especially with a ewe or a mare, we are at the barn the last thing before we go to bed, at least once in the middle of the night, and well before daylight in the morning. It is a sort of joke here that we have almost never had anything born in the middle of the night. And yet somebody must get up and go out anyway. With motherhood, you don't argue probabilities.

I set the alarm, but always wake up before it goes off. Some part of the mind is given to the barn, these times, and you can't put it to sleep. For a few minutes after I wake up, I lie there wondering where I will get the will and the energy to drag myself out of bed again. Anxiety takes care of that: maybe the ewe has started into labor, and is in trouble. But it isn't just anxiety. It is curiosity too, and the eagerness for new life that goes with motherhood. I want to see what nature and breeding and care and the passage of time have led to. If I open the barn door and hear a little bleat coming out of the darkness, I will be glad to be awake. My liking for that always returns with a force that surprises me.

These are bad times for motherhood – a kind of biological drudgery, some say, using up women who could do better things. Thoreau may have been the first to assert that people should not belong to farm animals, but the idea is now established doctrine with many farmers – and it has received amendments to the effect that people should not belong to children, or to each other. But we all have to belong to something, if only to the idea that we should not belong to anything. We all have to be used up by something. And though I will never be a mother, I am glad to be used up by motherhood and what it leads to, just as – most of the time – I gladly belong to my wife, my children, and several head of cattle, sheep, and horses. What better way to be used up? How else to be a farmer?

There are good arguments against female animals that need help in giving birth; I know what they are, and have gone over them many times. And yet – if the ordeal is not too painful or too long, and if it succeeds – I always wind up a little grateful to the ones that need help. Then I get to take part, get to go through the process another time, and I invariably come away from it feeling instructed and awed and pleased.

My wife and son and I find the heifer in a far corner of the field. In maybe two hours of labor she has managed to give birth to one small foot. We know how it has been with her. Time and again she has lain down and heaved at her burden, and got up and turned and smelled the ground. She is a heifer – how does she know that something is supposed to *be* there?

It takes some doing even for the three of us to get her into the barn. Her orders are to be alone, and she does all in her power to obey. But finally we shut the door behind her and get her into a stall. She isn't wild; once she is confined it isn't even necessary to tie her. I wash in a bucket of icy water and soap my right hand and forearm. She is quiet now. And so are we humans – worried, and excited too, for if there is a chance for failure here, there is also a chance for success.

I loop a bale string onto the calf's exposed foot, knot the string short around a stick which my son then holds. I press my hand gently into the birth canal until I find the second foot and then, a little further on, a nose. I loop a string around the second foot, fasten on another stick for a handhold. And then we pull. The heifer stands and pulls against us for a few seconds, then gives up and goes down. We brace ourselves the best we can into our work, pulling as the heifer pushes. Finally the head comes, and then, more easily, the rest.

We clear the calf's nose, help him to breathe, and then, because the heifer has not yet stood up, we lay him on the bedding in front of her. And what always seems to me the miracle of it begins. She has never calved before. If she ever saw another cow calve, she paid little attention. She has, as we humans say, no education and no experience. And yet she recognizes the calf as her own, and knows what to do for it. Some heifers don't, but most do, as this one does. Even before she gets up, she begins to lick it about the nose and face with loud, vigorous swipes of her tongue. And all the while she utters a kind of moan, meant to comfort, encourage, and reassure – or so I understand it.

How does she know so much? How did all this come about? Instinct. Evolution. I know those words. I understand the logic of the survival of the fittest: good mothering instincts have survived because bad mothers lost their calves: the good traits triumphed, the bad perished. But how come some are fit in the first place? What prepared in the mind of the first cow or ewe or mare – or, for that matter, in the mind of the first human mother – this intricate, careful, passionate welcome to the newborn? I don't know. I don't think anybody does. I distrust any mortal who claims to know. We call these animals dumb brutes, and so far as we can tell they are more or less dumb, and there are certainly times when those of us who live with them will seem to find evidence that they are plenty stupid. And yet, they are indisputably allied with intelligence more articulate and more refined than is to be found in any obstetrics textbook. What is one to make of it? Here is a dumb brute lying in dung and straw, licking her calf, and as always I am feeling honored to be associated with her.

The heifer has stood up now, and the calf is trying to stand, wobbling up onto its hind feet and knees, only to be knocked over by an exuberant caress of its mother's tongue. We have involved ourselves too much in this story by now to leave before the end, but we have our chores to finish too, and so to hasten things I lend a hand.

I help the calf onto his feet and maneuver him over to the heifer's flank. I am not supposed to be there, but her calf is, and so she accepts, or at least permits, my help. In these situations it sometimes seems to me that animals know that help is needed, and that they accept it with some kind of understanding. The thought moves me, but I am never sure, any more than I am sure what the cow means by the low moans she makes as the calf at last begins to nurse. To me, they sound like praise and encouragement – but how would I know?

Always when I hear that little smacking as the calf takes hold of the tit and swallows its first milk, I feel a pressure of laughter under my ribs. I am not sure what that means either. It certainly affirms more than the saved money value of the calf and the continued availability of beef. We all three feel it. We look at each other and grin with relief and satisfaction. Life is on its legs again, and we exult.

(1980)

Two Minds

Human orders – scientific, artistic, social, economic, and political – are fictions. They are untrue, not because they necessarily are false, but because they necessarily are incomplete. All of our human orders, however inclusive we may try to make them, turn out to be to some degree exclusive. And so we are always being surprised by something we find, too late, that we have excluded. Think of almost any political revolution or freedom movement or the ozone hole or mad cow disease or the events of September 11, 2001.

The present order, thus surprised, is then required to accommodate new knowledge and thus to be reordered. Thomas Kuhn described this process in *The Structure of Scientific Revolutions*.

But these surprises and changes obviously have their effect also on individual lives and on whole cultures. All of our fictions labor under an ever-failing need to be true. And this means that they labor under an obligation to be continuously revised.

Or, to put it another way, we humans necessarily make pictures in our minds of our places and our world. But we can do this only by selection, putting some things into the picture and leaving the rest out. And so we live in two landscapes, one superimposed upon the other.

First there is the cultural landscape made up of our own knowledge of where we are, of landmarks and memories, of patterns of use and travel, of remindings and meanings. The cultural landscape, among other things, is a pattern of exchanges of work, goods, and comforts among neighbors. It is the country we have in mind.

And then there is the actual landscape, which we can never fully know, which is always going to be to some degree a mystery, from time to time surprising us. These two landscapes are necessarily and irremediably different from each other. But there is danger in their difference; they can become *too* different. If the cultural landscape becomes too different from the actual landscape, then we will make practical errors that will be destructive of the actual landscape or of ourselves or of both.

You can learn this from the study of any landscape that is inhabited by humans, or from teachers such as Barry Lopez and Gary Nabhan, who have written on the traditional economies of the Arctic and the American Southwest. It is easier to understand, perhaps, when thinking about extreme landscapes: if the cultural landscapes come to be too much at odds with the actual landscapes of the Arctic or the desert, the penalties are apt to be swift and lethal. In more forgiving landscapes they will (perhaps) be slower, but finally just as dangerous.

In some temperate and well-watered areas, we humans have applied the most extreme industrial methods of landscape destruction. By disregarding the cultural landscape, and all values and protections that accrue therefrom to the actual landscape, the strip miners entirely destroy the actual landscape. Cropland erosion, caused by a serious incongruity between the cultural and the actual landscapes, is a slower form of destruction than strip mining, but given enough time, it too can be entirely destructive.

At present, in the United States and in much of the rest of the world, most of the cultural landscapes that still exist are hodge-podges of failing local memories, money-making schemes, ignorant plans, bucolic fantasies, misinformation, and the random facts that we now call 'information.' This is compounded by the outright destruction of innumerable burial sites and other sacred places, of natural and historical landmarks, and of entire actual landscapes. Moreover, we have enormous and increasing numbers of people who have no home landscape, though in every one of their economic acts they are affecting the actual landscapes of the world, mostly for the worse. This is a situation unprecedentedly disorderly and dangerous.

To be disconnected from any actual landscape is to be, in the practical or economic sense, without a home. To have no country carefully and practically in mind is to be without a culture. In such a situation, culture becomes purposeless and arbitrary, dividing into 'popular culture,' determined by commerce, advertising, and fashion, and 'high culture,' which is either social affectation, displaced cultural memory, or the merely aesthetic pursuits of artists and art lovers.

We are thus involved in a kind of lostness in which most people are participating more or less unconsciously in the destruction of the natural world, which is to say, the sources of their own lives. They are doing this unconsciously because they see or do very little of the actual destruction themselves, and they don't know, because they have no way to learn, how they are involved. At the same time, many of the same people fear and mourn the destruction, which they can't stop because they have no practical understanding of its causes.

Conservationists, scientists, philosophers, and others are telling us daily and hourly that our species is now behaving with colossal irrationality and that we had better become more rational. I agree as to the dimensions and danger of our irrationality. As to the possibility of curing it by rationality, or at least by the rationality of the rationalists, I have some doubts.

The trouble is not just in the way we are thinking; it is also in the way we, or anyhow we in the affluent parts of the world, are living. And it is going to be hard to define anybody's living as a series of simple choices between irrationality and rationality. Moreover, this is supposedly an age of reason; we are encouraged to believe that the governments and corporations of the affluent parts of the world are run by rational people using rational processes to make rational decisions. The dominant faith of the world in our time is in rationality. That in an age of reason, the human race, or the most wealthy and powerful parts of it, should be behaving with colossal irrationality ought to make us wonder if reason alone can lead us to do what is right.

It is often proposed, nowadays, that if we would only get rid of religion and other leftovers from our primitive past and become enlightened by scientific rationalism, we could invent the new values and ethics that are needed to preserve the natural world. This proposal is perfectly reasonable, and perfectly doubtful. It supposes that we can empirically know and rationally understand everything involved, which is exactly the supposition that has underwritten our transgressions against the natural world in the first place.

Obviously we need to use our intelligence. But how much intelligence have we got? And what sort of intelligence is it that we have? And how, at its best, does human intelligence work? In order to try to answer these questions I am going to suppose for a while that there are two different kinds of human mind: the Rational Mind and another, which, for want of a better term, I will call the Sympathetic Mind. I will say now, and try to keep myself reminded, that these terms are going to appear to be allegorical, too neat and too separate – though I need to say also that their separation was not invented by me.

The Rational Mind, without being anywhere perfectly embodied, is the mind all of us are supposed to be trying to have. It is the mind that the most powerful and influential people *think* they have. Our schools exist mainly to educate and propagate and authorize the Rational Mind. The Rational Mind is objective, analytical, and empirical; it makes itself up only by considering facts; it pursues truth by experimentation; it is uncorrupted by preconception, received authority, religious belief, or feeling. Its ideal products are the proven fact, the accurate prediction, and the 'informed decision.' It is, you might say, the official mind of science, industry, and government.

The Sympathetic Mind differs from the Rational Mind, not by being unreasonable, but by refusing to limit knowledge or reality to the scope of reason or factuality or experimentation, and by making reason the servant of things it considers precedent and higher.

The Rational Mind is motivated by the fear of being misled, of being wrong. Its purpose is to exclude everything that cannot empirically or experimentally be proven to be a fact.

The Sympathetic Mind is motivated by fear of error of a very different kind: the error of carelessness, of being unloving. Its purpose is to be considerate of whatever is present, to leave nothing out.

The Rational Mind is exclusive; the Sympathetic Mind, however failingly, wishes to be inclusive.

These two types certainly don't exhaust the taxonomy of minds. They are merely the two that the intellectual fashions of our age have most deliberately separated and thrown into opposition.

My purpose here is to argue in defense of the Sympathetic Mind. But my objection is not to the use of reason or to reasonability. I am objecting to the exclusiveness of the Rational Mind, which has limited itself to a selection of mental functions such as the empirical methodologies of analysis and experimentation and the attitudes of objectivity and realism. In order to go into business on its own, it has in effect withdrawn from all of human life that involves feeling, affection, familiarity, reverence, faith, and loyalty. The separability of the Rational Mind is not only the dominant fiction but also the master superstition of the modern age.

The Sympathetic Mind is under the influence of certain inborn or at least fundamental likes and dislikes. Its impulse is toward wholeness. It is moved by affection for its home place, the local topography, the local memories, and the local creatures. It hates estrangement, dismemberment, and disfigurement. The Rational Mind tolerates all these things 'in pursuit of truth' or in pursuit of money – which, in modern practice, have become nearly the same pursuit.

I am objecting to the failure of the rationalist enterprise of 'objective science' or 'pure science' or 'the disinterested pursuit of truth' to prevent massive damage both to nature and to human economy. The Rational Mind does not confess its complicity in the equation: knowledge = power = money = damage. Even so, the alliance of academic science, government, and the corporate economy, and their unifying pattern of sanctions and rewards, is obvious enough. We have resisted, so far, a state religion, but we are in danger of having both a corporate state and a state science, which some people, in both the sciences and the arts, would like to establish as a state religion.

The Rational Mind is the lowest common denominator of the government-corporation-university axis. It is the fiction that makes high intellectual ability the unquestioning servant of bad work and bad law.

Under the reign of the Rational Mind, there is no firewall between contemporary science and contemporary industry or economic development. It is entirely imaginable, for instance, that a young person might go into biology because of love for plants and animals. But such a young person had better be careful, for there is nothing to prevent knowledge gained for love of the creatures from being used to destroy them for the love of money.

Now some biologists, who have striven all their lives to embody perfectly the Rational Mind, have become concerned, even passionately concerned, about the loss of 'biological diversity,' and they are determined to do something about it. This is usually presented as a merely logical development from ignorance to realization to action. But so far it is only comedy. The Rational Mind, which has been destroying biological diversity by 'figuring out' some things, now proposes to save what is left of biological diversity by 'figuring out' some more things. It does what it has always done before: it defines the problem as a big problem calling for a big solution; it calls in the world-class experts; it invokes science, technology, and large grants of money; it propagandizes and organizes and 'gears up for a major effort.' The comedy here is in the failure of these rationalists to see that as soon as they have become passionately concerned they have stepped outside the dry, objective, geometrical territory claimed by the Rational Mind, and have entered the still mysterious homeland of the Sympathetic Mind, watered by unpredictable rains and by real sweat and real tears.

The Sympathetic Mind would not forget that so-called environmental problems have causes that are in part political and therefore have remedies that are in part political. But it would not try to solve these problems merely by large-scale political protections of 'the environment.' It knows that they must be solved ultimately by correcting the way people use their home places and local landscapes. Politically, but also by local economic improvements, it would stop colonialism in all its forms, domestic and foreign, corporate and governmental. Its first political principle is that landscapes should not be used by people who do not live in them and share their fate. If that principle were strictly applied, we would have far less need for the principle of 'environmental protection.'

The Sympathetic Mind understands the vital importance of the cultural landscape. The Rational Mind, by contrast, honors no cultural landscape, and therefore has no protective loyalty or affection for any actual landscape.

The definitive practical aim of the Sympathetic Mind is to adapt local economies to local landscapes. This is necessarily the work of local cultures. It cannot be done as a world-scale *feat* of science, industry, and government. This will seem a bitter bite to the optimists of scientific rationalism, which is scornful of limits and proud of its usurpations. But the science of the Sympathetic Mind is occupied precisely with the study of limits, both natural and human.

The Rational Mind does not work from any sense of geographical whereabouts or social connection or from any basis in cultural tradition or principle or character. It does not see itself as existing or working within a context. The Rational Mind doesn't think there is a context until it gets there. Its principle is to be 'objective' – which is to say, unremembering and disloyal. It works within narrow mental boundaries that it draws for itself, as directed by the requirements of its profession or academic specialty or its ambition or its desire for power or profit, thus allowing for the 'trade-off' and the 'externalization' of costs and effects. Even when working outdoors, it is an indoor mind.

The Sympathetic Mind, even when working indoors, is an outdoor mind. It lives within an abounding and unbounded reality, always partly mysterious, in which everything matters, in which we humans are therefore returned to our ancient need for thanksgiving, prayer, and propitiation, in which we meet again and again the ancient question: How does one become worthy to use what must be used?

Whereas the Rational Mind is the mind of analysis, explanation, and manipulation, the Sympathetic Mind is the mind of our creatureliness.

Creatureliness denotes what Wallace Stevens called 'the instinctive integrations which are the reasons for living.' In our creatureliness we forget the little or much that we know about the optic nerve and the light-sensitive cell, and *we see*; we forget whatever we know about the physiology of the brain, and *we think*; we forget what we know of anatomy, the nervous system, the gastrointestinal tract, and *we work, eat, and sleep*. We forget the theories and therapies of 'human relationships,' and we merely love the people we love, and even try to love the others. If we have any sense, we forget the fashionable determinisms, and we tell our children, 'Be good. Be careful. Mind your manners. Be kind.'

The Sympathetic Mind leaves the world whole, or it attempts always to do so. It looks upon people and other creatures as whole beings. It does not parcel them out into functions and uses.

The Rational Mind, by contrast, has rested its work for a long time on the proposition that all creatures are machines. This works as a sort of strainer to eliminate impurities such as affection, familiarity, and loyalty from the pursuit of knowledge, power, and profit. This machine-system assures the objectivity of the Rational Mind, which is itself understood as a machine, but it fails to account for a number of things, including the Rational Mind's own worries and enthusiasms. Why should a machine be bothered by the extinction of other machines? Would even an 'intelligent' computer grieve over the disappearance of the Carolina parakeet?

The Rational Mind is preoccupied with the search for a sure way to avoid risk, loss, and suffering. For the Rational Mind, experience is likely to consist of a sequence of bad surprises and therefore must be booked as a 'loss.' That is why, to rationalists, the past and the present are so readily expendable or destructible in favor of the future, the era of no loss.

But the Sympathetic Mind accepts loss and suffering as the price, willingly paid, of its sympathy and affection – its wholeness.

The Rational Mind attempts endlessly to inform itself against its ruin by facts, experiments, projections, scoutings of 'alternatives,' hedgings against the unknown.

The Sympathetic Mind is informed by experience, by tradition-borne stories of the experiences of others, by familiarity, by compassion, by commitment, by faith.

The Sympathetic Mind is preeminently a faithful mind, taking knowingly and willingly the risks required by faith. The Rational Mind, ever in need of certainty, is always in doubt, always looking for a better way, asking, testing, disbelieving in everything but its own sufficiency to its own needs, which its experience and its own methods continually disprove. It is a skeptical, fearful, suspicious mind, and always a disappointed one, awaiting the supreme truth or discovery it expects of itself, which of itself it cannot provide.

To show how these two minds work, let us place them within the dilemma of a familiar story. Here is the parable of the lost sheep from the Gospel of St. Matthew: 'If a man have an hundred sheep, and one of them be gone astray, doth he not leave the ninety and nine, and goeth into the mountains, and seeketh that which is gone astray? And if so be that he find it, verily I say unto you, he rejoiceth more of that sheep, than of the ninety and nine which went not astray.'

This parable is the product of an eminently sympathetic mind, but for the moment that need not distract us. The dilemma is practical enough, and we can see readily how the two kinds of mind would deal with it.

The rationalist, we may be sure, has a hundred sheep because he has a plan for that many. The one who has gone astray has escaped not only from the flock but also from the plan. That this particular sheep should stray off in this particular place at this particular time, though it is perfectly in keeping with the nature of sheep and the nature of the world, is not at all in keeping with a rational plan. What is to be done? Well, it certainly would not be rational to leave the ninety and nine, exposed as they would then be to further whims of nature, in order to search for the one. Wouldn't it be best to consider the lost sheep a 'trade-off' for the safety of the ninety-nine? Having thus agreed to his loss, the doctrinaire rationalist would then work his way through a series of reasonable questions. What would be an 'acceptable risk'? What would be an 'acceptable loss'? Would it not be good to do some experiments to determine how often sheep may be expected to get lost? If one sheep is likely to get lost every so often, then would it not be better to have perhaps 110 sheep? Or should one insure the flock against such expectable losses? The annual insurance premium would equal the market value of how many sheep? What is likely to be the cost of the labor of looking for one lost sheep after quitting time? How much time spent looking would equal the market value of the lost sheep? Should not one think of splicing a few firefly genes into one's sheep so that strayed sheep would glow in the dark? And so on.

But (leaving aside the theological import of the parable) the shepherd is a shepherd because he embodies the Sympathetic Mind. Because he is a man of sympathy, a man devoted to the care of sheep, a man who knows the nature of sheep and of the world, the shepherd of the parable is not surprised or baffled by his problem. He does not hang back to argue over risks, trade-offs, actuarial data, or market values. He does not quibble over fractions. He goes without hesitating to hunt for the lost sheep because he has committed himself to the care of the whole hundred, because he understands his work as the fulfillment of his whole trust, because he loves the sheep, and because he knows or imagines what it is to be lost. He does what he does on behalf of the whole flock because he wants to preserve himself as a whole shepherd.

He also does what he does because he has a particular affection for that particular sheep. To the Rational Mind, all sheep are the same; any one is the same as any other. They are interchangeable, like coins or clones or machine parts or members of 'the work force.' To the Sympathetic Mind, each one is different from every other. Each one is an individual whose value is never entirely reducible to market value.

The Rational Mind can and will rationalize any trade-off. The Sympathetic Mind can rationalize none. Thus we have not only the parable of the ninety and nine, but also the Buddhist vow to save all sentient beings. The parable and the vow are utterly alien to the rationalism of modern science, politics, and industry. To the Rational Mind, they 'don't make sense' because they deal with hardship and risk merely by acknowledgment and acceptance. Their very point is to require a human being's suffering to involve itself in the suffering of other creatures, including that of other human beings.

The Rational Mind conceives of itself as eminently practical, and is given to boasting about its competence in dealing with 'reality.' But if you want to hire somebody to take care of your hundred sheep, I think you had better look past the 'animal scientist' and hire the shepherd of the parable, if you can still find him anywhere. For it will continue to be more reasonable, from the point of view of the Rational Mind, to trade off the lost sheep for the sake of the sheep you have left – until only one is left.

If you think I have allowed my argument to carry me entirely into fantasy and irrelevance, then let me quote an up-to-date story that follows pretty closely the outline of Christ's parable. This is from an article by Bernard E. Rollin in *Christian Century*, December 19–26, 2001, p. 26:

> A young man was working for a company that operated a large, total-confinement swine farm. One day he detected symptoms of a disease among some of the feeder pigs. As a teen, he had raised pigs himself . . . so he knew how to treat the animals. But the company's policy was to kill any diseased animals with a blow to the head – the profit margin was considered too low to allow for treatment of individual animals. So the employee decided to come in on his own time, with his own medicine, and he cured the animals. The management's response was to fire him on the spot for violating company policy.

The young worker in the hog factory is a direct cultural descend-ant of the shepherd in the parable, just about opposite and perhaps incomprehensible to the 'practical' rationalist. But the practical implications are still the same. Would you rather have your pigs cared for by a young man who had compassion for them or by one who would indifferently knock them in the head? Which of the two would be most likely to prevent the disease in the first place? Compassion, of course, is the crux of the issue. For 'company policy' must exclude compassion; if compassion were to be admitted to con-sideration, such a 'farm' could not exist. And yet one imagines that even the hardheaded realists of 'management' must occasionally violate company policy by wondering at night what they would do if *all* the pigs got sick. (I suppose they would kill them all, collect the insurance, and move on. Perhaps all that has been foreseen and pre-pared for in the business plan, and there is no need, after all, to lie awake and worry.)

But what of the compassionate young man? The next sentence of Mr. Rollin's account says: 'Soon the young man left agriculture for good . . .' We need to pause here to try to understand the significance of his departure.

Like a strip mine, a hog factory exists in utter indifference to the landscape. Its purpose, as an animal *factory*, is to exclude from consid-eration both the nature of the place where it is and the nature of hogs. That it is a factory means that it could be in *any* place, and that the hog is a 'unit of production.' But the young man evidently was farm-raised. He evidently had in his mind at least the memory of an actual place and at least the remnants of its cultural landscape. In that land-scape, things were respected according to their nature, which made compassion possible when their nature was violated. That this young man was fired from his job for showing compassion is strictly logical, for the explicit purpose of the hog factory is to violate nature. And then, logically enough, the young man 'left agriculture for good.' But when you exclude compassion from agriculture, what have you done? Have you not removed something ultimately of the greatest practical worth? I believe so. But this is one of the Rational Mind's world-scale experiments that has not yet been completed.

The Sympathetic Mind is a freedom-loving mind because it knows, given the inevitable discrepancies between the cultural and the actual landscapes, that everybody involved must be free to change. The idea that science and industry and government can discover for the rest of us the ultimate truths of nature and human nature, which then can be infallibly used to regulate our life, is wrong. The true work of the sciences and the arts is to keep all of us moving, in our own lives in our own places, between the cultural and the actual landscapes, making the always necessary and the forever unfinished corrections.

When the Rational Mind establishes a 'farm,' the result is bad farming. There is a remarkable difference between a hog factory, which exists only for the sake of its economic product, and a good farm, which exists for many reasons, including the pleasure of the farm family, their affection for their home, their satisfaction in their good work – in short, their patriotism. Such a farm yields its economic product as a sort of side effect of the health of a flourishing place in which things live according to their nature. The hog factory attempts to be a totally rational, which is to say a totally economic, enterprise. It strips away from animal life and human work every purpose, every benefit too, that is not economic. It comes about as the result of a long effort on the part of 'scientific agriculture' to remove the Sympathetic Mind from all agricultural landscapes and replace it with the Rational Mind. And so good-bye to the shepherd of the parable, and to compassionate young men who leave agriculture for good. Good-bye to the cultural landscape. Good-bye to the actual landscape. These have all been dispensed with by the Rational Mind, to be replaced by a totalitarian economy with its neat, logical concepts of world-as-factory and life-as-commodity. This is an economy excluding all decisions but 'informed decisions,' purporting to reduce the possibility of loss.

Nothing so entices and burdens the Rational Mind as its need, and its self-imposed responsibility, to make 'informed decisions.' It is certainly possible for a mind to be informed – in several ways, too. And it is certainly possible for an informed mind to make decisions on the basis of all that has informed it. But that such decisions are 'informed decisions' – in the sense that 'informed decisions' are predictably right, or even that they are reliably better than uninformed decisions – is open to doubt.

The ideal of the 'informed decision' forces 'decision makers' into a thicket of facts, figures, studies, tests, and 'projections.' It requires long and uneasy pondering of 'cost-benefit ratios' – the costs and benefits, often, of abominations. The problem is that decisions all have to do with the future, and all the actual knowledge we have is of the past. It is impossible to make a decision, however well-informed it may be, that is assuredly right, because it is impossible to know what will happen. It is only possible to know or guess that some things *may* happen, and many things that have happened have not been foreseen.

Moreover, having made an 'informed decision,' even one that turns out well, there is no way absolutely to determine whether or not it was a better decision than another decision that one might have made instead. It is not possible to compare a decision that one made with a decision that one did not make. There are no 'controls,' no 'replication plots,' in experience.

The Rational Mind is under relentless pressure to justify governmental and corporate acts on an ever-increasing scale of power, extent, and influence. Given that pressure, it may be not so very surprising that the Rational Mind should have a remarkable tendency toward superstition. Reaching their mental limits, which, as humans, they must do soon enough, the rationalists begin to base their thinking on principles that are sometimes astonishingly unsound: 'Creatures are machines' or 'Knowledge is good' or 'Growth is good' or 'Science will find the answer' or 'A rising tide lifts all boats.' Or they approach the future with a stupefying array of computers, models, statistics, projections, calculations, cost-benefit analyses, experts, and even better computers – which of course cannot foretell the end of a horse race any better than Bertie Wooster.

And so the great weakness of the Rational Mind, contrary to its protestations, is a sort of carelessness or abandonment that takes the form of high-stakes gambling – as when, with optimism and fanfare, without foreknowledge or self-doubt or caution, nuclear physicists or chemists or genetic engineers release their products into the whole world, making the whole world their laboratory.

Or the great innovators and decision makers build huge airplanes whose loads of fuel make them, in effect, flying bombs. And they build the World Trade Center, forgetting apparently the B-25 bomber that crashed into the seventy-ninth floor of the Empire State Building in 1945. And then on September 11, 2001, some enemies – of a kind we well knew we had and evidently had decided to ignore – captured two huge airplanes and flew them, as bombs, into the two towers of the World Trade Center. In retrospect, we may doubt that these shaping decisions were properly informed, just as we may doubt that the expensive 'intelligence' that is supposed to foresee and prevent such disasters is sufficiently intelligent.

The decisions, if the great innovators and decision makers were given to reading poetry, might have been informed by James Laughlin's poem 'Above the City,' which was written soon after the B-25 crashed into the Empire State Building:

> You know our office on the 18th
> floor of the Salmon Tower looks
> right out on the
>
> Empire State & it just happened
> we were finishing up some
> late invoices on
>
> a new book that Saturday morning
> when a bomber roared through the
> mist and crashed
>
> flames poured from the windows
> into the drifting clouds & sirens
> screamed down in

> the streets below it was unearthly
> but you know the strangest thing
> we realized that
>
> none of us were much surprised be-
> cause we'd always known that those
> two Paragons of
>
> Progress sooner or later would per-
> form before our eyes this demon-
> stration of their
> true relationship

It is tempting now to call this poem 'prophetic.' But it is so only in the sense that it is insightful; it perceives the implicit contradiction between tall buildings and airplanes. This contradiction was readily apparent also to the terrorists of September 11, but evidently invisible within the mist of technological euphoria that had surrounded the great innovators and decision makers.

In the several dimensions of its horror the destruction of the World Trade Center exceeds imagination, and that tells us something. But as a physical event it is as comprehensible as $1 + 1$, and that tells us something else.

Now that terrorism has established itself among us as an inescapable consideration, even the great decision makers are beginning to see that we are surrounded by the results of great decisions not adequately informed. We have built many nuclear power plants, each one a potential catastrophe, that will have to be protected, not only against their inherent liabilities and dangers, but against terrorist attack. And we have made, in effect, one thing of our food supply system, and that will have to be protected (if possible) from bioterrorism. These are by no means the only examples of the way we have exposed ourselves to catastrophic harm and great expense by our informed, rational acceptance of the normalcy of bigness and centralization.

After September 11, it can no longer be believed that science, technology, and industry are only good or that they serve only one 'side.' That never has been more than a progressivist and commercial superstition. Any power that belongs to one side belongs, for worse as well as better, to all sides, as indifferent as the sun that rises 'on the evil and on the good.' Only in the narrowest view of history can the scientists who worked on the nuclear bomb be said to have worked for democracy and freedom. They worked inescapably also for the enemies of democracy and freedom. If terrorists get possession of a nuclear bomb and use it, then the scientists of the bomb will be seen to have worked also for terrorism. There is (so far as I can now see) nothing at all that the Rational Mind can do, after the fact, to make this truth less true or less frightening. This predicament cries out for a different kind of mind before and after the fact: a mind faithful and compassionate that will not rationalize about the 'good use' of destructive power, but will repudiate *any* use of it.

Freedom also is neutral, of course, and serves evil as well as good. But freedom rests on the power of good – by free speech, for instance – to correct evil. A great destructive power simply prevents this small decency of freedom. There is no way to correct a nuclear explosion.

In the midst of the dangers of the Rational Mind's achievement of bigness and centralization, the Sympathetic Mind is as hard-pressed as a pacifist in the midst of a war. There is no greater violence that ends violence, and no greater bigness with which to solve the problems of bigness. All that the Sympathetic Mind can do is maintain its difference, preserve its own integrity, and attempt to see the possibility of something better.

The Sympathetic Mind, as the mind of our creatureliness, accepts life in this world for what it is: mortal, partial, fallible, complexly dependent, entailing many responsibilities toward ourselves, our places, and our fellow beings. Above all, it understands itself as limited. It knows without embarrassment its own irreducible ignorance, especially of the future. It deals with the issue of the future, not by knowing what is going to happen, but by knowing – within limits – what to expect, and what should be required, of itself, of its neighbors, and of its place. Its decisions are informed by its culture, its experience, its understanding of nature. Because it is aware of its limits and its ignorance, it is alert to issues of scale. The Sympathetic Mind knows from experience – not with the brain only, but with the body – that danger increases with height, temperature, speed, and power. It knows by common sense and instinct that the way to protect a building from being hit by an airplane is to make it shorter; that the way to keep a nuclear power plant from becoming a weapon is not to build it; that the way to increase the security of a national food supply is to increase the agricultural self-sufficiency of states, regions, and local communities.

Because it is the mind of our wholeness, our involvement with all things beyond ourselves, the Sympathetic Mind is alert as well to the issues of propriety, of the fittingness of our artifacts to their places and to our own circumstances, needs, and hopes. It is preoccupied, in other words, with the fidelity or the truthfulness of the cultural landscape to the actual landscape.

I know I am not the only one reminded by the World Trade Center of the Tower of Babel: 'let us build . . . a tower, whose top may reach unto heaven; and let us make us a name, lest we be scattered abroad upon the face of the whole earth.' All extremely tall buildings have made me think of the Tower of Babel, and this started a long time before September, 11, 2001, for reasons that have become much clearer to me now that 'those two Paragons of / progress' have demonstrated again 'their true relationship.'

Like all such gigantic buildings, from Babel onward, the World Trade Center was built without reference to its own landscape or to any other. And the reason in this instance is not far to find. The World Trade Center had no reference to a landscape because world trade, as now practiced, has none. World trade now exists to exploit indifferently the landscapes of the world, and to gather the profits to centers whence they may be distributed to the world's wealthiest people. World trade needs centers precisely to prevent the world's wealth from being 'scattered abroad upon the face of the whole earth.' Such centers, like the 'global free market' and the 'global village,' are utopias, 'no-places.' They need to be no-places, because they respect no places and are loyal to no place.

As for the problem of building on Manhattan Island, the Rational Mind has reduced that also to a simple economic principle: land is expensive but air is cheap; therefore, build in the air. In the early 1960s my family and I lived on the Lower West Side, not far uptown from what would become the site of the World Trade Center. The area was run down, already under the judgment of 'development.' But once, obviously, it had been a coherent, thriving local neighborhood of residential apartments and flats, small shops and stores, where merchants and customers knew one another and neighbors were known to neighbors. Walking from our building to the Battery was a pleasant thing to do because one had the sense of being in a real place that kept both the signs of its old human history and the memory of its geographical identity. The last time I went there, the place had been utterly dis-placed by the World Trade Center.

Exactly the same feat of displacement is characteristic of the air transportation industry, which exists to free travel from all considerations of place. Air travel reduces place to space in order to traverse it in the shortest possible time. And like gigantic buildings, gigantic airports must destroy their places and become no-places in order to exist.

People of the modern world, who have accepted the dominance and the value system of the Rational Mind, do not object, it seems, to this displacement, or to the consequent disconnection of themselves from neighborhoods and from the landscapes that support them, or to their own anonymity within crowds of strangers. These things, according to cliché, free one from the suffocating intimacies of rural or small town life. And yet we now are obliged to notice that placelessness, centralization, gigantic scale, crowdedness, and anonymity are conditions virtually made to order for terrorists.

It is wrong to say, as some always do, that catastrophes are 'acts of God' or divine punishments. But it is not wrong to ask if they may not be the result of our misreading of reality or our own nature, and if some correction may not be needed. My own belief is that the Rational Mind has been performing impressively within the narrowly drawn boundaries of what it provably knows, but it has been doing badly in dealing with the things of which it is ignorant: the future, the mysterious wholeness and multiplicity of the natural world, the needs of human souls, and even the real bases of the human economy in nature, skill, kindness, and trust. Increasingly, it seeks to justify itself with intellectual superstitions, public falsehoods, secrecy, and mistaken hopes, responding to its failures and bad surprises with (as the terrorists intend) terror and with ever grosser applications of power.

But the Rational Mind is caught, nevertheless, in cross-purposes that are becoming harder to ignore. It is altogether probable that there is an executive of an air-polluting industry who has a beloved child who suffers from asthma caused by air pollution. In such a situation the Sympathetic Mind cries, 'Stop! Change your life! Quit your job! At least try to discover the cause of the harm and *do* something about it!' And here the Rational Mind must either give way to the Sympathetic Mind, or it must recite the conventional excuse that is a confession of its failure: 'There is nothing to be done. This is the way things are. It is inevitable.'

The same sort of contradiction now exists between national security and the global economy. Our government, having long ago abandoned any thought of economic self-sufficiency, having ceded a significant measure of national sovereignty to the World Trade Organization, and now terrified by terrorism, is obliged to police the global economy against the transportation of contraband weapons, which can be detected if the meshes of the surveillance network are fine enough, and also against the transportation of diseases, which cannot be detected. This too will be excused, at least for a while, by the plea of inevitability, never mind that this is the result of a conflict of policies and of 'informed decisions.' Meanwhile, there is probably no landscape in the world that is not threatened with abuse or destruction as a result of somebody's notion of trade or somebody's notion of security.

When the Rational Mind undertakes to work on a large scale, it works clumsily. It inevitably does damage, and it cannot exempt even itself or its own from the damage it does. You cannot help to pollute the world's only atmosphere and exempt your asthmatic child. You cannot make allies and enemies of the same people at the same time. Finally the idea of the trade-off fails. When the proposed trade-off is on the scale of the whole world – the natural world for world trade, world peace for national security – it can fail only into world disaster.

The Rational Mind, while spectacularly succeeding in some things, fails completely when it tries to deal in materialist terms with the part of reality that is spiritual. Religion and the language of religion deal approximately and awkwardly enough with this reality, but the Rational Mind, though it apparently cannot resist the attempt, cannot deal with it at all.

But most of the most important laws for the conduct of human life probably are religious in origin – laws such as these: Be merciful, be forgiving, love your neighbors, be hospitable to strangers, be kind to other creatures, take care of the helpless, love your enemies. We must, in short, love and care for one another and the other creatures. We are allowed to make no exceptions. Every person's obligation toward the Creation is summed up in two words from Genesis 2:15: 'Keep it.'

It is impossible, I believe, to make a neat thing of this set of instructions. It is impossible to disentangle its various obligations into a list of discrete items. Selfishness, or even 'enlightened self-interest,' cannot find a place to poke in its awl. One's obligation to oneself cannot be isolated from one's obligation to everything else. The whole thing is balanced on the verb *to love*. Love for oneself finds its only efficacy in love for everything else. Even loving one's enemy has become a strategy of self-love as the technology of death has grown greater. And this the terrorists have discovered and have accepted: the death of your enemy is your own death. The whole network of inter-dependence and obligation is a neatly set trap. Love does not let us escape from it; it turns the trap itself into the means and fact of our only freedom.

This condition of lawfulness and this set of laws did not originate in the Rational Mind, and could not have done so. The Rational Mind reduces our complex obligation to care for one another to issues of justice, forgetting the readiness with which we and our governments reduce justice, in turn, to revenge; and forgetting that even justice is intolerable without mercy, forgiveness, and love.

Justice is a rational procedure. Mercy is not a procedure and it is not rational. It is a kind of freedom that comes from sympathy, which is to say imagination – the *felt* knowledge of what it is to be another person or another creature. It is free because it does not have to be just. Justice is desirable, of course, but it is virtually the opposite of mercy. Mercy, says the Epistle of James, 'rejoiceth against judgment.'

As for the law requiring us to 'keep' the given or the natural world (to go in search of the lost sheep, to save all sentient beings), the Rational Mind, despite the reasonable arguments made by some ecologists and biologists, cannot cover that distance either. In response to the proposition that we are responsible for the health of all the world, the Rational Mind begins to insist upon exceptions and trade-offs. It begins to designate the profit-yielding parts of the world that may 'safely' be destroyed, and those unprofitable parts that may be preserved as 'natural' or 'wild.' It divides the domestic from the wild, the human from the natural. It conceives of a natural place as a place where no humans live. Places where humans live are not natu-ral, and the nature of such places must be reduced to comprehensibility, which is to say destroyed as they naturally are. The Rational Mind, convinced of the need to preserve 'biological diversity,' wants to pre-serve it in 'nature preserves.' It cannot conceive or tolerate the possibility of preserving biological diversity in the whole world, or of an economic harmony between humans and a world that by nature exceeds human comprehension.

It is because of the world's ultimately indecipherable webwork of vital connections, dependences, and obligations, and because ultimately our response to it must be loving beyond knowing, that the works of the Rational Mind are ultimately disappointing even to some rationalists.

When the Rational Mind fails not only into bewilderment but into irrationality and catastrophe, as it repeatedly does, that is because it has so isolated itself within its exclusive terms that it goes beyond its limits without knowing it.

Finally the human mind must accept the limits of sympathy, which paradoxically will enlarge it beyond the limits of rationality, but nevertheless will limit it. It must find its freedom and its satisfaction by working within its limits, on a scale much smaller than the Rational Mind will easily accept, for the Rational Mind continually longs to extend its limits by technology. But the safe competence of human work extends no further, ever, than our ability to think and love at the same time.

Obviously, we *can* work on a gigantic scale, but just as obviously we cannot foresee the gigantic catastrophes to which gigantic works are vulnerable, any more than we can foresee the natural and human consequences of such work. We can develop a global economy, but only on the conditions that it will not be loving in its effects on its human and natural sources, and that it will risk global economic collapse. We can build gigantic works of architecture too, but only with the likelihood that the gathering of the economic means to do so will generate somewhere the will to destroy what we have built.

The efficacy of a law is in the ability of people to obey it. The larger the scale of work, the smaller will be the number of people who can obey the law that we should be loving toward the world, even those places and creatures that we must use. You will see the problem if you imagine that you are one of the many, or if you *are* one of the many, who can find no work except in a destructive industry. Whether or not it is economic slavery to have no choice of jobs, it certainly is moral slavery to have no choice but to do what is wrong.

And so conservationists have not done enough when they conserve wilderness or biological diversity. They also must conserve the possibilities of peace and good work, and to do that they must help to make a good economy. To succeed, they must help to give more and more people everywhere in the world the opportunity to do work that is both a living and a loving. This, I think, cannot be accomplished by the Rational Mind. It will require the full employment of the Sympathetic Mind – *all* the little intelligence we have.

(2002)

The Prejudice Against Country People

On June 21, 2001, Richard Lewontin, a respected Harvard scientist, published in *The New York Review of Books* an article on genetic engineering and the controversy about it. In the latter part of his article, Mr. Lewontin turns away from his announced premise of scientific objectivity to attack, in a markedly personal way, the critics of industrial agriculture and biotechnology who are trying to defend small farmers against exploitation by global agribusiness.

He criticizes Vandana Shiva, the Indian scientist and defender of the traditional agricultures of the Third World, for her appeal to 'religious morality,' and calls her a 'cheerleader.' He speaks of some of her allies as 'a bunch of Luddites,' and he says that all such people are under the influence 'of a false nostalgia for an idyllic life never experienced.' He says that present efforts to save 'the independent family farmer . . . are a hundred years too late, and GMOs [genetically modified organisms] are the wrong target.' One would have thought, Mr. Lewontin says wearily, that 'industrial capitalism . . . has become so much the basis of European and American life that any truly popular new romantic movement against it would be inconceivable.'

Mr. Lewontin is a smart man, but I don't think he understands how conventional, how utterly trite and thoughtless, is his reaction to Ms. Shiva and other advocates of agricultural practices that are biologically sound and economically just. Apologists for industrialism seldom feel any need to notice their agrarian critics, but when a little dog snaps at the heels of a big dog long enough, now and again the big dog will have to condescend. On such occasions, the big dog *always* says what Mr. Lewontin has said in his article: You are a bunch of Luddites; you are a bunch of romantics motivated by nostalgia for a past that never existed; it is too late; there is no escape. The best-loved proposition is the last: Whatever happens is inevitable; it all has been determined by economics and technology.

This is not scientific objectivity or science or scholarship. It is the luxury politics of an academic islander.

The problem for Mr. Lewontin and others like him is that the faith in industrial agriculture as an eternal pillar of human society is getting harder to maintain, not because of the attacks of its opponents but because of the increasingly manifest failures of industrial agriculture itself: massive soil erosion, soil degradation, genetic impoverishment, ecological damage, pollution by toxic chemicals, pollution by animal factory wastes, depletion of aquifers, runaway subsidies, the spread of pests and diseases by the long-distance transportation of food, mad cow disease, indifferent cruelty to animals, the many human sufferings associated with agricultural depression, exploitation of 'cheap' labor, the abuse of migrant workers. And now, after the catastrophe of September 11, the media have begun to notice what critics of industrial capitalism have always known: the corporate food supply is highly vulnerable to acts of biological warfare.

That these problems exist and are serious is indisputable. So why are they so little noticed by politicians of influence, by people in the media, by university scientists and intellectuals? An increasing number of people alerted to the problems will answer immediately: Because far too many of those people are far too dependent on agribusiness contributions, advertising, and grants. That is true, but another reason that needs to be considered is modern society's widespread prejudice against country people. This prejudice is not easy to explain, in view of modern society's continuing dependence upon rural sustenance, but its existence also is indisputable.

Mr. Lewontin's condescension toward country people and their problems is not an aberration either in our society or in *The New York Review of Books*. On June 29, 2000, that magazine published this sentence: 'At worst, [Rebecca West] had a mind that was closed and cold, like a small town lawyer's, prizing facts but estranged from imaginative truth.' And on December 20, 2001, it published this: 'The Gridiron dinner, as the affair is known, drags on for about five hours, enlivened mainly by the speeches of the politicians, whose ghostwriters in

recent years have consistently outdone the journalists in the sharp
ness and grace of their wit (leaving journalists from the provinces
with a strong impulse to follow the groundhogs back into their holes).'

It is possible to imagine that some readers will ascribe my indigna-
tion at those sentences to the paranoia of an advocate for the losing
side. But I would ask those readers to imagine a reputable journal
nowadays that would attribute closed, cold minds to *Jewish* lawyers,
or speak of *black* journalists wanting to follow the groundhogs into
their holes. This, it seems to me, would pretty effectively dissipate
the ha-ha.

Disparagements of farmers, of small towns, of anything identifiable as 'provincial' can be found everywhere: in comic strips, TV
shows, newspaper editorials, literary magazines, and so on. A few
years ago, *The New Republic* affirmed the necessity of the decline of
family farms in a cover article entitled 'The Idiocy of Rural Life.'
And I remember a Kentucky high school basketball cheer that
instructed the opposing team:

> Go back, go back, go back to the woods.
> Your coach is a farmer and your team's no good.

I believe it is a fact, proven by their rapidly diminishing numbers and
economic power, that the world's small farmers and other 'provincial' people have about the same status now as enemy civilians in
wartime. They are the objects of small, 'humane' consideration, but
if they are damaged or destroyed 'collaterally,' then 'we very much
regret it' but they were in the way – and, by implication, not quite as
human as 'we' are. The industrial and corporate powers, abetted and
excused by their many dependants in government and the universities, are perpetrating a sort of economic genocide – less bloody than
military genocide, to be sure, but just as arrogant, foolish, and ruthless, and perhaps more effective in ridding the world of a kind of
human life. The small farmers and the people of small towns are
understood as occupying the bottom step of the economic stairway
and deservedly falling from it because they are rural, which is to say

not metropolitan or cosmopolitan, which is to say socially, intellectually, and culturally inferior to 'us.'

Am I trying to argue that all small farmers are superior or that they are all good farmers or that they live the 'idyllic life'? I certainly am not. And that is my point. The sentimental stereotype is just as damaging as the negative one. The image of the farmer as the salt of the earth, independent son of the soil, and child of nature is a sort of lantern slide projected over the image of the farmer as simpleton, hick, or redneck. Both images serve to obliterate any concept of farming as an ancient, useful, honorable vocation, requiring admirable intelligence and skill, a complex local culture, great patience and endurance, and moral responsibilities of the gravest kind.

I am not trying to attribute any virtues or characteristics to farmers or rural people as a category. I am only saying what black people, Jews, and others have said many times before: These stereotypes don't fit. They don't work. Of course, some small-town lawyers have minds that are 'closed and cold,' but some, too, have minds that are open and warm. And some 'provincial' journalists may be comparable to groundhogs, I suppose, though I know of none to whom that simile exactly applies, but some too are brilliant and brave and eminently useful. I am thinking, for example, of Tom and Pat Gish, publishers of *The Mountain Eagle* in Whitesburg, Kentucky, who for many decades have opposed the coal companies whenever necessary and have unflinchingly suffered the penalties, including arson. Do I think the Gishes would be intimidated by the frivolous wit of ghostwriters at the Gridiron dinner? I do not.

I have been attentive all my life to the doings of small-town lawyers and 'provincial' journalists, and I could name several of both sorts who have not been admirable, but I could name several also who have been heroes among those who wish to be just. I can say, too, that, having lived both in great metropolitan centers of culture and in a small farming community, I have seen few things dumber and tackier – or more provincial – than this half-scared, half-witted urban contempt for 'provinciality.'

•

The stereotype of the farmer as rustic simpleton or uncouth redneck is, like most stereotypes, easily refuted: all you have to do is compare it with a number of real people. But the stereotype of the small farmer as obsolete human clinging to an obsolete kind of life, though equally false, is harder to deal with because it comes from a more complicated prejudice, entrenched in superstition and a kind of insanity.

The prejudice begins in the idea that work is bad, and that manual work outdoors is the worst work of all. The superstition is that since all work is bad, all 'labor-saving' is good. The insanity is in the ultimately suicidal pillage of the natural world and the land-using cultures on which human society depends for its life.

The industrialization of agriculture has replaced working people with machines and chemicals. The people thus replaced have, supposedly, gone into the 'better' work of offices or factories. But in all the enterprises of the industrial economy, as in industrial war, we finally reach the end of the desk jobs, the indoor work, the glamour of forcing nature to submission by pushbuttons and levers, and we come to the unsheltered use of the body. Somebody, finally, must work in the mud and the snow, build and mend the pasture fences, help the calving cow.

Now, in the United States, the despised work of agriculture is done by the still-surviving and always struggling small farmers, and by many Mexican and Central American migrant laborers who live and work a half step, if that, above slavery. The work of the farmland, in other words, is now accomplished by two kinds of oppression, and most people do not notice, or if they notice they do not care. If they are invited to care, they are likely to excuse themselves by answers long available in the 'public consciousness': Farmers are better off when they lose their farms. They are improved by being freed of the 'mind-numbing work' of farming. Mexican migrant field hands, like Third World workers in sweatshops, are being improved by our low regard and low wages. And besides, however objectionable from the standpoint of 'nostalgia,' the dispossession of farmers and their replacement by machines, chemicals, and oppressed migrants is 'inevitable,' and it is 'too late' for correction.

Such talk, it seems to me, descends pretty directly from the old pro-slavery rhetoric: slavery was an improvement over 'savagery,' the slaves were happy in their promotion, slavery was sanctioned by God. The moral difference is not impressive.

But the prejudice against rural people is not merely an offense against justice and common decency. It also obscures or distorts perception of issues and problems of the greatest practical urgency. The unacknowledged question beneath the dismissal of the agrarian small farmers is this: What is the best way to farm – not anywhere or everywhere, but in every one of the Earth's fragile localities? What is the best way to farm *this* farm? In *this* ecosystem? For *this* farmer? For *this* community? For *these* consumers? For the next seven generations? In a time of terrorism? To answer those questions, we will have to go beyond our preconceptions about farmers and other 'provincial' people. And we will have to give up a significant amount of scientific objectivity, too. That is because the standards required to measure the qualities of farming are not just scientific or economic or social or cultural, but all of those, employed all together.

This line of questioning finally must encounter such issues as preference, taste, and appearance. What kind of farming and what kind of food do you *like*? How should a good steak or tomato *taste*? What does a good farm or good crop look like? Is this farm landscape healthful enough? Is it beautiful enough? Are health and beauty, as applied to landscapes, synonymous?

With such questions, we leave objective science and all other specialized disciplines behind, and we come to something like an undepartmented criticism or connoisseurship that is at once communal and personal. Even though we obviously must answer our questions about farming with all the intellectual power we have, we must not fail to answer them also with affection. I mean the complex, never-completed affection for our land and our neighbors that is true patriotism.

(2001)

Faustian Economics

The general reaction to the apparent end of the era of cheap fossil fuel, as to other readily foreseeable curtailments, has been to delay any sort of reckoning. The strategies of delay, so far, have been a sort of willed oblivion, or visions of large profits to the manufacturers of such 'biofuels' as ethanol from corn or switchgrass, or the familiar unscientific faith that 'science will find an answer.' The dominant response, in short, is a dogged belief that what we call 'the American way of life' will prove somehow indestructible. We will keep on consuming, spending, wasting, and driving, as before, at any cost to anything and everybody but ourselves.

This belief was always indefensible – the real names of global warming are 'waste' and 'greed' – and by now it is manifestly foolish. But foolishness on this scale looks disturbingly like a sort of national insanity. We seem to have come to a collective delusion of grandeur, insisting that all of us are 'free' to be as conspicuously greedy and wasteful as the most corrupt of kings and queens. (Perhaps by devoting more and more of our already abused cropland to fuel production, we will at last cure ourselves of obesity and become fashionably skeletal, hungry but – Thank God! – still driving.)

The problem with us is not only prodigal extravagance, but also an assumed godly limitlessness. We have obscured the issue by refusing to see that limitlessness is a godly trait. We have insistently, and with relief, defined ourselves as animals or as 'higher animals.' But to define ourselves as animals, given our specifically human powers and desires, is to define ourselves as *limitless* animals – which of course is a contradiction in terms. Any definition is a limit, which is why the God of Exodus refuses to define Himself: 'I am that I am.'

Even so, that we have founded our present society upon delusional assumptions of limitlessness is easy enough to demonstrate.

A recent 'summit' in Louisville, Kentucky, was entitled 'Unbridled Energy: The Industrialization of Kentucky's Energy Resources.' Its subjects were 'clean-coal generation, biofuels, and other cutting-edge applications,' the conversion of coal to 'liquid fuels,' and the likelihood that all this will be 'environmentally friendly.' These hopes, which 'can create jobs and boost the nation's security,' are to be supported by government 'loan guarantees . . . investment tax credits and other tax breaks.' Such talk we recognize as completely conventional. It is, in fact, a tissue of clichés that is now the common tongue of promoters, politicians, and journalists. This language does not allow for any question about the *net* good of anything proposed. The entire contraption of 'Unbridled Energy' is supported only by a rote optimism: 'The United States has 250 billion tons of recoverable coal reserves – enough to last 100 years even at double the current rate of consumption.'* We humans have inhabited the earth for many thousands of years, and now we can look forward to surviving for another hundred by doubling our consumption of coal? *This* is national security? The world-ending fire of industrial fundamentalism may already be burning in our furnaces and engines, but if it will burn for a hundred more years, that will be fine. Surely it would be better to intend straightforwardly to contain the fire and eventually put it out? But once greed has been made an honorable motive, then you have an economy without limits, a contradiction in terms. This supposed economy has no plan for temperance or thrift or the ecological law of return. It will do anything. It is monstrous by definition.†

In keeping with our unrestrained consumptiveness, the commonly accepted basis of our present economy is the fantastical possibility of limitless growth, limitless wants, limitless wealth, limitless natural resources, limitless energy, and limitless debt. The idea of a limitless economy implies and requires a doctrine of general human limitlessness: *all* are entitled to pursue without limit

---

* *Louisville Courier-Journal*, October 21, 2006.
† This is abundantly demonstrated by the suddenly ubiquitous rationalizations of 'clean' and 'safe' nuclear energy, ignoring the continuing problem of undisposable waste.

whatever they conceive as desirable – a license that classifies the most exalted Christian capitalist with the lowliest pornographer.

This fantasy of limitlessness perhaps arose from the coincidence of the industrial revolution with the suddenly exploitable resources of the 'new world.' Or perhaps it comes from the contrary apprehension of the world's 'smallness,' made possible by modern astronomy and high-speed transportation. Fear of the smallness of our world and its life may lead to a kind of claustrophobia and thence, with apparent reasonableness, to a desire for the 'freedom' of limitlessness. But this desire paradoxically reduces everything. The life of this world *is* small to those who think it is, and the desire to enlarge it makes it smaller, and can reduce it finally to nothing.

However it came about, this credo of limitlessness clearly implies a principled wish, not only for limitless possessions, but also for limitless knowledge, limitless science, limitless technology, and limitless progress. And necessarily it must lead to limitless violence, waste, war, and destruction. That it should finally produce a crowning cult of political limitlessness is only a matter of mad logic.

The normalization of the doctrine of limitlessness has produced a sort of moral minimalism: the desire to be 'efficient' at any cost, to be unencumbered by complexity. The minimization of neighborliness, respect, reverence, responsibility, accountability, and self-subordination – this is the 'culture' of which our present leaders and heroes are the spoiled children.

Our national faith so far has been 'There's always more.' Our true religion is a sort of autistic industrialism. People of intelligence and ability seem now to be genuinely embarrassed by any solution to any problem that does not involve high technology, a great expenditure of energy, or a big machine. Thus an X marked on a paper ballot no longer fulfills our idea of voting. One problem with this state of affairs is that the work now most needing to be done – that of neighborliness and caretaking – cannot be done by remote control with the greatest power on the largest scale. A second problem is that the economic fantasy of limitlessness in a limited world calls fearfully into question the value of our monetary wealth, which does not reliably stand for the real wealth of land, resources, and workmanship, but instead wastes and depletes it.

That human limitlessness is a fantasy means, obviously, that its life expectancy is limited. There is now a growing perception, and not just among a few experts, that we are entering a time of inescapable limits. We are not likely to be granted another world to plunder in compensation for our pillage of this one. Nor are we likely to believe much longer in our ability to outsmart, by means of science and technology, our economic stupidity. The hope that we can cure the ills of industrialism by the homeopathy of more technology seems at last to be losing status. We are, in short, coming under pressure to understand ourselves as limited creatures in a limited world.

This constraint, however, is not the condemnation it may seem. On the contrary, it returns us to our real condition and to our human heritage, from which our self-definition as limitless animals has for too long cut us off. Every cultural and religious tradition that I know about, while fully acknowledging our animal nature, defines us specifically as *humans* – that is, as animals (if the word still applies) capable of living, not only within natural limits, but also within cultural limits, self-imposed. As earthly creatures we live, because we must, within natural limits, which we may describe by such names as 'earth' or 'ecosystem' or 'watershed' or 'place' or 'neighborhood.' But as humans we may elect to respond to this necessary placement by the self-restraints implied in neighborliness, stewardship, thrift, temperance, generosity, care, kindness, friendship, loyalty, and love.

In our limitless selfishness, we have tried to define 'freedom,' for example, as an escape from all restraint. But, as my friend Bert Hornback has explained in his book *The Wisdom in Words*, 'free' is etymologically related to 'friend.' These words come from the same Germanic and Sanskrit roots, which carry the sense of 'dear' or 'beloved.'* We set our friends free by our love for them, with the implied restraints of faithfulness or loyalty. This suggests that our

* Bert Hornback, *The Wisdom in Words* (Louisville: Bellarmine University Press, 2004), p. 10.

'identity' is located not in the impulse of selfhood but in deliberately maintained connections.

Thinking of our predicament has sent me back again to Christopher Marlowe's *Tragical History of Doctor Faustus*. This is a play of the Renaissance: Faustus, a man of learning, longs to possess 'all nature's treasury,' to 'Ransack the ocean . . . / And search all corners of the new-found world . . .'* To assuage his thirst for knowledge and power, he deeds his soul to Lucifer, receiving in compensation for twenty-four years the services of the subdevil Mephistophilis, nominally his slave but in fact his master. Having the subject of limitlessness in mind, I was astonished on this reading to come upon Mephistophilis' description of hell. When Faustus asks, 'How comes it then that thou art out of hell?' Mephistophilis replies, 'Why, this is hell, nor am I out of it.'† A few pages later he explains:

> Hell hath no limits, nor is circumscribed
> In one self place, but where we [the damned] are is hell,
> And where hell is must we ever be.‡

For those who reject heaven, hell is everywhere, and thus is limitless. For them, even the thought of heaven is hell.

It is only appropriate, then, that Mephistophilis rejects any conventional limit: 'Tut, Faustus, marriage is but a ceremonial toy. If thou lovest me, think no more of it.'§ Continuing this theme, for Faustus' pleasure the devils present a sort of pageant of the seven deadly sins, three of which – Pride, Wrath, and Gluttony – describe themselves as orphans, disdaining the restraints of parental or filial love.

* Marlowe, *The Tragical History of Doctor Faustus*, scene 1, lines 77, 85–86.
† Ibid., scene 3, line 77.
‡ Ibid., scene 5, lines 123–25.
§ Ibid., scene 5, lines 152–53.

Seventy or so years later, and with the issue of the human defini-tion more than ever in doubt, John Milton in Book VII of *Paradise Lost* returns again to a consideration of our urge to know. To Adam's request to be told the story of creation, the 'affable Archangel' Raphael agrees 'to answer thy desire / Of knowledge *within bounds* [my emphasis] . . . ,'* explaining that

> Knowledge is as food, and needs no less
> Her temperance over appetite, to know
> In measure what the mind may well contain;
> Oppresses else with surfeit, and soon turns
> Wisdom to folly, as nourishment to wind.†

Raphael is saying, with angelic circumlocution, that knowledge without wisdom, limitless knowledge, is not worth a fart; he is not a humorless archangel. But he also is saying that knowledge without measure, knowledge that the human mind cannot appropriately use, is mortally dangerous.

I am well aware of what I risk in bringing this language of religion into what is normally a scientific discussion – if economics is in fact a science. I do so because I doubt that we can define our present problems adequately, let alone solve them, without some recourse to our cultural heritage. We are, after all, trying now to deal with the failure of scientists, technicians, and politicians to 'think up' a ver-sion of human continuance that is economically probable and ecologically responsible, or perhaps even imaginable. If we go back into our tradition, we are going to find a concern with religion, which at a minimum shatters the selfish context of the individual life and thus forces a consideration of what human beings are and ought to be.

This concern persists at least as late as our Declaration of Independence, which holds as 'self-evident, that all men are created

---

* Milton, *Paradise Lost*, bk. 7, lines 119–20.
† Ibid., bk. 7, lines 126–30.

equal; that they are endowed by their Creator with certain inaliena-
ble rights . . .' Thus among our political roots we have still our old
preoccupation with our definition as humans, which in the
Declaration is wisely assigned to our Creator; our rights and
the rights of all humans are not granted by any human government
but are innate, belonging to us by birth. This insistence comes, not
from the fear of death or even extinction, but from the ancient fear,
readily documentable in our cultural tradition, that in order to survive we might become inhuman or monstrous.

Our cultural tradition is in large part the record of our continuing
effort to understand ourselves as beings specifically human – to say
that, as humans, we must do certain things and we must not do certain things. We must have limits or we will cease to exist as humans;
perhaps we will cease to exist, period. At times, for example, some of
us humans have thought that human beings, properly so-called, did
not make war against civilian populations, or hold prisoners without
a fair trial, or use torture for any reason.

Some of us would-be humans have thought too that we should
not be free at anybody else's expense. And yet in the phrase 'free
market,' the word 'free' has come to mean unlimited economic
power for some, with the necessary consequence of economic
powerlessness for others. Several years ago, after I had spoken at a
meeting, two earnest and obviously troubled young veterinarians
approached me with a question: How could they practice veterinary medicine without serious economic damage to the farmers
who were their clients? Underlying their question was the fact that
for a long time veterinary help for a sheep or a pig has been likely to
cost more than the animal is worth. I had to answer that, in my
opinion, so long as their practice relied heavily on selling patented
drugs, they had no choice, since the market for medicinal drugs was
entirely controlled by the drug companies, whereas most farmers
had no control at all over the market for agricultural products. My
questioners were asking in effect if a predatory economy can have a
beneficent result. The answer usually is No. And that is because

there is an absolute discontinuity between the economy of the seller of medicines and the economy of the buyer, as there is in the health industry as a whole. The drug industry is interested in the survival of patients, we have to suppose, because surviving patients will continue to consume drugs.

Now let us consider a contrary example. Recently at another meeting I talked for some time with an elderly, some would say old-fashioned, farmer from Nebraska. Unable to farm any longer himself, he had rented his land to a younger farmer on the basis of what he called 'crop share' instead of a price paid or owed in advance. Thus, as the old farmer said of his renter, 'If he has a good year, I have a good year. If he has a bad year, I have a bad one.' This is what I would call community economy. It is a sharing of fate. It assures an economic continuity and a common interest between the two partners to the trade. This is as far as possible from the economy in which the young veterinarians were caught, in which the economically powerful are limitlessly 'free' to trade to the disadvantage, and ultimately the ruin, of the powerless.

It is this economy of community destruction that, wittingly or unwittingly, most scientists and technicians have served for the last two hundred years. These scientists and technicians have justified themselves by the proposition that they are the vanguard of progress, enlarging human knowledge and power. Thus have they romanticized both themselves and the predatory enterprises that they have served.

As a consequence, our great need now is for sciences and technologies of limits, of domesticity, of what Wes Jackson of the Land Institute in Salina, Kansas, has called 'homecoming.' These would be specifically human sciences and technologies, working, as the best humans always have worked, within self-imposed limits. The limits would be, as they always have been, the accepted contexts of places, communities, and neighborhoods, both natural and human.

I know that the idea of such limitations will horrify some people, maybe most people, for we have long encouraged ourselves to feel at home on 'the cutting edges' of knowledge and power or on some 'frontier' of human experience. But I know too that we are talking now in the presence of much evidence that improvement by outward expansion may no longer be a good idea, if it ever was. It was not a good idea for the farmers who 'leveraged' secure acreage to buy more during the 1970s. It has proved tragically to be a bad idea in a number of recent wars. If it is a good idea in the form of corporate gigantism, then we must ask, For whom? Faustus, who wants all knowledge and all the world for himself, is a man supremely lonely and finally doomed. I don't think Marlowe was kidding. I don't think Satan is kidding when he says in *Paradise Lost*, 'myself am Hell.'*

If the idea of appropriate limitation seems unacceptable to us, that may be because, like Marlowe's Faustus and Milton's Satan, we confuse limits with confinement. But that, as I think Marlowe and Milton and others were trying to tell us, is a great and potentially a fatal mistake. Satan's fault, as Milton understood it and perhaps with some sympathy, was precisely that he could not tolerate his proper limitation; he could not subordinate himself to anything whatsoever. Faustus' error was his unwillingness to remain 'Faustus, and a man.'† In our age of the world it is not rare to find writers, critics, and teachers of literature, as well as scientists and technicians, who regard Satan's and Faustus' defiance as salutary and heroic.

On the contrary, our human and earthly limits, properly understood, are not confinements, but rather are inducements to formal elaboration and elegance, to *fullness* of relationship and meaning. Perhaps our most serious cultural loss in recent centuries is the knowledge that some things, though limited, can be inexhaustible. For example, an ecosystem, even that of a working forest or farm, so long as it remains ecologically intact, is inexhaustible. A small place, as I know from my own experience, can provide opportunities of work and learning, and a fund of beauty, solace, and pleasure – in

---

* Ibid., bk. 4, line 75.
† Marlowe, *Doctor Faustus*, scene 1, line 23.

addition to its difficulties – that cannot be exhausted in a lifetime or in generations.

To recover from our disease of limitlessness, we will have to give up the idea that we have a right to be godlike animals, that we are at least potentially omniscient and omnipotent, ready to discover 'the secret of the universe.' We will have to start over, with a different and much older premise: the naturalness and, for creatures of limited intelligence, the necessity of limits. We must learn again to ask how we can make the most of what we are, what we have, what we have been given. If we always have a theoretically better substitute available from somebody or someplace else, we will never make the most of anything. It is hard enough to make the most of one life. If we each had two lives, we would not make much of either. One of my best teachers said of people in general: 'They'll never be worth a damn as long as they've got two choices.'

To deal with the problems, which after all are inescapable, of living with limited intelligence in a limited world, I suggest that we may have to remove some of the emphasis we have lately placed on science and technology and have a new look at the arts. For an art does not propose to enlarge itself by limitless extension, but rather to enrich itself within bounds that are accepted prior to the work.

It is the artists, not the scientists, who have dealt unremittingly with the problem of limits. A painting, however large, must finally be bounded by a frame or a wall. A composer or playwright must reckon, at a minimum, with the capacity of an audience to sit still and pay attention. A story, once begun, must end somewhere within the limits of the writer's and the reader's memory. And of course the arts characteristically impose limits that are artificial: the five acts of a play, or the fourteen lines of a sonnet. Within these limits artists achieve elaborations of pattern, of sustaining relationships of parts with one another and with the whole, that may be astonishingly complex. Probably most of us can name a painting, a piece of music, a poem or play or story that still grows in meaning and remains fresh after many years of familiarity.

We know by now that a natural ecosystem survives by the same sort of formal intricacy, ever-changing, inexhaustible, and perhaps finally unknowable. We know further that if we want to make our economic landscapes sustainably and abundantly productive, we must do so by maintaining in them a living formal complexity something like that of natural ecosystems. We can do this only by raising to the highest level our mastery of the arts of agriculture, animal husbandry, forestry, and, ultimately, the art of living.

It is true that insofar as scientific experiments must be conducted within carefully observed limits, scientists also are artists. But in science one experiment, whether it succeeds or fails, is logically followed by another in a theoretically infinite progression. According to the underlying myth of modern science, this progression is always replacing the smaller knowledge of the past with the larger knowledge of the present, which will be replaced by the yet larger knowledge of the future.

In the arts, by contrast, no limitless sequence of works is ever implied or looked for. No work of art is necessarily followed by a second work that is necessarily better. Given the methodologies of science, the law of gravity and the genome were bound to be discovered by somebody; the identity of the discoverer is incidental. But in the arts there are no second chances. We must assume that we had one chance each for *The Divine Comedy* and *King Lear*. If Dante and Shakespeare had died before they wrote those poems, nobody ever would have written them.

The same is true of our arts of land use, our economic arts, which are our arts of living. With these it is once-for-all. We will have no chance to redo our experiments with bad agriculture leading to soil loss. The Appalachian mountains and forests we have destroyed for coal are gone forever. It is now and forevermore too late to use thriftily the first half of the world's supply of petroleum. In the art of living we can only start again with what remains.

As we confront the phenomenon of 'peak oil,' we are really confronting the end of our customary delusion of 'more.' Whichever way we turn, from now on, we are going to find a limit beyond which there will be no more. To hit these limits at top speed is not a rational choice. To start slowing down, with the idea of avoiding catastrophe, *is* a rational choice, and a viable one if we can recover the necessary political sanity. Of course it makes sense to consider alternative energy sources, provided *they* make sense. But also we will have to reexamine the economic structures of our life, and conform them to the tolerances and limits of our earthly places. Where there is no more, our one choice is to make the most and the best of what we have.

(2006)

Quantity versus Form[*]

1

My family and I had a good friend I will call Lily. Lily was industrious and generous, a good neighbor. She was especially well loved by her neighbors' children and grandchildren, though she had no children of her own. She lived a long time, surviving her husband by many years. At last, permanently ill and debilitated, she had to leave the small house that she and her husband had bought in their latter years and go to the nursing home. My brother, who was her lawyer, never until then much needed, arranged for the sale of her house and all her worldly goods.

I went to visit her a day or two after the sale. She was bedfast, sick and in some pain, but perfectly clear in her mind. We talked of the past and of several of our old neighbors, long gone. And then, speaking of the sale of her possessions, she said, 'I'm all finished now. Everything is done.'

She said this so cheerfully that I asked her, 'Lily, is it a load off your mind?'

She said, 'Well, Wendell, it hurt me. I laid here the night when I knew it was all gone, and I could *see* it all, all the things I'd cared for so long. But, yes, it is a load off my mind.'

I was so moved and impressed by what she said that I wrote it down. She had lived her life and met her hardships bravely and cheerfully, and now she faced her death fully aware and responsible and

* Written originally for a conference, 'Evidence-Based, Opinion-Based, and Real World Agriculture and Medicine,' convened by Charlie Sing at Emigrant, Montana, October 10–15, 2004.

with what seemed to me a completed grace. I didn't then and I don't now see how she could have been more admirable.

The last time I saw Lily she was in the hospital, where the inevitable course of her illness had taken her. By then, in addition to a seriously afflicted heart, she had not recovered from a bout of pneumonia, and because of osteoporosis she had several broken bones. She was as ill probably as a living creature can be and in great pain. She was dying. But in talking with the resident physician, I discovered that he had taken her off her pain medication to increase her appetite in the hope, he said, of 'getting her back on her feet.'

And so a life in every sense complete had to suffer at its end this addendum of useless and meaningless pain. I don't think this episode is unusual or anomalous at the present time. The doctor's stupidity and cowardice are in fact much mitigated by being perfectly conventional. The medical industry now instructs us all that longevity is a good in itself. Plain facts and simple mercy, moreover, are readily obscured by the supposed altruism of the intent to 'heal.'

I am obliged now to say that I am by no means an advocate of euthanasia or 'assisted suicide.' My purpose here is only to notice that the ideal of a whole or a complete life, as expressed in Psalm 128 or in Tiresias' foretelling of the death of Odysseus, now appears to have been replaced by the ideal merely of a *long* life. And I do not believe that these two ideals can be reconciled.

As a man growing old, I have not been able to free my mind of the story of Lily's last days or of other stories like it that I know, and I have not been able to think of them without fear. This fear is only somewhat personal. It is also a cultural fear, the fear that something valuable and necessary to our life is being lost.

To clarify my thoughts I have been in need of some further example, and recently the associations of reading led me to Robert Southey's account of the Battle of Trafalgar in his biography of Lord Nelson. I am by conviction a pacifist, but that does not prevent me from being moved and instructed by the story of a military hero. What impresses me in Southey's account is the substantial evidence that Nelson went into the battle both expecting and fully prepared to die.

He expected to die because he had refused any suggestion that he should enter the battle in disguise in order to save himself. Instead, he would wear, Southey wrote, 'as usual, his Admiral's frockcoat, bearing on the left breast four stars of the different orders with which he was invested.' He thus made himself the prime target of the engagement; he would live and fight as himself, though it meant that he would die unmistakably as himself. As for his decorations: 'In honor I gained them, and in honor I will die with them.' And before the battle he wrote out a prayer, asking for a British victory but also for humanity afterward toward the enemy. 'For myself individually,' he wrote, 'I commit my life to Him who made me . . .'

At the end of his account, published in 1813, eight years after the battle, Southey wrote of the admiral's death a verdict undoubtedly not so remarkable then as the succeeding two centuries have made it: 'There was reason to suppose, from the appearance upon opening the body, that in the course of nature he might have attained, like his father, to a good old age. Yet he cannot be said to have fallen prematurely whose work was done . . .'

Nelson was killed at the age of forty-seven, which would seem to us in our time to be a life cut 'tragically short.' But Southey credited to that life a formal completeness that had little to do with its extent and much to do with its accomplishments and with Nelson's own sense of its completeness: 'Thank God, I have done my duty.'

The issue of the form of a lived life is difficult, for the form as opposed to the measurable extent of a life has as much to do with inward consciousness as with verifiable marks left on the world. But we are already in the thick of the problem when we have noticed that there does seem to be such a thing as a good life; that a good life consists, in part at least, of doing well; and that this possibility is an ancient one, having apparently little to do with the progress of science or how much a person knows. And so we must ask how it is that one does not have to know everything in order to do well.

The answer, apparently, is that one does so by accepting formal constraints. We are excused from the necessity of creating the universe, and most of us will not have even to command a fleet in a great battle. We come to form, we in-form our lives, by accepting the obvious limits imposed by our talents and circumstances, by nature and mortality, and thus by getting the scale right. Form permits us to live and work gracefully within our limits.

In *The Soil and Health*, his light-giving book of 1947, Sir Albert Howard wrote:

> It needs a more refined perception to recognize throughout this stupendous wealth of varying shapes and forms the principle of stability. Yet this principle dominates. It dominates by means of an ever-recurring cycle, a cycle which, repeating itself silently and ceaselessly, ensures the continuation of living matter. This cycle is constituted of the successive and repeated processes of birth, growth, maturity, death, and decay.

Following, as he said, 'an eastern religion,' Howard speaks of this cycle as 'The Wheel of Life.' The life of nature depends upon the uninterrupted turning of this wheel. Howard's work rested upon his conviction, obviously correct, that a farm needed to incorporate within its own working the entire revolution of the wheel of life, so that it too might remain endlessly alive and productive by obeying 'Nature's law of return.' When, thirty years ago, I wrote in a poem, 'The farm is an infinite form,' this is what I meant.

The wheel of life is a form. It is a natural form, and it can become an artistic form insofar as the art of farming and the work of a farm can be made to conform to it. It can be made a form also of the art of living, but that, I think, requires an additional step. The wheel of human – that is, of *fully* human – life would consist over the generations of birth, growth, maturity, *ripeness*, death, and decay.

'Ripeness' is implicit in the examples of Lord Nelson and my friend Lily, but the term itself comes from act V, scene 2, of *King Lear*, in which Edgar says to his father:

> Men must endure
> Their going hence, even as their coming hither.
> Ripeness is all.

By 'ripeness' Edgar means a perfect readiness for death, and his sentence echoes 'The readiness is all' in act V, scene 2, of *Hamlet*. In the wheel of human life, 'ripeness' adds to the idea of biological growth the growth in a living soul of the knowledge of time and eternity in preparation for death. And after the addition of 'ripeness,' 'decay' acquires the further sense of the 'plowing in' of experience and memory, building up the cultural humus. The art of living thus is practiced not only by individuals, but by whole communities or societies. It is the work of the long-term education of a people. Its purpose, we may say, is to make life conform gracefully both to its natural course and to its worldly limits. And this is in fulfillment of what Vermont Chief Justice Jeffrey L. Amestoy says is 'our common responsibility . . . to imagine humanity the heart can recognize.'

What is or what should be the goal of our life and work? This is a fearful question and it ought to be fearfully answered. Probably it should not be answered for anybody in particular by anybody else in particular. But the ancient norm or ideal seems to have been a life in which you perceived your calling, faithfully followed it, and did your work with satisfaction; married, made a home, and raised a family; associated generously with neighbors; ate and drank with pleasure the produce of your local landscape; grew old seeing yourself replaced by your children or younger neighbors, but continuing in old age to be useful; and finally died a good or a holy death surrounded by loved ones.

Now we seem to have lost any such thought of a completed life. We no longer imagine death as an appropriate end or as a welcome deliverance from pain or grief or weariness. Death now apparently is understood, and especially by those who have placed themselves in charge of it, as a punishment for growing old, to be delayed at any cost.

We seem to be living now with the single expectation that there should and will always be more of everything, including 'life expectancy.' This insatiable desire for more is the result of an overwhelming sense of incompleteness, which is the result of the insatiable desire for more. This is the wheel of death. It is the revolving of this wheel that now drives technological progress. The more superficial and unsatisfying our lives become, the faster we need to progress. When you are skating on thin ice, speed up.

The medical industry's invariable unction about life-saving, healing, and the extended life expectancy badly needs a meeting on open ground with tragedy, absurdity, and moral horror. To wish for a longer life is to wish implicitly for an extension of the possibility that one's life may become a burden or even a curse. And what are we to think when a criminal becomes a medical emergency by the beneficence of nature, is accorded the full panoply of technological mercy, and is soon back in practice? The moral horror comes when the suffering or dementia of an overly extended life is reduced to another statistical verification of the 'miracle' of modern medicine; or when a mental disease, such as the inability to face death or an ungovernable greed for more of everything, is exploited for profit.

Perhaps there is nobody now who has not benefited in some urgently personal way from the technology of the modern medical industry. To disregard the benefit is a falsehood, and to be ungrateful is inexcusable. But even gratitude does not free us of the obligation to be critical when criticism is needed. And there can be no doubt that the rapid development of industrial technology in medicine – and, as I am about to show, in agriculture – is much in need of criticism. We need to study with great concern the effects of introducing the mechanical and chemical procedures and quantitative standards of industry into the organic world and into the care of creatures. If this has given us benefits, it has also charged us and our world with costs that, typically, have been ignored by the accountants of progress. There is never, at best, an exact fit between the organic world and industrial technology. At worst, there is contradiction, opposition, and serious damage.

Industrial technology tends to obscure or destroy the sense of appropriate scale and of propriety of application. The standard of performance tends to be set by the capacity of the technology rather than the individual nature of places and creatures. Industrial technology, instead of adapting itself to life, attempts to adapt life to itself by treating life as merely a mechanical or chemical process, and thus it inhibits the operation of love, imagination, familiarity, compassion, fear, and awe. It reduces responsibility to routine, and work to 'processing.' It destroys the worker's knowledge of what is being worked upon.

2

The opposition of quantity and form in agriculture is not so immediately painful as in medicine, but it is more obvious. The medical industry has lifted the 'norm' of life expectancy out of reach by proposing to extend longevity ad infinitum. Likewise, agricultural science, agribusiness, and the food industry propose to increase production ad infinitum, and this is their only aim. They will increase production by any means and at any cost, even at the cost of future productivity, for they have no functioning idea of ecological or agricultural or human limits. And since the agricultural economy is controlled by agribusiness and the food industry, their fixation on quantity is too easily communicated to farmers.

The art of farming, as I said earlier, fashions the farm's cycle of productivity so that it conforms to the wheel of life. That is Sir Albert Howard's language. In Wes Jackson's language, the art of farming is to mimic on the farm the self-renewing processes of the local ecosystem. But that is not all. The art of farming is also the art of living on a farm. The form of a farm is partly in its embodied consciousness of ecological obligation, and thus in its annual cycle of work, but it is also in the arrangement of fields and buildings in relation to the life of the farm's human family whose focus is the household. There is thus a convergence or even a coincidence between the form of a farm and the form of a farming life. The art of sustaining fertility and the art of living on a farm are mutually enhancing and mutually reinforcing.

A long view of an old agricultural landscape, in America and even more in Europe, would show how fencerows and fields have conformed over time both to natural topography and to human use, and how the location of dwellings, barns, and outbuildings reveals the established daily and seasonal patterns of work. In talking now about such farms in such landscapes, we are talking mostly about the past. Such farms were highly diversified and formally complex, and sometimes they were impressively sensitive (though perhaps no farm can ever be sensitive enough) both to the requirements of the place and to human need. The pursuit of higher and higher productivity has replaced those complex forms with the form (if it can be called that) of a straight line. The minimal formality of the straight line is even further attenuated because the line really is an arrow pointing toward nothing at all that is present, but toward the goal of even more production in the future. The line, it is proposed, will go on and on from one record yield to another. And the line of this determination is marked on the ground by longer and longer rows, which is to say larger and larger farms.

The exclusive standard of productivity destroys the formal integrity of a farm just as the exclusive standard of longevity destroys the formal integrity of a life. The quest for higher and higher production on farms leads almost inevitably to specialization, ignoring the natural impulsion toward diversity; specialization in turn obliterates local proprieties of scale and proportion and obscures any sense of human connection. Driven by fashion, debt, and bad science, the desire for more overrides completely the idea of a home or a home place or a home economy or a home community. The desire for quantity replaces the desire for wholeness or holiness or health. The sense of right proportion and scale cannot survive the loss of the sense of relationship, of the parts to one another and to the whole. The result, inevitably, is ugliness, violence, and waste.

Those of us who have watched, and have cared, have seen the old diverse and complex farm homesteads dissolving into an oversimplified, overcapitalized, market-determined agriculture that destroys farms and farmers. The fences, the fencerow plants and animals, the woodlots, the ponds and wetlands, the pastures and hayfields, the grassed waterways all disappear. The farm buildings go from disuse to neglect to decay and finally to fire and the bulldozer. The farmhouse is rented, dishonored, neglected until it too goes down and disappears. A neighborhood of home places, a diverse and comely farmed landscape, is thus replaced by a mechanical and chemical, entirely patented agricultural desert. And this is a typical reductionist blunder, the success story of a sort of materialist fundamentalism.

By indulging a limitless desire for a supposedly limitless quantity, one gives up all the things that are most desirable. One abandons any hope of the formal completeness, grace, and beauty that come only by subordinating one's life to the whole of which it is a part, and thus one is condemned to the life of a fragment, forever unfinished and incomplete, forever greedy. One loses, that is, the sense of human life as an artifact, a part made imaginatively whole.

(2004)

Word and Flesh

Toward the end of *As You Like It*, Orlando says: 'I can live no longer by thinking.' He is ready to marry Rosalind. It is time for incarnation. Having thought too much, he is at one of the limits of human experience, or of human sanity. If his love does put on flesh, we know he must sooner or later arrive at the opposite limit, at which he will say, 'I can live no longer without thinking.' Thought – even consciousness – seems to live between these limits: the abstract and the particular, the word and the flesh.

All public movements of thought quickly produce a language that works as a code, useless to the extent that it is abstract. It is readily evident, for example, that you can't conduct a relationship with another person in terms of the rhetoric of the civil rights movement or the women's movement – as useful as those rhetorics may initially have been to personal relationships.

The same is true of the environment movement. The favorite adjective of this movement now seems to be 'planetary.' This word is used, properly enough, to refer to the interdependence of places, and to the recognition, which is desirable and growing, that no place on the earth can be completely healthy until all places are.

But the word 'planetary' also refers to an abstract anxiety or an abstract passion that is desperate and useless exactly to the extent that it is abstract. How, after all, can anybody – any particular body – do anything to heal a planet? The suggestion that anybody could do so is preposterous. The heroes of abstraction keep galloping in on their white horses to save the planet – and they keep falling off in front of the grandstand.

What we need, obviously, is a more intelligent – which is to say, a more accurate – description of the problem. The description of a problem as planetary arouses a motivation for which, of necessity, there is no employment. The adjective 'planetary' describes a problem in such a way that it cannot be solved. In fact, though we now have serious problems nearly everywhere on the planet, we have no problem that can accurately be described as planetary. And, short of the total annihilation of the human race, there is no planetary solution.

There are also no national, state, or county problems, and no national, state, or county solutions. That will-o'-the-wisp, the large-scale solution to the large-scale problem, which is so dear to governments, universities, and corporations, serves mostly to distract people from the small, private problems that they may, in fact, have the power to solve.

The problems, if we describe them accurately, are all private and small. Or they are so initially.

The problems are our lives. In the 'developed' countries, at least, the large problems occur because all of us are living either partly wrong or almost entirely wrong. It was not just the greed of corporate shareholders and the hubris of corporate executives that put the fate of Prince William Sound into one ship; it was also our demand that energy be cheap and plentiful.

The economies of our communities and households are wrong. The answers to the human problems of ecology are to be found in economy. And the answers to the problems of economy are to be found in culture and in character. To fail to see this is to go on dividing the world falsely between guilty producers and innocent consumers.

The planetary versions – the heroic versions – of our problems have attracted great intelligence. But these problems, as they are caused and suffered in our lives, our households, and our communities, have attracted very little intelligence.

There are some notable exceptions. A few people have learned to do a few things better. But it is discouraging to reflect that, though we have been talking about most of our problems for decades, we are still mainly *talking* about them. The civil rights movement has not given us better communities. The women's movement has not given us better marriages or better households. The environment movement has not changed our parasitic relationship to nature.

We have failed to produce new examples of good home and community economies, and we have nearly completed the destruction of the examples we once had. Without examples, we are left with theory and the bureaucracy and meddling that come with theory. We change our principles, our thoughts, and our words, but these are changes made in the air. Our lives go on unchanged.

For the most part, the subcultures, the countercultures, the dissenters, and the opponents continue mindlessly – or perhaps just helplessly – to follow the pattern of the dominant society in its extravagance, its wastefulness, its dependencies, and its addictions. The old problem remains: How do you get intelligence *out* of an institution or an organization?

My small community in Kentucky has lived and dwindled for at least a century under the influence of four kinds of organizations: governments, corporations, schools, and churches – all of which are distant (either actually or in interest), centralized, and consequently abstract in their concerns.

Governments and corporations (except for employees) have no presence in our community at all, which is perhaps fortunate for us, but we nevertheless feel the indifference or the contempt of governments and corporations for communities such as ours.

We have had no school of our own for nearly thirty years. The school system takes our young people, prepares them for 'the world of tomorrow' – which it does not expect to take place in any rural area – and gives back 'expert' (that is, extremely generalized) ideas.

The church is present in the town. We have two churches. But both have been used by their denominations, for almost a century, to provide training and income for student ministers, who do not stay long enough even to become disillusioned.

For a long time, then, the minds that have most influenced our town have not been *of* the town and so have not tried even to perceive, much less to honor, the good possibilities that are there. They have not wondered on what terms a good and conserving life might be lived there. In this my community is not unique but is like almost every other neighborhood in our country and in the 'developed' world.

The question that *must* be addressed, therefore, is not how to care for the planet, but how to care for each of the planet's millions of human and natural neighborhoods, each of its millions of small pieces and parcels of land, each one of which is in some precious way different from all the others. Our understandable wish to preserve the planet must somehow be reduced to the scale of our competence – that is, to the wish to preserve all of its humble households and neighborhoods.

What can accomplish this reduction? I will say again, without overweening hope but with certainty nonetheless, that only love can do it. Only love can bring intelligence out of the institutions and organizations, where it aggrandizes itself, into the presence of the work that must be done.

Love is never abstract. It does not adhere to the universe or the planet or the nation or the institution or the profession, but to the singular sparrows of the street, the lilies of the field, 'the least of these my brethren.' Love is not, by its own desire, heroic. It is heroic only when compelled to be. It exists by its willingness to be anonymous, humble, and unrewarded.

The older love becomes, the more clearly it understands its involvement in partiality, imperfection, suffering, and mortality. Even so, it longs for incarnation. It can live no longer by thinking.

And yet to put on flesh and do the flesh's work, it must think.

In his essay on Kipling, George Orwell wrote: 'All left-wing parties in the highly industrialized countries are at bottom a sham, because they make it their business to fight against something which they do not really wish to destroy. They have internationalist aims, and at the same time they struggle to keep up a standard of life with which those aims are incompatible. We all live by robbing Asiatic coolies, and those of us who are "enlightened" all maintain that those coolies ought to be set free; but our standard of living, and hence our "enlightenment," demands that the robbery shall continue.'

This statement of Orwell's is clearly applicable to our situation now; all we need to do is change a few nouns. The religion and the environmentalism of the highly industrialized countries are at bottom a sham, because they make it their business to fight against something that they do not really wish to destroy. We all live by robbing nature, but our standard of living demands that the robbery shall continue.

We must achieve the character and acquire the skills to live much poorer than we do. We must waste less. We must do more for ourselves and each other. It is either that or continue merely to think and talk about changes that we are inviting catastrophe to make.

The great obstacle is simply this: the conviction that we cannot change because we are dependent on what is wrong. But that is the addict's excuse, and we know that it will not do.

How dependent, in fact, are we? How dependent are our neighborhoods and communities? How might our dependences be reduced? To answer these questions will require better thoughts and better deeds than we have been capable of so far.

We must have the sense and the courage, for example, to see that the ability to transport food for hundreds or thousands of miles does not necessarily mean that we are well off. It means that the food supply is more vulnerable and more costly than a local food supply would be. It means that consumers do not control or influence the healthfulness of their food supply and that they are at the mercy of the people who have the control and influence. It means that, in eating, people are using large quantities of petroleum that other people in another time are almost certain to need.

Our most serious problem, perhaps, is that we have become a nation of fantasists. We believe, apparently, in the infinite availability of finite resources. We persist in land-use methods that reduce the potentially infinite power of soil fertility to a finite quantity, which we then proceed to waste as if it were an infinite quantity. We have an economy that depends not on the quality and quantity of necessary goods and services but on the moods of a few stockbrokers. We believe that democratic freedom can be preserved by people ignorant of the history of democracy and indifferent to the responsibilities of freedom.

Our leaders have been for many years as oblivious to the realities and dangers of their time as were George III and Lord North. They believe that the difference between war and peace is still the overriding political difference – when, in fact, the difference has diminished to the point of insignificance. How would you describe the difference between modern war and modern industry – between, say, bombing and strip mining, or between chemical warfare and chemical manufacturing? The difference seems to be only that in war the victimization of humans is directly intentional and in industry it is 'accepted' as a 'trade-off.'

Were the catastrophes of Love Canal, Bhopal, Chernobyl, and the *Exxon Valdez* episodes of war or of peace? They were, in fact, peacetime acts of aggression, intentional to the extent that the risks were known and ignored.

We are involved unremittingly in a war not against 'foreign enemies,' but against the world, against our freedom, and indeed against our existence. Our so-called industrial accidents should be looked upon as revenges of Nature. We forget that Nature is necessarily party to all our enterprises and that she imposes conditions of her own.

Now she is plainly saying to us: 'If you put the fates of whole communities or cities or regions or ecosystems at risk in single ships or factories or power plants, then I will furnish the drunk or the fool or the imbecile who will make the necessary small mistake.'

(1989)

Why I Am Not Going to Buy
a Computer

Like almost everybody else, I am hooked to the energy corporations, which I do not admire. I hope to become less hooked to them. In my work, I try to be as little hooked to them as possible. As a farmer, I do almost all of my work with horses. As a writer, I work with a pencil or a pen and a piece of paper.

My wife types my work on a Royal standard typewriter bought new in 1956 and as good now as it was then. As she types, she sees things that are wrong and marks them with small checks in the margins. She is my best critic because she is the one most familiar with my habitual errors and weaknesses. She also understands, sometimes better than I do, what *ought* to be said. We have, I think, a literary cottage industry that works well and pleasantly. I do not see anything wrong with it.

A number of people, by now, have told me that I could greatly improve things by buying a computer. My answer is that I am not going to do it. I have several reasons, and they are good ones.

The first is the one I mentioned at the beginning. I would hate to think that my work as a writer could not be done without a direct dependence on strip-mined coal. How could I write conscientiously against the rape of nature if I were, in the act of writing, implicated in the rape? For the same reason, it matters to me that my writing is done in the daytime, without electric light.

I do not admire the computer manufacturers a great deal more than I admire the energy industries. I have seen their advertisements, attempting to seduce struggling or failing farmers into the belief that they can solve their problems by buying yet another piece of expensive equipment. I am familiar with their propaganda campaigns that have put computers into public schools in need of books.

That computers are expected to become as common as TV sets in 'the future' does not impress me or matter to me. I do not own a TV set. I do not see that computers are bringing us one step nearer to anything that does matter to me: peace, economic justice, ecological health, political honesty, family and community stability, good work.

What would a computer cost me? More money, for one thing, than I can afford, and more than I wish to pay to people whom I do not admire. But the cost would not be just monetary. It is well understood that technological innovation always requires the discarding of the 'old model' – the 'old model' in this case being not just our old Royal standard, but my wife, my critic, my closest reader, my fellow worker. Thus (and I think this is typical of present-day technological innovation), what would be superseded would be not only something, but somebody. In order to be technologically up-to-date as a writer, I would have to sacrifice an association that I am dependent upon and that I treasure.

My final and perhaps my best reason for not owning a computer is that I do not wish to fool myself. I disbelieve, and therefore strongly resent, the assertion that I or anybody else could write better or more easily with a computer than with a pencil. I do not see why I should not be as scientific about this as the next fellow: when somebody has used a computer to write work that is demonstrably better than Dante's, and when this better is demonstrably attributable to the use of a computer, then I will speak of computers with a more respectful tone of voice, though I still will not buy one.

To make myself as plain as I can, I should give my standards for technological innovation in my own work. They are as follows:

1. The new tool should be cheaper than the one it replaces.
2. It should be at least as small in scale as the one it replaces.
3. It should do work that is clearly and demonstrably better than the one it replaces.
4. It should use less energy than the one it replaces.
5. If possible, it should use some form of solar energy, such as that of the body.

6. It should be repairable by a person of ordinary intelligence, provided that he or she has the necessary tools.
7. It should be purchasable and repairable as near to home as possible.
8. It should come from a small, privately owned shop or store that will take it back for maintenance and repair.
9. It should not replace or disrupt anything good that already exists, and this includes family and community relationships.

After the foregoing essay, first published in the *New England Review and Bread Loaf Quarterly*, was reprinted in *Harper's*, the *Harper's* editors published the following letters in response and permitted me a reply. W. B.

LETTERS

Wendell Berry provides writers enslaved by the computer with a handy alternative: Wife – a low-tech energy-saving device. Drop a pile of handwritten notes on Wife and you get back a finished manuscript, edited while it was typed. What computer can do that? Wife meets all of Berry's uncompromising standards for technological innovation: she's cheap, repairable near home, and good for the family structure. Best of all, Wife is politically correct because she breaks a writer's 'direct dependence on strip-mined coal.'

 History teaches us that Wife can also be used to beat rugs and wash clothes by hand, thus eliminating the need for the vacuum cleaner and washing machine, two more nasty machines that threaten the act of writing.

Gordon Inkeles
Miranda, Calif.

I have no quarrel with Berry because he prefers to write with pencil and paper; that is his choice. But he implies that I and others are somehow impure because we choose to write on a computer. I do not admire the

*energy corporations, either. Their shortcoming is not that they produce
electricity but how they go about it. They are poorly managed because
they are blind to long-term consequences. To solve this problem,
wouldn't it make more sense to correct the precise error they are making
rather than simply ignore their product? I would be happy to join Berry
in a protest against strip mining, but I intend to keep plugging this
computer into the wall with a clear conscience.*

*James Rhoads
Battle Creek, Mich.*

*I enjoyed reading Berry's declaration of intent never to buy a personal
computer in the same way that I enjoy reading about the belief systems
of unfamiliar tribal cultures. I tried to imagine a tool that would meet
Berry's criteria for superiority to his old manual typewriter. The clear
winner is the quill pen. It is cheaper, smaller, more energy-efficient,
human-powered, easily repaired, and non-disruptive of existing
relationships.*

*Berry also requires that this tool must be 'clearly and demonstrably
better' than the one it replaces. But surely we all recognize by now
that 'better' is in the mind of the beholder. To the quill pen aficionado, the
benefits obtained from elegant calligraphy might well outweigh all others.*

*I have no particular desire to see Berry use a word processor; if he
doesn't like computers, that's fine with me. However, I do object to his
portrayal of this reluctance as a moral virtue. Many of us have found
that computers can be an invaluable tool in the fight to protect our
environment. In addition to helping me write, my personal computer
gives me access to up-to-the-minute reports on the workings of the EPA
and the nuclear industry. I participate in electronic bulletin boards on
which environmental activists discuss strategy and warn each other
about urgent legislative issues. Perhaps Berry feels that the Sierra Club
should eschew modern printing technology, which is highly wasteful of
energy, in favor of having its members hand-copy the club's magazines
and other mailings each month?*

*Nathaniel S. Borenstein
Pittsburgh, Pa.*

The value of a computer to a writer is that it is a tool not for generating ideas but for typing and editing words. It is cheaper than a secretary (or a wife!) and arguably more fuel-efficient. And it enables spouses who are not inclined to provide free labor more time to concentrate on their own work.

We should support alternatives both to coal-generated electricity and to IBM-style technocracy. But I am reluctant to entertain alternatives that presuppose the traditional subservience of one class to another. Let the PCs come and the wives and servants go seek more meaningful work.

Toby Koosman
Knoxville, Tenn.

Berry asks how he could write conscientiously against the rape of nature if in the act of writing on a computer he was implicated in the rape. I find it ironic that a writer who sees the underlying connectedness of things would allow his diatribe against computers to be published in a magazine that carries ads for the National Rural Electric Cooperative Association, Marlboro, Phillips Petroleum, McDonnell Douglas, and yes, even Smith-Corona. If Berry rests comfortably at night, he must be using sleeping pills.

Bradley C. Johnson
Grand Forks, N.D.

WENDELL BERRY REPLIES

The foregoing letters surprised me with the intensity of the feelings they expressed. According to the writers' testimony, there is nothing wrong with their computers; they are utterly satisfied with them and all that they stand for. My correspondents are certain that I am wrong and that I am, moreover, on the losing side, a side already relegated to the dustbin of history. And yet they grow huffy and condescending over my tiny dissent. What are they so anxious about?

I can only conclude that I have scratched the skin of a technological fundamentalism that, like other fundamentalisms, wishes to monopolize a whole society and, therefore, cannot tolerate the smallest difference of opinion. At the slightest hint of a threat to their complacency, they repeat, like a chorus of toads, the notes sounded by their leaders in industry. The past was gloomy, drudgery-ridden, servile, meaningless, and slow. The present, thanks only to purchasable products, is meaningful, bright, lively, centralized, and fast. The future, thanks only to more purchasable products, is going to be even better. Thus consumers become salesmen, and the world is made safer for corporations.

I am also surprised by the meanness with which two of these writers refer to my wife. In order to imply that I am a tyrant, they suggest by both direct statement and innuendo that she is subservient, characterless, and stupid – a mere 'device' easily forced to provide meaningless 'free labor.' I understand that it is impossible to make an adequate public defense of one's private life and so I will only point out that there are a number of kinder possibilities that my critics have disdained to imagine: that my wife may do this work because she wants to and likes to; that she may find some use and some meaning in it; that she may not work for nothing. These gentlemen obviously think themselves feminists of the most correct and principled sort, and yet they do not hesitate to stereotype and insult, on the basis of one fact, a woman they do not know. They are audacious and irresponsible gossips.

In his letter, Bradley C. Johnson rushes past the possibility of sense in what I said in my essay by implying that I am or ought to be a fanatic. That I am a person of this century and am implicated in many practices that I regret is fully acknowledged at the beginning of my essay. I did not say that I proposed to end forthwith all my involvement in harmful technology, for I do not know how to do that. I said merely that I want to limit such involvement, and to a certain extent I do know how to do that. If some technology does damage to the world – as two of the above letters seem to agree that it does – then why is it not reasonable, and indeed moral, to try to limit one's use of that technology? *Of course*, I think that I am right to do this.

I would not think so, obviously, if I agreed with Nathaniel S. Borenstein that '"better" is in the mind of the beholder.' But if he truly believes this, I do not see why he bothers with his personal computer's 'up-to-the-minute reports on the workings of the EPA and the nuclear industry' or why he wishes to be warned about 'urgent legislative issues.' According to his system, the 'better' in a bureaucratic, industrial, or legislative mind is as good as the 'better' in his. His mind apparently is being subverted by an objective standard of some sort, and he had better look out.

Borenstein does not say what he does after his computer has drummed him awake. I assume from his letter that he must send donations to conservation organizations and letters to officials. Like James Rhoads, at any rate, he has a clear conscience. But this is what is wrong with the conservation movement. It has a clear conscience. The guilty are always other people, and the wrong is always somewhere else. That is why Borenstein finds his 'electronic bulletin board' so handy. To the conservation movement, it is only production that causes environmental degradation; the consumption that supports the production is rarely acknowledged to be at fault. The ideal of the run-of-the-mill conservationist is to impose restraints upon production without limiting consumption or burdening the consciences of consumers.

But virtually all of our consumption now is extravagant, and virtually all of it consumes the world. It is not beside the point that most electrical power comes from strip-mined coal. The history of the exploitation of the Appalachian coal fields is long, and it is available to readers. I do not see how anyone can read it and plug in any appliance with a clear conscience. If Rhoads can do so, that does not mean that his conscience is clear; it means that his conscience is not working.

To the extent that we consume, in our present circumstances, we are guilty. To the extent that we guilty consumers are conservationists, we are absurd. But what can we do? Must we go on writing letters to politicians and donating to conservation organizations until the majority of our fellow citizens agree with us? Or can we do something directly to solve our share of the problem?

I am a conservationist. I believe wholeheartedly in putting pressure on the politicians and in maintaining the conservation organizations. But I wrote my little essay partly in distrust of centralization. I don't think that the government and the conservation organizations alone will ever make us a conserving society. Why do I need a centralized computer system to alert me to environmental crises? That I live every hour of every day in an environmental crisis I know from all my senses. Why then is not my first duty to reduce, so far as I can, my own consumption?

Finally, it seems to me that none of my correspondents recognizes the innovativeness of my essay. If the use of a computer is a new idea, then a newer idea is not to use one.

(1987)

Feminism, the Body, and the Machine

Some time ago *Harper's* reprinted a short essay of mine in which I gave some of my reasons for refusing to buy a computer. Until that time, the vast numbers of people who disagree with my writings had mostly ignored them. An unusual number of people, however, neglected to ignore my insensitivity to the wonders of computer enhancement. Some of us, it seems, would be better off if we would just realize that this is already the best of all possible worlds, and is going to get even better if we will just buy the right equipment.

Harper's published only five of the letters the editors received in response to my essay, and they published only negative letters. But of the twenty letters received by the *Harper's* editors, who forwarded copies to me, three were favorable. This I look upon as extremely gratifying. If these letters may be taken as a fair sample, then one in seven of *Harper's* readers agreed with me. If I had guessed beforehand, I would have guessed that my supporters would have been fewer than one in a thousand. And so I suppose, after further reflection, that my surprise at the intensity of the attacks on me is mistaken. There are more of us than I thought. Maybe there is even a 'significant number' of us.

Only one of the negative letters seemed to me to have much intelligence in it. That one was from R. N. Neff of Arlington, Virginia, who scored a direct hit: 'Not to be obtuse, but being willing to bare my illiterate soul for all to see, is there indeed a "work demonstrably better than Dante's" . . . which was written on a Royal standard typewriter?' I like this retort so well that I am tempted to count it a favorable response, raising the total to four. The rest of the negative replies, like the five published ones, were more feeling than intelligent. Some of them, indeed, might be fairly described as exclamatory.

One of the letter writers described me as 'a fool' and 'doubly a fool,' but fortunately misspelled my name, leaving me a speck of hope that I am not the 'Wendell Barry' he was talking about. Two others accused me of self-righteousness, by which they seem to have meant that they think they are righter than I think I am. And another accused me of being more concerned about my own moral purity than with 'any ecological effect,' thereby making the sort of razor-sharp philosophical distinction that could cause a person to be elected president.

But most of my attackers deal in feelings either feminist or techno-logical, or both. The feelings expressed seem to be representative of what the state of public feeling currently permits to be felt, and of what public rhetoric currently permits to be said. The feelings, that is, are similar enough, from one letter to another, to be thought representative, and as representative letters they have an interest greater than the quarrel that occasioned them.

Without exception, the feminist letters accuse me of exploiting my wife, and they do not scruple to allow the most insulting implica-tions of their indictment to fall upon my wife. They fail entirely to see that my essay does not give any support to their accusation – or if they see it, they do not care. My essay, in fact, does not characterize my wife beyond saying that she types my manuscripts and tells me what she thinks about them. It does not say what her motives are, how much work she does, or whether or how she is paid. Aside from saying that she is my wife and that I value the help she gives me with my work, it says nothing about our marriage. It says nothing about our economy.

There is no way, then, to escape the conclusion that my wife and I are subjected in these letters to a condemnation by category. My offense is that I am a man who receives some help from his wife; my wife's offense is that she is a woman who does some work for her husband – which work, according to her critics and mine, makes her a drudge, exploited by a conventional subservience. And my detractors have, as I say, no evidence to support any of this. Their accusation rests on a syllogism of the flimsiest sort: my wife helps me in my work, some wives who have helped their husbands in their work have been exploited, therefore my wife is exploited.

This, of course, outrages justice to about the same extent that it insults intelligence. Any respectable system of justice exists in part as a protection against such accusations. In a just society nobody is expected to plead guilty to a general indictment, because in a just society nobody can be convicted on a general indictment. What is required for a just conviction is a particular accusation that can be *proved*. My accusers have made no such accusation against me.

That feminists or any other advocates of human liberty and dignity should resort to insult and injustice is regrettable. It is equally regrettable that all of the feminist attacks on my essay implicitly deny the validity of two decent and probably necessary possibilities: marriage as a state of mutual help, and the household as an economy.

Marriage, in what is evidently its most popular version, is now on the one hand an intimate 'relationship' involving (ideally) two successful careerists in the same bed, and on the other hand a sort of private political system in which rights and interests must be constantly asserted and defended. Marriage, in other words, has now taken the form of divorce: a prolonged and impassioned negotiation as to how things shall be divided. During their understandably temporary association, the 'married' couple will typically consume a large quantity of merchandise and a large portion of each other.

The modern household is the place where the consumptive couple do their consuming. Nothing productive is done there. Such work as is done there is done at the expense of the resident couple or family, and to the profit of suppliers of energy and household technology. For entertainment, the inmates consume television or purchase other consumable diversion elsewhere.

There are, however, still some married couples who understand themselves as belonging to their marriage, to each other, and to their children. What they have they have in common, and so, to them, helping each other does not seem merely to damage their ability to compete against each other. To them, 'mine' is not so powerful or necessary a pronoun as 'ours.'

This sort of marriage usually has at its heart a household that is to some extent productive. The couple, that is, makes around itself a household economy that involves the work of both wife and husband, that gives them a measure of economic independence and self-protection, a measure of self-employment, a measure of freedom, as well as a common ground and a common satisfaction. Such a household economy may employ the disciplines and skills of housewifery, of carpentry and other trades of building and maintenance, of gardening and other branches of subsistence agriculture, and even of woodlot management and wood-cutting. It may also involve a 'cottage industry' of some kind, such as a small literary enterprise.

It is obvious how much skill and industry either partner may put into such a household and what a good economic result such work may have, and yet it is a kind of work now frequently held in contempt. Men in general were the first to hold it in contempt as they departed from it for the sake of the professional salary or the hourly wage, and now it is held in contempt by such feminists as those who attacked my essay. Thus farm wives who help to run the kind of household economy that I have described are apt to be asked by feminists, and with great condescension, 'But what do you *do*?' By this they invariably mean that there is something better to do than to make one's marriage and household, and by better they invariably mean 'employment outside the home.'

I know that I am in dangerous territory, and so I had better be plain: what I have to say about marriage and household I mean to apply to men as much as to women. I do not believe that there is anything better to do than to make one's marriage and household, whether one is a man or a woman. I do not believe that 'employment outside the home' is as valuable or important or satisfying as employment at home, for either men or women. It is clear to me from my experience as a teacher, for example, that children need an ordinary daily association with *both* parents. They need to see their parents at work; they need, at first, to play at the work they see their parents doing, and then they need to work with their parents. It does not matter so much that this working together should be what is called 'quality time,' but it matters a great deal that the work done should have the dignity of economic value.

I should say too that I understand how fortunate I have been in being able to do an appreciable part of my work at home. I know that in many marriages both husband and wife are now finding it necessary to work away from home. This issue, of course, is troubled by the question of what is meant by 'necessary,' but it is true that a family living that not so long ago was ordinarily supplied by one job now routinely requires two or more. My interest is not to quarrel with individuals, men or women, who work away from home, but rather to ask why we should consider this general working away from home to be a desirable state of things, either for people or for marriage, for our society or for our country.

If I had written in my essay that my wife worked as a typist and editor for a publisher, doing the same work that she does for me, no feminists, I daresay, would have written to *Harper's* to attack me for exploiting her – even though, for all they knew, I might have forced her to do such work in order to keep me in gambling money. It would have been assumed as a matter of course that if she had a job away from home she was a 'liberated woman,' possessed of a dignity that no home could confer upon her.

As I have said before, I understand that one cannot construct an adequate public defense of a private life. Anything that I might say here about my marriage would be immediately (and rightly) suspect on the ground that it would be only *my* testimony. But for the sake of argument, let us suppose that whatever work my wife does, as a member of our marriage and household, she does both as a full economic partner and as her own boss, and let us suppose that the economy we have is adequate to our needs. Why, granting that supposition, should anyone assume that my wife would increase her freedom or dignity or satisfaction by becoming the employee of a boss, who would be in turn also a corporate underling and in no sense a partner?

Why would any woman who would refuse, properly, to take the marital vow of obedience (on the ground, presumably, that subservience to a mere human being is beneath human dignity) then regard as 'liberating' a job that puts her under the authority of a boss (man or woman) whose authority specifically requires and expects obedience? It is easy enough to see why women came to object to the role of Blondie, a mostly decorative custodian of a degraded, consumptive modern household, preoccupied with clothes, shopping, gossip, and outwitting her husband. But are we to assume that one may fittingly cease to be Blondie by becoming Dagwood? Is the life of a corporate underling – even acknowledging that corporate underlings are well paid – an acceptable end to our quest for human dignity and worth? It is clear enough by now that one does not cease to be an underling by reaching 'the top.' Corporate life is composed only of lower underlings and higher underlings. Bosses are everywhere, and all the bosses are underlings. This is invariably revealed when the time comes for accepting responsibility for something unpleasant, such as the Exxon fiasco in Prince William Sound, for which certain lower underlings are blamed but no higher underling is responsible. The underlings at the top, like telephone operators, have authority and power, but no responsibility.

And the oppressiveness of some of this office work defies belief. Edward Mendelson (in the *New Republic*, February 22, 1988) speaks of 'the office worker whose computer keystrokes are monitored by the central computer in the personnel office, and who will be fired if the keystrokes-per-minute figure doesn't match the corporate quota.' (Mr. Mendelson does not say what form of drudgery this worker is being saved from.) And what are we to say of the diversely skilled country housewife who now bores the same six holes day after day on an assembly line? What higher form of womanhood or humanity is she evolving toward?

How, I am asking, can women improve themselves by submitting to the same specialization, degradation, trivialization, and tyrannization of work that men have submitted to? And that question is made legitimate by another: How have men improved themselves by submitting to it? The answer is that men have not, and women cannot, improve themselves by submitting to it.

Women have complained, justly, about the behavior of 'macho' men. But despite their he-man pretensions and their captivation by masculine heroes of sports, war, and the Old West, most men are now entirely accustomed to obeying and currying the favor of their bosses. Because of this, of course, they hate their jobs – they mutter, 'Thank God it's Friday' and 'Pretty good for Monday' – but they do as they are told. They are more compliant than most housewives have been. Their characters combine feudal submissiveness with modern helplessness. They have accepted almost without protest, and often with relief, their dispossession of any usable property and, with that, their loss of economic independence and their consequent subordination to bosses. They have submitted to the destruction of the household economy and thus of the household, to the loss of home employment and self-employment, to the disintegration of their families and communities, to the desecration and pillage of their country, and they have continued abjectly to believe, obey, and vote for the people who have most eagerly abetted this ruin and who have most profited from it. These men, moreover, are helpless to do anything for themselves or anyone else without money, and so for money they do whatever they are told. They know that their ability to be useful is precisely defined by their willingness to be somebody else's tool. Is it any wonder that they talk tough and worship athletes and cowboys? Is it any wonder that some of them are violent?

It is clear that women cannot justly be excluded from the daily fracas by which the industrial economy divides the spoils of society and nature, but their inclusion is a poor justice and no reason for applause. The enterprise is as devastating with women in it as it was before. There is no sign that women are exerting a 'civilizing influence' upon it. To have an equal part in our juggernaut of national vandalism is to be a vandal. To call this vandalism 'liberation' is to prolong, and even ratify, a dangerous confusion that was once principally masculine.

A broader, deeper criticism is necessary. The problem is not just the exploitation of women by men. A greater problem is that women and men alike are consenting to an economy that exploits women and men and everything else.

Another decent possibility my critics implicitly deny is that of work as a gift. Not one of them supposed that my wife may be a consulting engineer who helps me in her spare time out of the goodness of her heart; instead they suppose that she is 'a household drudge.' But what appears to infuriate them the most is their supposition that she works for nothing. They assume – and this is the orthodox assumption of the industrial economy – that the only help worth giving is not given at all, but sold. Love, friendship, neighborliness, compassion, duty – what are they? We are realists. We will be most happy to receive your check.

The various reductions I have been describing are fairly directly the results of the ongoing revolution of applied science known as 'technological progress.' This revolution has provided the means by which both the productive and the consumptive capacities of people could be detached from household and community and made to serve other people's purely economic ends. It has provided as well a glamor of newness, ease, and affluence that made it seductive even to those who suffered most from it. In its more recent history especially, this revolution has been successful in putting unheard-of quantities of consumer goods and services within the reach of ordinary people. But the technical means of this popular 'affluence' has at the same time made possible the gathering of the real property and the real power of the country into fewer and fewer hands.

Some people would like to think that this long sequence of industrial innovations has changed human life and even human nature in fundamental ways. Perhaps it has – but, arguably, almost always for the worse. I know that 'technological progress' can be defended, but I observe that the defenses are invariably quantitative – catalogs of statistics on the ownership of automobiles and television sets, for example, or on the increase of life expectancy – and I see that these statistics are always kept carefully apart from the related statistics of soil loss, pollution, social disintegration, and so forth. That is to say, there is never an effort to determine the *net* result of this progress. The voice of its defenders is not that of the responsible bookkeeper, but that of the propagandist or salesman, who says that the net gain is more than 100 percent – that the thing we have bought has perfectly replaced everything it has cost, and added a great deal more: 'You just can't lose!' We thus have got rich by spending, just as the advertisers have told us we would, and the best of all possible worlds is getting better every day.

The statistics of life expectancy are favorites of the industrial apologists, because they are perhaps the hardest to argue with. Nevertheless, this emphasis on longevity is an excellent example of the way the isolated aims of the industrial mind reduce and distort human life, and also the way statistics corrupt the truth. A long life has indeed always been thought desirable; everything that is alive apparently wishes to continue to live. But until our own time, that sentence would have been qualified: long life is desirable and everything wishes to live *up to a point*. Past a certain point, and in certain conditions, death becomes preferable to life. Moreover, it was generally agreed that a good life was preferable to one that was merely long, and that the goodness of a life could not be determined by its length. The statisticians of longevity ignore good in both its senses; they do not ask if the prolonged life is virtuous, or if it is satisfactory. If the life is that of a vicious criminal, or if it is inched out in a veritable hell of captivity within the medical industry, no matter – both become statistics to 'prove' the good luck of living in our time.

But in general, apart from its own highly specialized standards of quantity and efficiency, 'technological progress' has produced a social and ecological decline. Industrial war, except by the most fanatically narrow standards, is worse than war used to be. Industrial agriculture, except by the standards of quantity and mechanical efficiency, diminishes everything it affects. Industrial workmanship is certainly worse than traditional workmanship, and is getting shoddier every day. After forty-odd years, the evidence is everywhere that television, far from proving a great tool of education, is a tool of stupefaction and disintegration. Industrial education has abandoned the old duty of passing on the cultural and intellectual inheritance in favor of baby-sitting and career preparation.

After several generations of 'technological progress,' in fact, we have become a people who *cannot* think about anything important. How far down in the natural order do we have to go to find creatures who raise their young as indifferently as industrial humans now do? Even the English sparrows do not let loose into the streets young sparrows who have no notion of their identity or their adult responsibilities. When else in history would you find 'educated' people who know more about sports than about the history of their country, or uneducated people who do not know the stories of their families and communities?

To ask a still more obvious question, what is the purpose of this technological progress? What higher aim do we think it is serving? Surely the aim cannot be the integrity or happiness of our families, which we have made subordinate to the education system, the television industry, and the consumer economy. Surely it cannot be the integrity or health of our communities, which we esteem even less than we esteem our families. Surely it cannot be love of our country, for we are far more concerned about the desecration of the flag than we are about the desecration of our land. Surely it cannot be the love of God, which counts for at least as little in the daily order of business as the love of family, community, and country.

The higher aims of 'technological progress' are money and ease. And this exalted greed for money and ease is disguised and justified by an obscure, cultish faith in 'the future.' We do as we do, we say, 'for the sake of the future' or 'to make a better future for our children.' How we can hope to make a good future by doing badly in the present, we do not say. We cannot think about the future, of course, for the future does not exist: the existence of the future is an article of faith. We can be assured only that, if there is to be a future, the good of it is already implicit in the good things of the present. We do not need to plan or devise a 'world of the future'; if we take care of the world of the present, the future will have received full justice from us. A good future is implicit in the soils, forests, grasslands, marshes, deserts, mountains, rivers, lakes, and oceans that we have now, and in the good things of human culture that we have now; the only valid 'futurology' available to us is to take care of those things. We have no need to contrive and dabble at 'the future of the human race'; we have the same pressing need that we have always had – to love, care for, and teach our children.

And so the question of the desirability of adopting any technological innovation is a question with two possible answers – not one, as has been commonly assumed. If one's motives are money, ease, and haste to arrive in a technologically determined future, then the answer is foregone, and there is, in fact, no question, and no thought. If one's motive is the love of family, community, country, and God, then one will have to think, and one may have to decide that the proposed innovation is undesirable.

The question of how to end or reduce dependence on some of the technological innovations already adopted is a baffling one. At least, it baffles me. I have not been able to see, for example, how people living in the country, where there is no public transportation, can give up their automobiles without becoming less useful to each other. And this is because, owing largely to the influence of the automobile, we live too far from each other, and from the things we need, to be able to get about by any other means. Of course, you *could* do without an automobile, but to do so you would have to disconnect yourself from many obligations. Nothing I have so far been able to think about this problem has satisfied me.

But if we have paid attention to the influence of the automobile on country communities, we know that the desirability of technological innovation is an issue that requires thinking about, and we should have acquired some ability to think about it. Thus if I am partly a writer, and I am offered an expensive machine to help me write, I ought to ask whether or not such a machine is desirable.

I should ask, in the first place, whether or not I wish to purchase a solution to a problem that I do not have. I acknowledge that, as a writer, I need a lot of help. And I have received an abundance of the best of help from my wife, from other members of my family, from friends, from teachers, from editors, and sometimes from readers. These people have helped me out of love or friendship, and perhaps in exchange for some help that I have given them. I suppose I should leave open the possibility that I need more help than I am getting, but I would certainly be ungrateful and greedy to think so.

But a computer, I am told, offers a kind of help that you can't get from other humans; a computer will help you to write faster, easier, and more. For a while, it seemed to me that every university professor I met told me this. Do I, then, want to write faster, easier, and more? No. My standards are not speed, ease, and quantity. I have already left behind too much evidence that, writing with a pencil, I have written too fast, too easily, and too much. I would like to be a *better* writer, and for that I need help from other humans, not a machine.

The professors who recommended speed, ease, and quantity to me were, of course, quoting the standards of their universities. The chief concern of the industrial system, which is to say the present university system, is to cheapen work by increasing volume. But implicit in the professors' recommendation was the idea that one needs to be up with the times. The pace-setting academic intellectuals have lately had a great hankering to be up with the times. They don't worry about keeping up with the Joneses: as intellectuals, they know that they are supposed to be Nonconformists and Independent Thinkers living at the Cutting Edge of Human Thought. And so they are all a-dither to keep up with the times – which means adopting the latest technological innovations as soon as the Joneses do.

Do I wish to keep up with the times? No.

My wish simply is to live my life as fully as I can. In both our work and our leisure, I think, we should be so employed. And in our time this means that we must save ourselves from the products that we are asked to buy in order, ultimately, to replace ourselves.

The danger most immediately to be feared in 'technological progress' is the degradation and obsolescence of the body. Implicit in the technological revolution from the beginning has been a new version of an old dualism, one always destructive, and now more destructive than ever. For many centuries there have been people who looked upon the body, as upon the natural world, as an encumbrance of the soul, and so have hated the body, as they have hated the natural world, and longed to be free of it. They have seen the body as intolerably imperfect by spiritual standards. More recently, since the beginning of the technological revolution, more and more people have looked upon the body, along with the rest of the natural creation, as intolerably imperfect by mechanical standards. They see the body as an encumbrance of the mind – the mind, that is, as reduced to a set of mechanical ideas that can be implemented in machines – and so they hate it and long to be free of it. The body has limits that the machine does not have; therefore, remove the body from the machine so that the machine can continue as an unlimited idea.

It is odd that simply because of its 'sexual freedom' our time should be considered extraordinarily physical. In fact, our 'sexual revolution' is mostly an industrial phenomenon, in which the body is used as an idea of pleasure or a pleasure machine with the aim of 'freeing' natural pleasure from natural consequence. Like any other industrial enterprise, industrial sexuality seeks to conquer nature by exploiting it and ignoring the consequences, by denying any connection between nature and spirit or body and soul, and by evading social responsibility. The spiritual, physical, and economic costs of this 'freedom' are immense, and are characteristically belittled or ignored. The diseases of sexual irresponsibility are regarded as a technological problem and an affront to liberty. Industrial sex, characteristically, establishes its freeness and goodness by an industrial accounting, dutifully toting up numbers of 'sexual partners,' orgasms, and so on, with the inevitable industrial implication that the body is somehow a limit on the idea of sex, which will be a great deal more abundant as soon as it can be done by robots.

This hatred of the body and of the body's life in the natural world, always inherent in the technological revolution (and sometimes explicitly and vengefully so), is of concern to an artist because art, like sexual love, is of the body. Like sexual love, art is of the mind and spirit also, but it is made with the body and it appeals to the senses. To reduce or shortcut the intimacy of the body's involvement in the making of a work of art (that is, of any artifice, anything made by art) inevitably risks reducing the work of art and the art itself. In addition to the reasons I gave previously, which I still believe are good reasons, I am not going to use a computer because I don't want to diminish or distort my bodily involvement in my work. I don't want to deny myself the *pleasure* of bodily involvement in my work, for that pleasure seems to me to be the sign of an indispensable integrity.

At first glance, writing may seem not nearly so much an art of the body as, say, dancing or gardening or carpentry. And yet language is the most intimately physical of all the artistic means. We have it palpably in our mouths; it is our *langue*, our tongue. Writing it, we shape it with our hands. Reading aloud what we have written – as we must do, if we are writing carefully – our language passes in at the eyes, out at the mouth, in at the ears; the words are immersed and steeped in the senses of the body before they make sense in the mind. They *cannot* make sense in the mind until they have made sense in the body. Does shaping one's words with one's own hand impart character and quality to them, as does speaking them with one's own tongue to the satisfaction of one's own ear? There is no way to prove that it does. On the other hand, there is no way to prove that it does not, and I believe that it does.

The act of writing language down is not so insistently tangible an act as the act of building a house or playing the violin. But to the extent that it is tangible, I love the tangibility of it. The computer apologists, it seems to me, have greatly underrated the value of the handwritten manuscript as an artifact. I don't mean that a writer should be a fine calligrapher and write for exhibition, but rather that handwriting has a valuable influence on the work so written. I am certainly no calligrapher, but my handwritten pages have a home-made, handmade look to them that both pleases me in itself and suggests the possibility of ready correction. It looks hospitable to improvement. As the longhand is transformed into typescript and then into galley proofs and the printed page, it seems increasingly to resist improvement. More and more spunk is required to mar the clean, final-looking lines of type. I have the notion – again not provable – that the longer I keep a piece of work in longhand, the better it will be.

To me, also, there is a significant difference between ready correction and easy correction. Much is made of the ease of correction in computer work, owing to the insubstantiality of the light-image on the screen; one presses a button and the old version disappears, to be replaced by the new. But because of the substantiality of paper and the consequent difficulty involved, one does not handwrite or typewrite a new page every time a correction is made. A handwritten or typewritten page therefore is usually to some degree a palimpsest; it contains parts and relics of its own history – erasures, passages crossed out, interlineations – suggesting that there is something to go back to as well as something to go forward to. The light-text on the computer screen, by contrast, is an artifact typical of what can only be called the industrial present, a present absolute. A computer destroys the sense of historical succession, just as do other forms of mechanization. The well-crafted table or cabinet embodies the memory of (because it embodies respect for) the tree it was made of and the forest in which the tree stood. The work of certain potters embodies the memory that the clay was dug from the earth. Certain farms contain hospitably the remnants and reminders of the forest or prairie that preceded them. It is possible even for towns and cities to remember farms and forests or prairies. All good human work remembers its history. The best writing, even when printed, is full of intimations that it is the present version of earlier versions of itself, and that its maker inherited the work and the ways of earlier makers. It thus keeps, even in print, a suggestion of the quality of the handwritten page; it is a palimpsest.

Something of this undoubtedly carries over into industrial products. The plastic Clorox jug has a shape and a loop for the forefinger that recalls the stoneware jug that went before it. But something vital is missing. It embodies no memory of its source or sources in the earth or of any human hand involved in its shaping. Or look at a large factory or a power plant or an airport, and see if you can imagine – even if you know – what was there before. In such things the materials of the world have entered a kind of orphanhood.

It would be uncharitable and foolish of me to suggest that nothing good will ever be written on a computer. Some of my best friends have computers. I have only said that a computer cannot help you to write *better*, and I stand by that. (In fact, I know a publisher who says that under the influence of computers – or of the immaculate copy that computers produce – many writers are now writing worse.) But I do say that in using computers writers are flirting with a radical separation of mind and body, the elimination of the work of the body from the work of the mind. The text on the computer screen, and the computer printout too, has a sterile, untouched, factorymade look, like that of a plastic whistle or a new car. The body does not do work like that. The body *characterizes* everything it touches. What it makes it traces over with the marks of its pulses and breathings, its excitements, hesitations, flaws, and mistakes. On its good work, it leaves the marks of skill, care, and love persisting through hesitations, flaws, and mistakes. And to those of us who love and honor the life of the body in this world, these marks are precious things, necessities of life.

But writing is of the body in yet another way. It is preeminently a walker's art. It can be done on foot and at large. The beauty of its traditional equipment is simplicity. And cheapness. Going off to the woods, I take a pencil and some paper (*any* paper – a small notebook, an old envelope, a piece of a feed sack), and I am as well equipped for my work as the president of IBM. I am also free, for the time being at least, of everything that IBM is hooked to. My thoughts will not be coming to me from the power structure or the power grid, but from another direction and way entirely. My mind is free to go with my feet.

I know that there are some people, perhaps many, to whom you cannot appeal on behalf of the body. To them, disembodiment is a goal, and they long for the realm of pure mind – or pure machine; the difference is negligible. Their departure from their bodies, obviously, is much to be desired, but the rest of us had better be warned: they are going to cause a lot of dangerous commotion on their way out.

Some of my critics were happy to say that my refusal to use a computer would not do any good. I have argued, and am convinced, that it will at least do *me* some good, and that it may involve me in the preservation of some cultural goods. But what they meant was real, practical, public good. They meant that the materials and energy I save by not buying a computer will not be 'significant.' They meant that no individual's restraint in the use of technology or energy will be 'significant.' That is true.

But each one of us, by 'insignificant' individual abuse of the world, contributes to a general abuse that is devastating. And if I were one of thousands or millions of people who could afford a piece of equipment, even one for which they had a conceivable 'need,' and yet did not buy it, *that* would be 'significant,' Why, then, should I hesitate for even a moment to be one, even the first one, of that 'significant' number? Thoreau gave the definitive reply to the folly of 'significant numbers' a long time ago: Why should anybody wait to do what is right until everybody does it? It is not 'significant' to love your own children or to eat your own dinner, either. But normal humans will not wait to love or eat until it is mandated by an act of Congress.

One of my correspondents asked where one is to draw the line. That question returns me to the bewilderment I mentioned earlier: I am unsure where the line ought to be drawn, or how to draw it. But it is an intelligent question, worth losing some sleep over.

I know how to draw the line only where it is easy to draw. It is easy – it is even a luxury – to deny oneself the use of a television set, and I zealously practice that form of self-denial. Every time I see television (at other people's houses), I am more inclined to congratulate myself on my deprivation. I have no doubt, as I have said, that I am better off without a computer. I joyfully deny myself a motorboat, a camping van, an off-road vehicle, and every other kind of recreational machinery. I have, and want, no 'second home.' I suffer very comfortably the lack of colas, TV dinners, and other counterfeit foods and beverages.

I am, however, still in bondage to the automobile industry and the energy companies, which have nothing to recommend them except our dependence on them. I still fly on airplanes, which have nothing to recommend them but speed; they are inconvenient, uncomfortable, undependable, ugly, stinky, and scary. I still cut my wood with a chainsaw, which has nothing to recommend it but speed, and has all the faults of an airplane, except it does not fly.

It is plain to me that the line ought to be drawn without fail wherever it can be drawn easily. And it ought to be easy (though many do not find it so) to refuse to buy what one does not need. If you are already solving your problem with the equipment you have – a pencil, say – why solve it with something more expensive and more damaging? If you don't have a problem, why pay for a solution? If you love the freedom and elegance of simple tools, why encumber yourself with something complicated?

And yet, if we are ever again to have a world fit and pleasant for little children, we are surely going to have to draw the line where it is *not* easily drawn. We are going to have to learn to give up things that we have learned (in only few years, after all) to 'need.' I am not an optimist; I am afraid that I won't live long enough to escape my bondage to the machines. Nevertheless, on every day left to me I will search my mind and circumstances for the means of escape. And I am not without hope. I knew a man who, in the age of chainsaws, went right on cutting his wood with a handsaw and an axe. He was a healthier and a saner man than I am. I shall let his memory trouble my thoughts.

(1989)

Family Work

For those of us who have wished to raise our food and our children at home, it is easy enough to state the ideal. Growing our own food, unlike buying it, is a complex activity, and it affects deeply the shape and value of our lives. We like the thought that the outdoor work that improves our health should produce food of excellent quality that, in turn, also improves and safeguards our health. We like no less the thought that the home production of food can improve the quality of family life. Not only do we intend to give our children better food than we can buy for them at the store, or than they will buy for themselves from vending machines or burger joints, we also know that growing and preparing food at home can provide family work – work for everybody. And by thus elaborating household chores and obligations, we hope to strengthen the bonds of interest, loyalty, affection, and cooperation that keep families together.

Forty years ago, for most of our people, whether they lived in the country or in town, this was less an ideal than a necessity, enforced both by tradition and by need. As is often so, it was only after family life and family work became (allegedly) unnecessary that we began to think of them as 'ideals.'

As ideals, they are threatened; as they have become (even allegedly) unnecessary, they have become by the same token less possible. I do not mean to imply that I think the ideal is any less valuable than it ever was, or that it is – in reality, in the long run – less necessary. Nor do I think that less possible means impossible.

I do think that the ideal is more difficult now than it was. We are trying to uphold it now mainly by will, without much help from necessity, and with no help at all from custom or public value. For most people now do seem to think that family life and family work are unnecessary, and this thought has been institutionalized in our economy and in our public values. Never before has private life been so preyed upon by public life. How can we preserve family life – if by that we mean, as I think we must, *home* life – when our attention is so forcibly drawn away from home?

We know the causes well enough.

Automobiles and several decades of supposedly cheap fuel have put longer and longer distances between home and work, household and daily needs.

TV and other media have learned to suggest with increasing subtlety and callousness – especially, and most wickedly, to children – that it is better to consume than to produce, to buy than to grow or to make, to 'go out' than to stay home. If you have a TV, your children will be subjected almost from the cradle to an overwhelming insinuation that all worth experiencing is somewhere else and that all worth having must be bought. The purpose is blatantly to supplant the joy and beauty of health with cosmetics, clothes, cars, and ready-made desserts. There is clearly too narrow a limit on how much money can be made from health, but the profitability of disease – especially disease of spirit or character – has so far, for profiteers, no visible limit.

Another cause, and one that seems particularly regrettable, is public education. The idea that the public should be educated is altogether salutary, and since we insist on making this education compulsory we ought, in reason, to reconcile ourselves to the likelihood that it will be mainly poor. I am not nearly so much concerned about its quality as I am about its *length*. My impression is that the chief, if unadmitted, purpose of the school system is to keep children away from home as much as possible. Parents want their children kept out of their hair; education is merely a by-product, not overly prized. In many places, thanks to school consolidation, two hours or more of travel time have been added to the school day. For my own children the regular school day from the first grade – counting from the time they went to catch the bus until they came home – was nine hours. An extracurricular activity would lengthen the day to eleven hours or more. This is not education, but a form of incarceration. Why should anyone be surprised if, under these circumstances, children should become 'disruptive' or even 'ineducable'?

If public education is to have any meaning or value at all, then public education *must* be supplemented by home education. I know this from my own experience as a college teacher. What can you teach a student whose entire education has been public, whose daily family life for twenty years has consisted of four or five hours of TV, who has never read a book for pleasure or even *seen* a book so read; whose only work has been schoolwork, who has never learned to perform any essential task? Not much, so far as I could tell.

We can see clearly enough at least a couple of solutions.

We can get rid of the television set. As soon as we see that the TV cord is a vacuum line, pumping life and meaning out of the household, we can unplug it. What a grand and neglected privilege it is to be shed of the glibness, the gleeful idiocy, the idiotic gravity, the unctuous or lubricious greed of those public faces and voices!

And we can try to make our homes centers of attention and interest. Getting rid of the TV, we understand, is not just a practical act, but also a symbolical one: we thus turn our backs on the invitation to consume; we shut out the racket of consumption. The ensuing silence is an invitation to our homes, to our own places and lives, to come into being. And we begin to recognize a truth disguised or denied by TV and all that it speaks and stands for: no life and no place is destitute; all have possibilities of productivity and pleasure, rest and work, solitude and conviviality that belong particularly to themselves. These possibilities exist everywhere, in the country or in the city, it makes no difference. All that is necessary is the time and the inner quietness to look for them, the sense to recognize them, and the grace to welcome them. They are now most often lived out in home gardens and kitchens, libraries, and workrooms. But they are beginning to be worked out, too, in little parks, in vacant lots, in neighborhood streets. Where we live is also a place where our interest and our effort can be. But they can't be there by the means and modes of consumption. If we consume nothing but what we buy, we are living in 'the economy,' in 'television land,' not at home. It is productivity that rights the balance, and brings us home. Any way at all of joining and using the air and light and weather of your own place – even if it is only a window box, even if it is only an opened window – is a making and a having that you cannot get from TV or government or school.

That local productivity, however small, is a gift. If we are parents we cannot help but see it as a gift to our children – and the *best* of gifts. How will it be received?

Well, not ideally. Sometimes it will be received gratefully enough. But sometimes indifferently, and sometimes resentfully.

According to my observation, one of the likeliest results of a wholesome diet of home-raised, home-cooked food is a heightened relish for cokes and hot dogs. And if you 'deprive' your children of TV at home, they are going to watch it with something like rapture away from home. And obligations, jobs, and chores at home will almost certainly cause your child to wish, sometimes at least, to be somewhere else, watching TV.

Because, of course, parents are not the only ones raising their children. They are being raised also by their schools and by their friends and by the parents of their friends. Some of this outside raising is good, some is not. It is, anyhow, unavoidable.

What this means, I think, is about what it has always meant. Children, no matter how nurtured at home, must be risked to the world. And parenthood is not an exact science, but a vexed privilege and a blessed trial, absolutely necessary and not altogether possible.

If your children spurn your healthful meals in favor of those concocted by some reincarnation of Col. Sanders, Long John Silver, or the Royal Family of Burger; if they flee from books to a friend's house to watch TV, if your old-fashioned notions and ways embarrass them in front of their friends – does that mean you are a failure?

It may. And what parent has not considered that possibility? I know, at least, that I have considered it – and have wailed and gnashed my teeth, found fault, laid blame, preached and ranted. In weaker moments, I have even blamed myself.

But I have thought, too, that the term of human judgment is longer than parenthood, that the upbringing we give our children is not just for their childhood but for all their lives. And it is surely the *duty* of the older generation to be embarrassingly old-fashioned, for the claims of the 'newness' of any younger generation are mostly frivolous. The young are born to the human condition more than to their time, and they face mainly the same trials and obligations as their elders have faced.

The real failure is to give in. If we make our house a household instead of a motel, provide healthy nourishment for mind and body, enforce moral distinctions and restraints, teach essential skills and disciplines and require their use, there is no certainty that we are providing our children a 'better life' that they will embrace wholeheartedly during childhood. But we are providing them a choice that they may make intelligently as adults.

(1980)

Rugged Individualism

The career of rugged individualism in America has run mostly to absurdity, tragic or comic. But it also has done us a certain amount of good. There was a streak of it in Thoreau, who went alone to jail in protest against the Mexican War. And that streak has continued in his successors who have suffered penalties for civil disobedience because of their perception that the law and the government were not always or necessarily right. This is individualism of a kind rugged enough, and it has been authenticated typically by its identification with a communal good.

The tragic version of rugged individualism is in the presumptive 'right' of individuals to do as they please, as if there were no God, no legitimate government, no community, no neighbors, and no posterity. This is most frequently understood as the right to do whatever one pleases with one's property. One's property, according to this formulation, is one's own absolutely.

Rugged individualism of this kind has cost us dearly in lost topsoil, in destroyed forests, in the increasing toxicity of the world, and in annihilated species. When property rights become absolute they are invariably destructive, for then they are used to justify not only the abuse of things of permanent value for the temporary benefit of legal owners, but also the appropriation and abuse of things to which the would-be owners have no rights at all, but which can belong only to the public or to the entire community of living creatures: the atmosphere, the water cycle, wilderness, ecosystems, the possibility of life.

This is made worse when great corporations are granted the status of 'persons,' who then can also become rugged individuals, insisting on their right to do whatever they please with their property. Because of the overwhelming wealth and influence of these 'persons,' the elected representatives and defenders of 'the people of the United

States' become instead the representatives and defenders of the corporations.

It has become ever more clear that this sort of individualism has never proposed or implied any protection of the rights of all individuals, but instead has promoted a ferocious scramble in which more and more of the rights of 'the people' have been gathered into the ownership of fewer and fewer of the greediest and most powerful 'persons.'

I have described so far what most of us would identify as the rugged individualism of the political right. Now let us have a look at the left. The rugged individualism of the left believes that an individual's body is a property belonging to that individual absolutely: the owners of bodies may, by right, use them as they please, as if there were no God, no legitimate government, no community, no neighbors, and no posterity. This supposed right is manifested in the democratizing of 'sexual liberation'; in the popular assumption that marriage has been 'privatized' and so made subordinate to the wishes of individuals; in the proposition that the individual is 'autonomous'; in the legitimation of abortion as birth control – in the denial, that is to say, that the community, the family, one's spouse, or even one's own soul might exercise a legitimate proprietary interest in the use one makes of one's body. And this too is tragic, for it sets us 'free' from responsibility and thus from the possibility of meaning. It makes unintelligible the self-sacrifice that sent Thoreau to jail.

The comedy begins when these two rugged (or 'autonomous') individualisms confront each other. Conservative individualism strongly supports 'family values' and abominates lust. But it does not dissociate itself from the profits accruing from the exercise of lust (and, in fact, of the other six deadly sins), which it encourages in its advertisements. The 'conservatives' of our day understand pride, lust, envy, anger, covetousness, gluttony, and sloth as virtues when they lead to profit or to political power. Only as unprofitable or unauthorized personal indulgences do they rank as sins, imperiling salvation of the soul, family values, and national security.

Liberal individualism, on the contrary, understands sin as a private matter. It strongly supports protecting 'the environment,' which is that part of the world which surrounds, at a safe distance, the privately owned body. 'The environment' does not include the economic landscapes of agriculture and forestry or their human communities, and it does not include the privately owned bodies of other people – all of which appear to have been bequeathed in fee simple to the corporate individualists.

Conservative rugged individualists and liberal rugged individualists believe alike that they should be 'free' to get as much as they can of whatever they want. Their major doctrinal difference is that they want (some of the time) different sorts of things.

'Every man for himself' is a doctrine for a feeding frenzy or for a panic in a burning nightclub, appropriate for sharks or hogs or perhaps a cascade of lemmings. A society wishing to endure must speak the language of caretaking, faith-keeping, kindness, neighborliness, and peace. That language is another precious resource that cannot be 'privatized.'

(2004)

Economy and Pleasure

To those who still uphold the traditions of religious and political thought that influenced the shaping of our society and the founding of our government, it is astonishing, and of course discouraging, to see economics now elevated to the position of ultimate justifier and explainer of all the affairs of our daily life, and competition enshrined as the sovereign principle and ideal of economics.

As thousands of small farms and small local businesses of all kinds falter and fail under the effects of adverse economic policies or live under the threat of what we complacently call 'scientific progress,' the economist sits in the calm of professorial tenure and government subsidy, commenting and explaining for the illumination of the press and the general public. If those who fail happen to be fellow humans, neighbors, children of God, and citizens of the republic, all that is outside the purview of the economist. As the farmers go under, as communities lose their economic supports, as all of rural America sits as if condemned in the shadow of the 'free market' and 'revolutionary science,' the economist announces pontifically to the press that 'there will be some winners and some losers' – as if that might justify and clarify everything, or anything. The sciences, one gathers, mindlessly serve economics, and the humanities defer abjectly to the sciences. All assume, apparently, that we are in the grip of the determination of economic laws that are the laws of the universe. The newspapers quote the economists as the ultimate authorities. We read their pronouncements, knowing that the last word has been said.

'Science,' President Reagan says, 'tells us that the breakthroughs in superconductivity bring us to the threshold of a new age.' He is speaking to 'a federal conference on the commercial applications of the new technology,' and we know that by 'science' he means scientists in the pay of corporations. 'It is our task at this conference,' he says, 'to herald in that new age with a rush.' A part of his program to accomplish this task is a proposal to 'relax' the antitrust laws.* Thus even the national executive and our legal system itself must now defer to the demands of 'the economy.' Whatever 'new age' is at hand at the moment must be heralded in 'with a rush' because of the profits available to those who will rush it in.

It seems that we have been reduced almost to a state of absolute economics, in which people and all other creatures and things may be considered purely as economic 'units,' or integers of production, and in which a human being may be dealt with, as John Ruskin put it, 'merely as a covetous machine.'† And the voices bitterest to hear are those saying that all this destructive work of mindless genius, money, and power is regrettable but cannot be helped.

Perhaps it cannot. Surely we would be fools if, having understood the logic of this terrible process, we assumed that it might not go on in its glutton's optimism until it achieves the catastrophe that is its logical end. But let us suppose that a remedy is possible. If so, perhaps the best beginning would be in understanding the falseness and silliness of the economic ideal of competition, which is destructive both of nature and of human nature because it is untrue to both.

The ideal of competition always implies, and in fact requires, that any community must be divided into a class of winners and a class of losers. This division is radically different from other social divisions: that of the more able and the less able, or that of the richer and the poorer, or even that of the rulers and the ruled. These latter divisions have existed throughout history and at times, at least, have been ameliorated by social and religious ideals that instructed the strong to help the weak. As a purely economic ideal, competition does not contain or imply any such instructions. In fact, the defenders of the ideal of competition have never known what to do with or for the losers. The losers simply accumulate in human dumps, like stores of industrial waste, until they gain enough misery and strength to

---

* 'Reagan calls for effort to find commercial uses for superconductors,' *Louisville Courier-Journal*, July 29, 1987, p. A3.

† John Ruskin, *Unto This Last* (Lincoln: University of Nebraska Press, 1967), p. 11.

overpower the winners. The idea that the displaced and dispossessed 'should seek retraining and get into another line of work' is, of course, utterly cynical; it is only the hand-washing practiced by officials and experts.* A loser, by definition, is somebody whom nobody knows what to do with. There is no limit to the damage and the suffering implicit in this willingness that losers should exist as a normal economic cost.

The danger of the ideal of competition is that it neither proposes nor implies any limits. It proposes simply to lower costs at any cost, and to raise profits at any cost. It does not hesitate at the destruction of the life of a family or the life of a community. It pits neighbor against neighbor as readily as it pits buyer against seller. Every transaction is *meant* to involve a winner and a loser. And for this reason the human economy is pitted without limit against nature. For in the unlimited competition of neighbor and neighbor, buyer and seller, all available means must be used; none may be spared.

I will be told that indeed there are limits to economic competitiveness as now practiced – that, for instance, one is not allowed to kill one's competitor. But, leaving aside the issue of whether or not murder would be acceptable as an economic means if the stakes were high enough, it is a fact that the destruction of life is a part of the daily business of economic competition as now practiced. If one person is willing to take another's property or to accept another's ruin as a normal result of economic enterprise, then he is willing to destroy that other person's life as it is and as it desires to be. That this person's biological existence has been spared seems merely incidental; it was spared because it was not worth anything. That this person is now 'free' to 'seek retraining and get into another line of work' signifies only that his life as it was has been destroyed.

But there is another implication in the limitlessness of the ideal of competition that is politically even more ominous: namely, that unlimited economic competitiveness proposes an unlimited concentration of economic power. Economic anarchy, like any other

---

* Reed Karaim, 'Loss of million farms in 14 years projected,' *Des Moines Register*, March 18, 1986, p. 1A.

free-for-all, tends inevitably toward dominance by the strongest. If it is normal for economic activity to divide the community into a class of winners and a class of losers, then the inescapable implication is that the class of winners will become ever smaller, the class of losers ever larger. And that, obviously, is now happening: the usable property of our country, once divided somewhat democratically, is owned by fewer and fewer people every year. That the president of the republic can, without fear, propose the 'relaxation' of antitrust laws in order to 'rush' the advent of a commercial 'new age' suggests not merely that we are 'rushing' toward plutocracy, but that this is now a permissible goal for the would-be winning class for which Mr. Reagan speaks and acts, and a burden acceptable to nearly everybody else.

Nowhere, I believe, has this grossly oversimplified version of economics made itself more at home than in the land-grant universities. The colleges of agriculture, for example, having presided over the now nearly completed destruction of their constituency – the farm people and the farm communities – are now scrambling to ally themselves more firmly than ever, not with 'the rural home and rural life'* that were, and are, their trust, but with the technocratic aims and corporate interests that are destroying the rural home and rural life. This, of course, is only a new intensification of an old alliance. The revolution that began with machines and chemicals proposes now to continue with automation, computers, and biotechnology. That this has been and is a revolution is undeniable. It has not been merely a 'scientific revolution,' as its proponents sometimes like to call it, but also an economic one, involving great and profound changes in property ownership and the distribution of real wealth. It has done by insidious tendency what the communist revolutions have done by fiat: it has dispossessed the people and usurped the power and integrity of community life.

This work has been done, and is still being done, under the heading of altruism: its aims, as its proponents never tire of repeating, are to 'serve agriculture' and to 'feed the world.' These aims, as stated,

---

* This is the language of the Hatch Act, *United States Code*, Section 361b.

are irreproachable; as pursued, they raise a number of doubts. Agriculture, it turns out, is to be served strictly according to the rules of competitive economics. The aim is 'to make farmers more competitive' and 'to make American agriculture more competitive.' Against whom, we must ask, are our farmers and our agriculture to be made more competitive? And we must answer, because we know: against other farmers, at home and abroad. Now, if the colleges of agriculture 'serve agriculture' by helping farmers to compete against one another, what do they propose to do to help the farmers who have been out-competed? Well, those people are not farmers any-more, and therefore are of no concern to the academic servants of agriculture. Besides, they are the beneficiaries of the inestimable lib-erty to 'seek retraining and get into another line of work.'

And so the colleges of agriculture, entrusted though they are to serve the rural home and rural life, give themselves over to a hysteri-cal rhetoric of 'change,' 'the future,' 'the frontiers of modern science,' 'competition,' 'the competitive edge,' 'the cutting edge,' 'early adop-tion,' and the like, as if there is nothing worth learning from the past and nothing worth preserving in the present. The idea of the teacher and scholar as one called upon to preserve and pass on a common cultural and natural birthright has been almost entirely replaced by the idea of the teacher and scholar as a developer of 'human capital' and a bestower of economic advantage. The ambition is to make the university an 'economic resource' in a competition for wealth and power that is local, national, and global. Of course, all this works directly against the rural home and rural life, because it works directly against community.

There is no denying that competitiveness is a part of the life both of an individual and of a community, or that, within limits, it is a use-ful and necessary part. But it is equally obvious that no individual can lead a good or a satisfying life under the rule of competition, and that no community can succeed except by limiting somehow the com-petitiveness of its members. One cannot maintain one's 'competitive edge' if one helps other people. The advantage of 'early adoption' would disappear – it would not be thought of – in a community that put a proper value on mutual help. Such advantages would not be thought of by people intent on loving their neighbors as themselves. And it is impossible to imagine that there can be any reconciliation between local and national competitiveness and global altruism. The ambition to 'feed the world' or 'feed the hungry,' rising as it does out of the death struggle of farmer with farmer, proposes not the filling of stomachs, but the engorgement of 'the bottom line.' The strangest of all the doctrines of the cult of competition, in which admittedly there must be losers as well as winners, is that the result of competition is inevitably good for everybody, that altruistic ends may be met by a system without altruistic motives or altruistic means.

In agriculture, competitiveness has been based throughout the industrial era on constantly accelerating technological change – the very *principle* of agricultural competitiveness is ever-accelerating change – and this has encouraged an ever-accelerating dependency on purchased products, products purchased ever farther from home. Community, however, aspires toward stability. It strives to balance change with constancy. That is why community life places such high value on neighborly love, marital fidelity, local loyalty, the integrity and continuity of family life, respect for the old, and instruction of the young. And a vital community draws its life, so far as possible, from local sources. It prefers to solve its problems, for example, by nonmonetary exchanges of help, not by buying things. A community cannot survive under the rule of competition.

But the land-grant universities, in espousing the economic determinism of the industrialists, have caught themselves in a logical absurdity that they may finally discover to be dangerous to themselves. If competitiveness is the economic norm, and the 'competitive edge' the only recognized social goal, then how can these institutions justify public support? Why, in other words, should the public be willing to permit a corporation to profit privately from research that has been subsidized publicly? Why should not the industries be required to afford their own research, and why should not the laws of competition and the free market – if indeed they perform as advertised – enable industries to do their own research a great deal more cheaply than the universities can do it?

The question that we finally come to is a practical one, though it is not one that is entirely answerable by empirical methods: Can a university, or a nation, *afford* this exclusive rule of competition, this purely economic economy? The great fault of this approach to things is that it is so drastically reductive; it does not permit us to live and work as human beings, as the best of our inheritance defines us. Rats and roaches live by competition under the law of supply and demand; it is the privilege of human beings to live under the laws of justice and mercy. It is impossible not to notice how little the proponents of the ideal of competition have to say about honesty, which is the fundamental economic virtue, and how *very* little they have to say about community, compassion, and mutual help.

But what the ideal of competition most flagrantly and disastrously excludes is affection. The affections, John Ruskin said, are 'an anomalous force, rendering every one of the ordinary political economist's calculations nugatory; while, even if he desired to introduce this new element into his estimates, he has no power of dealing with it; for the affections only become a true motive power when they ignore every other motive power and condition of political economy.' Thus, if we are sane, we do not dismiss or abandon our infant children or our aged parents because they are too young or too old to work. For human beings, affection is the ultimate motive, because the force that powers us, as Ruskin also said, is not 'steam, magnetism, or gravitation,' but 'a Soul.'

I would like now to attempt to talk about economy from the standpoint of affection – or, as I am going to call it, pleasure, advancing just a little beyond Ruskin's term, for pleasure is, so to speak, affection in action. There are obvious risks in approaching an economic problem by a way that is frankly emotional – to talk, for example, about the pleasures of nature and the pleasures of work. But these risks seem to me worth taking, for what I am trying to deal with here is the grief that we increasingly suffer as a result of the loss of those pleasures.

It is necessary, at the outset, to make a distinction between pleasure that is true or legitimate and pleasure that is not. We know that a pleasure can be as heavily debited as an economy. Some people undoubtedly thought it pleasant, for example, to have the most oner-ous tasks of their economy performed by black slaves. But this proved to be a pleasure that was temporary and dangerous. It lived by an enormous indebtedness that was inescapably to be paid not in money, but in misery, waste, and death. The pleasures of fossil fuel combus-tion and nuclear 'security' are, as we are beginning to see, similarly debited to the future. These pleasures are in every way analogous to the self-indulgent pleasures of individuals. They are pleasures that we are allowed to have merely to the extent that we can ignore or defer the logical consequences.

That there is pleasure in competition is not to be doubted. We know from childhood that winning is fun. But we probably begin to grow up when we begin to sympathize with the loser – that is, when we begin to understand that competition involves costs as well as benefits. Sometimes perhaps, as in the most innocent games, the benefits are all to the winner and the costs all to the loser. But when the competition is more serious, when the stakes are higher and greater power is used, then we know that the winner shares in the cost, sometimes disastrously. In war, for example, even the winner is a loser. And this is equally true of our present economy: in unlimited economic competition, the winners are losers; that they may appear to be winners is owing only to their temporary ability to charge their costs to other people or to nature.

But a victory over community or nature can be won only at everybody's cost. For example, we now have in the United States many landscapes that have been defeated – temporarily or permanently – by strip mining, by clear-cutting, by poisoning, by bad farming, or by vari-ous styles of 'development' that have subjugated their sites entirely to human purposes. These landscapes have been defeated for the benefit of what are assumed to be victorious landscapes: the suburban housing developments and the places of amusement (the park systems, the recreational wildernesses) of the winners – so far – in the economy. But these victorious landscapes and their human inhabitants are already paying the costs of their defeat of other landscapes: in air and water pollution, overcrowding, inflated prices, and various diseases of body and mind. Eventually, the cost will be paid in scarcity or want of necessary goods.

Is it possible to look beyond this all-consuming 'rush' of winning and losing to the possibility of countrysides, a nation of countrysides, in which use is not synonymous with defeat? It is. But in order to do so we must consider our pleasures. Since we all know, from our own and our nation's experience, of some pleasures that are canceled by their costs, and of some that result in unredeemable losses and miseries, it is natural to wonder if there may not be such phenomena as *net* pleasures, pleasures that are free or without a permanent cost. And we know that there are. These are the pleasures that we take in our own lives, our own wakefulness in this world, and in the company of other people and other creatures – pleasures innate in the Creation and in our own good work. It is in these pleasures that we possess the likeness to God that is spoken of in Genesis.

'This curious world we inhabit is more wonderful than convenient; more beautiful than it is useful; it is more to be admired and enjoyed than used.' Henry David Thoreau said that to his graduating class at Harvard in 1837. We may assume that to most of them it sounded odd, as to most of the Harvard graduating class of 1987 it undoubtedly still would. But perhaps we will be encouraged to take him seriously, if we recognize that this idea is not something that Thoreau made up out of thin air. When he uttered it, he may very well have been remembering Revelation 4:11: 'Thou art worthy, O Lord, to receive glory and honour and power: for thou hast created all things, and for thy pleasure they are and were created.' That God created 'all things' is in itself an uncomfortable thought, for in our workaday world we can hardly avoid preferring some things above others, and this makes it hard to imagine *not* doing so. That God created all things for His pleasure, and that they continue to exist because they please Him, is formidable doctrine indeed, as far as possible both from the 'anthropocentric' utilitarianism that some environmentalist critics claim to find in the Bible and from the grouchy spirituality of many Christians.

It would be foolish, probably, to suggest that God's pleasure in all things can be fully understood or appreciated by mere humans. The passage suggests, however, that our truest and profoundest religious experience may be the simple, unasking pleasure in the existence of other creatures that *is* possible to humans. It suggests that God's pleasure in all things must be respected by us in our use of things, and even in our displeasure in some things. It suggests too that we have an obligation to preserve God's pleasure in all things, and surely this means not only that we must not misuse or abuse anything, but also that there must be some things and some places that by common agreement we do not use at all, but leave wild. This bountiful and lovely thought that all creatures are pleasing to God – and potentially pleasing, therefore, to us – is unthinkable from the point of view of an economy divorced from pleasure, such as the one we have now, which completely discounts the capacity of people to be affectionate toward what they do and what they use and where they live and the other people and creatures with whom they live.

It may be argued that our whole society is more devoted to pleasure than any whole society ever was in the past, that we support in fact a great variety of pleasure industries and that these are thriving as never before. But that would seem only to prove my point. That there can be pleasure industries at all, exploiting our apparently limitless inability to be pleased, can only mean that our economy is divorced from pleasure and that pleasure is gone from our workplaces and our dwelling places. Our workplaces are more and more exclusively given over to production, and our dwelling places to consumption. And this accounts for the accelerating division of our country into defeated landscapes and victorious (but threatened) landscapes.

More and more, we take for granted that work must be destitute of pleasure. More and more, we assume that if we want to be pleased we must wait until evening, or the weekend, or vacation, or retirement. More and more, our farms and forests resemble our factories and offices, which in turn more and more resemble prisons – why else should we be so eager to escape them? We recognize defeated landscapes by the absence of pleasure from them. We are defeated at work because our work gives us no pleasure. We are defeated at home because we have no pleasant work there. We turn to the pleasure industries for relief from our defeat, and are again defeated, for the pleasure industries can thrive and grow only upon our dissatisfaction with them.

Where is our comfort but in the free, uninvolved, finally mysterious beauty and grace of this world that we did not make, that has no price? Where is our sanity but there? Where is our pleasure but in working and resting kindly in the presence of this world?

And in the right sort of economy, our pleasure would not be merely an addition or by-product or reward; it would be both an empowerment of our work and its indispensable measure. Pleasure, Ananda Coomaraswamy said, *perfects* work. In order to have leisure and pleasure, we have mechanized and automated and computerized our work. But what does this do but divide us ever more from our work and our products – and, in the process, from one another and the world? What have farmers done when they have mechanized and computerized their farms? They have removed themselves and their pleasure from their work.

I was fortunate, late in his life, to know Henry Besuden of Clark County, Kentucky, the premier Southdown sheep breeder and one of the great farmers of his time. He told me once that his first morning duty in the spring and early summer was to saddle his horse and ride across his pastures to see the condition of the grass when it was freshest from the moisture and coolness of the night. What he wanted to see in his pastures at that time of year, when his spring lambs would be fattening, was what he called 'bloom' – by which he meant not flowers, but a certain visible delectability. He recognized it, of course, by his delight in it. He was one of the best of the traditional livestockmen – the husbander or husband of his animals. As such, he was not interested in 'statistical indicators' of his flock's 'productivity.' He wanted his sheep to be pleased. If they were pleased with their pasture, they would eat eagerly, drink well, rest, and grow. He knew their pleasure by his own.

The nearly intolerable irony in our dissatisfaction is that we have removed pleasure from our work in order to remove 'drudgery' from our lives. If I could pick any rule of industrial economics to receive a thorough reexamination by our people, it would be the one that says that all hard physical work is 'drudgery' and not worth doing. There are of course many questions surrounding this issue: What is the work? In whose interest is it done? Where and in what circumstances is it done? How well and to what result is it done? In whose company is it done? How long does it last? And so forth. But this issue is personal and so needs to be reexamined by everybody. The argument, if it is that, can proceed only by personal testimony.

I can say, for example, that the tobacco harvest in my own home country involves the hardest work that I have done in any quantity. In most of the years of my life, from early boyhood until now, I have taken part in the tobacco cutting. This work usually occurs at some time between the last part of August and the first part of October. Usually the weather is hot; usually we are in a hurry. The work is extremely demanding, and often, because of the weather, it has the character of an emergency. Because all of the work still must be done by hand, this event has maintained much of its old character; it is very much the sort of thing the agriculture experts have had in mind when they have talked about freeing people from drudgery.

That the tobacco cutting *can* be drudgery is obvious. If there is too much of it, if it goes on too long, if one has no interest in it, if one cannot reconcile oneself to the misery involved in it, if one does not like or enjoy the company of one's fellow workers, then drudgery would be the proper name for it.

But for me, and I think for most of the men and women who have been my companions in this work, it has not been drudgery. None of us would say that we take pleasure in all of it all of the time, but we do take pleasure in it, and sometimes the pleasure can be intense and clear. Many of my dearest memories come from these times of hardest work.

The tobacco cutting is the most protracted social occasion of our year. Neighbors work together; they are together all day every day for weeks. The quiet of the work is not much interrupted by machine noises, and so there is much talk. There is the talk involved in the management of the work. There is incessant speculation about the weather. There is much laughter; because of the unrelenting difficulty of the work, everything funny or amusing is relished. And there are memories.

The crew to which I belong is the product of kinships and friendships going far back; my own earliest associations with it occurred nearly forty years ago. And so as we work we have before us not only the present crop and the present fields, but other crops and other fields that are remembered. The tobacco cutting is a sort of ritual of remembrance. Old stories are retold; the dead and the absent are remembered. Some of the best talk I have ever listened to I have heard during these times, and I am especially moved to think of the care that is sometimes taken to speak well – that is, to speak fittingly – of the dead and the absent. The conversation, one feels, is ancient. Such talk in barns and at row ends must go back without interruption to the first farmers. How long it may continue is now an uneasy question; not much longer perhaps, but we do not know. We only know that while it lasts it can carry us deeply into our shared life and the happiness of farming.

On many days we have had somebody's child or somebody's children with us, playing in the barn or around the patch while we worked, and these have been our best days. One of the most regrettable things about the industrialization of work is the segregation of children. As industrial work excludes the dead by social mobility and technological change, it excludes children by haste and danger. The small scale and the handwork of our tobacco cutting permit margins both temporal and spatial that accommodate the play of children. The children play at the grown-ups' work, as well as at their own play. In their play the children learn to work; they learn to know their elders and their country. And the presence of playing children means invariably that the grown-ups play too from time to time.

(I am perforce aware of the problems and the controversies about tobacco. I have spoken of the tobacco harvest here simply because it is the only remaining farm job in my part of the country that still involves a traditional neighborliness.)

Ultimately, in the argument about work and how it should be done, one has only one's pleasure to offer. It is possible, as I have learned again and again, to be in one's place, in such company, wild or domestic, and with such pleasure, that one cannot think of another place that one would prefer to be – or of another place at all. One does not miss or regret the past, or fear or long for the future. Being there is simply all, and is enough. Such times give one the chief standard and the chief reason for one's work.

Last December, when my granddaughter, Katie, had just turned five, she stayed with me one day while the rest of the family was away from home. In the afternoon we hitched a team of horses to the wagon and hauled a load of dirt for the barn floor. It was a cold day, but the sun was shining; we hauled our load of dirt over the tree-lined gravel lane beside the creek – a way well known to her mother and to my mother when they were children. As we went along, Katie drove the team for the first time in her life. She did very well, and she was proud of herself. She said that her mother would be proud of her, and I said that I was proud of her.

We completed our trip to the barn, unloaded our load of dirt, smoothed it over the barn floor, and wetted it down. By the time we started back up the creek road the sun had gone over the hill and the air had turned bitter. Katie sat close to me in the wagon, and we did not say anything for a long time. I did not say anything because I was afraid that Katie was not saying anything because she was cold and tired and miserable and perhaps homesick; it was impossible to hurry much, and I was unsure how I would comfort her.

But then, after a while, she said, 'Wendell, isn't it fun?'

(1988)

In Distrust of Movements

I must burden my readers as I have burdened myself with the knowledge that I speak from a local, some might say a provincial, point of view. When I try to identify myself to myself I realize that, in my most immediate reasons and affections, I am less than an American, less than a Kentuckian, less even than a Henry Countian, but am a man most involved with and concerned about my family, my neighbors, and the land that is daily under my feet. It is this involvement that defines my citizenship in the larger entities. And so I will remember, and I ask you to remember, that I am not trying to say what is thinkable everywhere, but rather what it is possible to think on the westward bank of the lower Kentucky River in the summer of 1998.

Over the last twenty-five or thirty years I have been making and remaking different versions of the same argument. It is not 'my' argument, really, but rather one that I inherited from a long line of familial, neighborly, literary, and scientific ancestors. We could call it 'the agrarian argument.' This argument can be summed up in as many ways as it can be made. One way to sum it up is to say that we humans can escape neither our dependence on nature nor our responsibility to nature – and that, precisely because of this condition of dependence *and* responsibility, we are also dependent upon and responsible for human culture.

Food, as I have argued at length, is both a natural (which is to say a divine) gift and a cultural product. Because we must *use* land and water and plants and animals to produce food, we are at once dependent on and responsible to what we use. We must know both how to use and how to care for what we use. This knowledge is the basis of human culture. If we do not know how to adapt our desires, our methods, and our technology to the nature of the places in which we are working, so as to make them productive *and to keep them so*, that is a cultural failure of the grossest and most dangerous kind. Poverty and starvation also can be cultural products – if the culture is wrong.

Though this argument, in my keeping, has lengthened and acquired branches, in its main assumptions it has stayed the same. What has changed – and I say this with a good deal of wonder and with much thankfulness – is the audience. Perhaps the audience will always include people who are not listening, or people who think the agrarian argument is merely an anachronism, a form of entertainment, or a nuisance to be waved away. But increasingly the audience also includes people who take this argument seriously, because they are involved in one or more of the tasks of agrarianism. They are trying to maintain a practical foothold on the earth for themselves or their families or their communities. They are trying to preserve and develop local land-based economies. They are trying to preserve or restore the health of local communities and ecosystems and watersheds. They are opposing the attempt of the great corporations to own and control all of Creation.

In short, the agrarian argument now has a significant number of friends. As the political and ecological abuses of the so-called global economy become more noticeable and more threatening, the agrarian argument is going to have more friends than it has now. This being so, maybe the advocate's task needs to change. Maybe now, instead of merely propounding (and repeating) the agrarian argument, the advocate must also try to see that this argument does not win friends too easily. I think, myself, that this is the case. The tasks of agrarianism that we have undertaken are not going to be finished for a long time. To preserve the remnants of agrarian life, to oppose the abuses of industrial land use and finally correct them, and to develop the locally adapted economies and cultures that are necessary to our survival will require many lifetimes of dedicated work. This work does not need friends with illusions. And so I would like to speak – in a friendly way, of course – out of my distrust of 'movements.'

I have had with my friend Wes Jackson a number of useful conversations about the necessity of getting out of movements – even movements that have seemed necessary and dear to us – when

they have lapsed into self-righteousness and self-betrayal, as movements seem almost invariably to do. People in movements too
readily learn to deny to others the rights and privileges they demand
for themselves. They too easily become unable to mean their own
language, as when a 'peace movement' becomes violent. They often
become too specialized, as if they cannot help taking refuge in the
pinhole vision of the industrial intellectuals. They almost always fail
to be radical enough, dealing finally in effects rather than causes. Or
they deal with single issues or single solutions, as if to assure themselves that they will not be radical enough.

And so I must declare my dissatisfaction with movements to promote soil conservation or clean water or clean air or wilderness
preservation or sustainable agriculture or community health or the
welfare of children. Worthy as these and other goals may be, they
cannot be achieved alone. They cannot be responsibly advocated
alone. I am dissatisfied with such efforts because they are too specialized, they are not comprehensive enough, they are not radical
enough, they virtually predict their own failure by implying that we
can remedy or control effects while leaving the causes in place.
Ultimately, I think, they are insincere; they propose that the trouble
is caused by *other* people; they would like to change policy but not
behavior.

The worst danger may be that a movement will lose its language
either to its own confusion about meaning and practice, or to
preemption by its enemies. I remember, for example, my naïve
confusion at learning that it was possible for advocates of organic
agriculture to look upon the 'organic method' as an end in itself. To
me, organic farming was attractive both as a way of conserving
nature and as a strategy of survival for small farmers. Imagine my
surprise in discovering that there could be huge 'organic' monocultures. And so I was somewhat prepared for the recent attempt
of the United States Department of Agriculture to appropriate the
'organic' label for food irradiation, genetic engineering, and other
desecrations by the corporate food economy. Once we allow our language to mean anything that anybody wants it to mean, it becomes
impossible to mean what we say. When 'homemade' ceases to mean

neither more nor less than 'made at home,' then it means anything, which is to say that it means nothing. The same decay is at work on words such as 'conservation,' 'sustainable,' 'safe,' 'natural,' 'healthful,' 'sanitary,' and 'organic.' The use of such words now requires the most exacting control of context and the use immediately of illustrative examples.

Real organic gardeners and farmers who market their produce locally are finding that, to a lot of people, 'organic' means something like 'trustworthy.' And so, for a while, it will be useful for us to talk about the meaning and the economic usefulness of trust and trustworthiness. But we must be careful. Sooner or later, Trust Us Global Foods, Inc., will be upon us, advertising safe, sanitary, natural food irradiation. And then we must be prepared to raise another standard and move on.

As you see, I have good reasons for declining to name the movement I think I am a part of. I call it The Nameless Movement for Better Ways of Doing – which I hope is too long and uncute to be used as a bumper sticker. I know that movements tend to die with their names and slogans, and I believe that this Nameless Movement needs to live on and on. I am reconciled to the likelihood that from time to time it will name itself and have slogans, but I am not going to use its slogans or call it by any of its names. After this, I intend to stop calling it The Nameless Movement for Better Ways of Doing, for fear it will become the NMBWD and acquire a headquarters and a budget and an inventory of T-shirts covered with language that in a few years will be mere spelling.

Let us suppose, then, that we have a Nameless Movement for Better Land Use and that we know we must try to keep it active, responsive, and intelligent for a long time. What must we do?

What we must do above all, I think, is try to see the problem in its full size and difficulty. If we are concerned about land abuse, then we must see that this is an economic problem. Every economy is, by definition, a land-using economy. If we are using our land wrong, then something is wrong with our economy. This is difficult. It becomes more difficult when we recognize that, in modern times, every one of us is a member of the economy of everybody else. Every one of us has given many proxies to the economy to use the land (and the air, the water, and other natural gifts) on our behalf. Adequately supervising those proxies is at present impossible; withdrawing them is for virtually all of us, as things now stand, unthinkable.

But if we are concerned about land abuse, we have begun an extensive work of economic criticism. Study of the history of land use (and any local history will do) informs us that we have had for a long time an economy that thrives by undermining its own foundations. Industrialism, which is the name of our economy, and which is now virtually the only economy of the world, has been from its beginnings in a state of riot. It is based squarely upon the principle of violence toward everything on which it depends, and it has not mattered whether the form of industrialism was communist or capitalist; the violence toward nature, human communities, traditional agricultures, and local economies has been constant. The bad news is coming in from all over the world. Can such an economy somehow be fixed without being radically changed? I don't think it can.

The Captains of Industry have always counseled the rest of us to 'be realistic.' Let us, therefore, be realistic. Is it realistic to assume that the present economy would be just fine if only it would stop poisoning the earth, air, and water, or if only it would stop soil erosion, or if only it would stop degrading watersheds and forest ecosystems, or if only it would stop seducing children, or if only it would quit buying politicians, or if only it would give women and favored minorities an equitable share of the loot? Realism, I think, is a very limited program, but it informs us at least that we should not look for bird eggs in a cuckoo clock.

Or we can show the hopelessness of single-issue causes and single-issue movements by following a line of thought such as this: We need a continuous supply of uncontaminated water. Therefore, we need (among other things) soil-and-water-conserving ways of agriculture and forestry that are not dependent on monoculture, toxic chemicals, or the indifference and violence that always accompany big-scale industrial enterprises on the land. Therefore, we need diversified, small-scale land economies that are dependent on people. Therefore, we need people with the knowledge, skills, motives, and attitudes required by diversified, small-scale land economies. And all this is clear and comfortable enough, until we recognize the question we have come to: *Where are the people?*

Well, all of us who live in the suffering rural landscapes of the United States know that most people are available to those landscapes only recreationally. We see them bicycling or boating or hiking or camping or hunting or fishing or driving along and looking around. They do not, in Mary Austin's phrase, 'summer and winter with the land.' They are unacquainted with the land's human and natural economies. Though people have not progressed beyond the need to eat food and drink water and wear clothes and live in houses, most people have progressed beyond the domestic arts – the husbandry and wifery of the world – by which those needful things are produced and conserved. In fact, the comparative few who still practice that necessary husbandry and wifery often are inclined to apologize for doing so, having been carefully taught in our education system that those arts are degrading and unworthy of people's talents. Educated minds, in the modern era, are unlikely to know anything about food and drink or clothing and shelter. In merely taking these things for granted, the modern educated mind reveals itself also to be as superstitious a mind as ever has existed in the world. What could be more superstitious than the idea that money brings forth food?

I am not suggesting, of course, that everybody ought to be a farmer or a forester. Heaven forbid! I *am* suggesting that most people now are living on the far side of a broken connection, and that this is potentially catastrophic. Most people are now fed, clothed, and sheltered from sources, in nature and in the work of other people, toward which they feel no gratitude and exercise no responsibility.

We are involved now in a profound failure of imagination. Most of us cannot imagine the wheat beyond the bread, or the farmer beyond the wheat, or the farm beyond the farmer, or the history (human or natural) beyond the farm. Most people cannot imagine the forest and the forest economy that produced their houses and furniture and paper; or the landscapes, the streams, and the weather that fill their pitchers and bathtubs and swimming pools with water. Most people appear to assume that when they have paid their money for these things they have entirely met their obligations. And that is, in fact, the conventional economic assumption. The problem is that it is possible to starve under the rule of the conventional economic assumption; some people are starving now under the rule of that assumption.

Money does not bring forth food. Neither does the technology of the food system. Food comes from nature and from the work of people. If the supply of food is to be continuous for a long time, then people must work in harmony with nature. That means that people must find the right answers to a lot of questions. The same rules apply to forestry and the possibility of a continuous supply of forest products.

People grow the food that people eat. People produce the lumber that people use. People care properly or improperly for the forests and the farms that are the sources of those goods. People are necessarily at both ends of the process. The economy, always obsessed with its need to sell products, thinks obsessively and exclusively of the consumer. It mostly takes for granted or ignores those who do the damaging or the restorative and preserving work of agriculture and forestry. The economy pays poorly for this work, with the unsurprising result that the work is mostly done poorly. But here we must ask a very realistic economic question: Can we afford to have this work done poorly? Those of us who know something about land stewardship know that we cannot afford to pay poorly for it, because that means simply that we will not get it. And we know that we cannot afford land use without land stewardship.

One way we could describe the task ahead of us is by saying that we need to enlarge the consciousness and the conscience of the economy. Our economy needs to know – and care – what it is doing. This is revolutionary, of course, if you have a taste for revolution, but it is also merely a matter of common sense. How could anybody seriously object to the possibility that the economy might eventually come to know what it is doing?

Undoubtedly some people will want to start a movement to bring this about. They probably will call it the Movement to Teach the

Economy What It Is Doing – the MTEWIID. Despite my very considerable uneasiness, I will agree to participate, but on three conditions.

My first condition is that this movement should begin by giving up all hope and belief in piecemeal, one-shot solutions. The present scientific quest for odorless hog manure should give us sufficient proof that the specialist is no longer with us. Even now, after centuries of reductionist propaganda, the world is still intricate and vast, as dark as it is light, a place of mystery, where we cannot do one thing without doing many things, or put two things together without putting many things together. Water quality, for example, cannot be improved without improving farming and forestry, but farming and forestry cannot be improved without improving the education of consumers – and so on.

The proper business of a human economy is to make one whole thing of ourselves and this world. To make ourselves into a practical wholeness with the land under our feet is maybe not altogether possible – how would *we* know? – but, as a goal, it at least carries us beyond *hubris*, beyond the utterly groundless assumption that we can subdivide our present great failure into a thousand separate problems that can be fixed by a thousand task forces of academic and bureaucratic specialists. That program has been given more than a fair chance to prove itself, and we ought to know by now that it won't work.

My second condition is that the people in this movement (the MTEWIID) should take full responsibility for themselves as members of the economy. If we are going to teach the economy what it is doing, then we need to learn what *we* are doing. This is going to have to be a private movement as well as a public one. If it is unrealistic to expect wasteful industries to be conservers, then obviously we must lead in part the public life of complainers, petitioners, protesters, advocates and supporters of stricter regulations and saner policies. But that is not enough. If it is unrealistic to expect a bad economy to try to become a good one, then *we* must go to work to build a good economy. It is appropriate that this duty should fall to us, for good economic behavior is more possible for us than it is for the great corporations with their miseducated managers and their greedy and oblivious stockholders. Because it is possible for us, we must try in every way we can to make good economic sense in our own lives, in our households, and in our communities. We must do more for ourselves and our neighbors. We must learn to spend our money with our friends and not with our enemies. But to do this, it is necessary to renew local economies, and revive the domestic arts. In seeking to change our economic use of the world, we are seeking inescapably to change our lives. The outward harmony that we desire between our economy and the world depends finally upon an inward harmony between our own hearts and the creative spirit that is the life of all creatures, a spirit as near us as our flesh and yet forever beyond the measures of this obsessively measuring age. We can grow good wheat and make good bread only if we understand that we do not live by bread alone.

My third condition is that this movement should content itself to be poor. We need to find cheap solutions, solutions within the reach of everybody, and the availability of a lot of money prevents the discovery of cheap solutions. The solutions of modern medicine and modern agriculture are all staggeringly expensive, and this is caused in part, and maybe altogether, by the availability of huge sums of money for medical and agricultural research.

Too much money, moreover, attracts administrators and experts as sugar attracts ants – look at what is happening in our universities. We should not envy rich movements that are organized and led by an alternative bureaucracy living on the problems it is supposed to solve. We want a movement that is a movement because it is advanced by all its members in their daily lives.

Now, having completed this very formidable list of the problems and difficulties, fears and fearful hopes that lie ahead of us, I am relieved to see that I have been preparing myself all along to end by saying something cheerful. What I have been talking about is the possibility of renewing human respect for this earth and all the good, useful, and beautiful things that come from it. I have made it clear, I hope, that I don't think this respect can be adequately enacted or conveyed by tipping our hats to nature or by representing natural loveliness in art or by prayers of thanksgiving or by preserving tracts of wilderness – though I recommend all those things. The respect I mean can be given only by using well the world's goods that are given to us. This good use, which renews respect – which is the only currency, so to speak, of respect – also renews our pleasure. The callings and disciplines that I have spoken of as the domestic arts are stationed all along the way from the farm to the prepared dinner, from the forest to the dinner table, from stewardship of the land to hospitality to friends and strangers. These arts are as demanding and gratifying, as instructive and as pleasing as the so-called fine arts. To learn them, to practice them, to honor and reward them is, I believe, our profoundest calling. Our reward is that they will enrich our lives and make us glad.

(1998)

In Defense of Literacy

In a country in which everybody goes to school, it may seem absurd to offer a defense of literacy, and yet I believe that such a defense is in order, and that the absurdity lies not in the defense, but in the necessity for it. The published illiteracies of the certified educated are on the increase. And the universities seem bent upon ratifying this state of things by declaring the acceptability in their graduates of adequate – that is to say, of mediocre – writing skills.

The schools, then, are following the general subservience to the 'practical,' as that term has been defined for us according to the benefit of corporations. By 'practicality' most users of the term now mean whatever will most predictably and most quickly make a profit. Teachers of English and literature have either submitted, or are expected to submit, along with teachers of the more 'practical' disciplines, to the doctrine that the purpose of education is the mass production of producers and consumers. This has forced our profession into a predicament that we will finally have to recognize as a perversion. As if awed by the ascendency of the 'practical' in our society, many of us secretly fear, and some of us are apparently ready to say, that if a student is not going to become a teacher of his language, he has no need to master it.

In other words, to keep pace with the specialization – and the dignity accorded to specialization – in other disciplines, we have begun to look upon and to teach our language and literature as specialties. But whereas specialization is of the nature of the applied sciences, it is a perversion of the disciplines of language and literature. When we understand and teach these as specialties, we submit willy-nilly to the assumption of the 'practical men' of business, and also apparently of education, that literacy is no more than an ornament: when one has become an efficient integer of the economy, *then* it is permissible, even desirable, to be able to talk about the latest novels. After all, the disciples of 'practicality' may someday find themselves stuck in conversation with an English teacher.

I may have oversimplified that line of thinking, but not much. There are two flaws in it. One is that, among the self-styled 'practical men,' the practical is synonymous with the immediate. The long-term effects of their values and their acts lie outside the boundaries of their interest. For such people a strip mine ceases to exist as soon as the coal has been extracted. Short-term practicality is long-term idiocy.

The other flaw is that language and literature are always *about* something else, and we have no way to predict or control what they may be about. They are about the world. We will understand the world, and preserve ourselves and our values in it, only insofar as we have a language that is alert and responsive to it, and careful of it. I mean that literally. When we give our plows such brand names as 'Sod Blaster,' we are imposing on their use conceptual limits that raise the likelihood that they will be used destructively. When we speak of man's 'war against nature,' or of a 'peace offensive,' we are accepting the limitations of a metaphor that suggests, and even proposes, violent solutions. When students ask for the right of 'participatory input' at the meetings of a faculty organization, they are thinking of democratic process, but they are *speaking* of a convocation of robots, and are thus devaluing the very traditions that they invoke.

Ignorance of books and the lack of a critical consciousness of language were safe enough in primitive societies with coherent oral traditions. In our society, which exists in an atmosphere of prepared, public language – language that is either written or being read – illiteracy is both a personal and a public danger. Think how constantly 'the average American' is surrounded by premeditated language, in newspapers and magazines, on signs and billboards, on TV and radio. He is forever being asked to buy or believe somebody else's line of goods. The line of goods is being sold, moreover, by men who are trained to make him buy it or believe it, whether or not he needs it or understands it or knows its value or wants it. This sort of selling is an honored profession among us. Parents who grow hysterical at the thought that their son might not cut his hair are *glad* to have him taught, and later employed, to lie about the quality of an automobile or the ability of a candidate.

What is our defense against this sort of language – this language-as-weapon? There is only one. We must know a better language. We must speak, and teach our children to speak, a language precise and articulate and lively enough to tell the truth about the world as we know it. And to do this we must know something of the roots and resources of our language; we must know its literature. The only defense against the worst is a knowledge of the best. By their ignorance people enfranchise their exploiters.

But to appreciate fully the necessity for the best sort of literacy we must consider not just the environment of prepared language in which most of us now pass most of our lives, but also the utter transience of most of this language, which is meant to be merely glanced at, or heard only once, or read once and thrown away. Such language is by definition, and often by calculation, not memorable; it is language meant to be replaced by what will immediately follow it, like that of shallow conversation between strangers. It cannot be pondered or effectively criticized. For those reasons an unmixed diet of it is destructive of the informed, resilient, critical intelligence that the best of our traditions have sought to create and to maintain – an intelligence that Jefferson held to be indispensable to the health and longevity of freedom. Such intelligence does not grow by bloating upon the ephemeral information and misinformation of the public media. It grows by returning again and again to the landmarks of its cultural birthright, the works that have proved worthy of devoted attention.

'Read not the Times. Read the Eternities,' Thoreau said. Ezra Pound wrote that 'literature is news that STAYS news.' In his lovely poem, 'The Island,' Edwin Muir spoke of man's inescapable cultural boundaries and of his consequent responsibility for his own sources and renewals:

Men are made of what is made,
The meat, the drink, the life, the corn,
Laid up by them, in them reborn.
And self-begotten cycles close
About our way; indigenous art
And simple spells make unafraid
The haunted labyrinths of the heart . . .

These men spoke of a truth that no society can afford to shirk for long: we are dependent, for understanding, and for consolation and hope, upon what we learn of ourselves from songs and stories. This has always been so, and it will not change.

I am saying, then, that literacy – the mastery of language and the knowledge of books – is not an ornament, but a necessity. It is impractical only by the standards of quick profit and easy power. Longer perspective will show that it alone can preserve in us the possibility of an accurate judgment of ourselves, and the possibilities of correction and renewal. Without it, we are adrift in the present, in the wreckage of yesterday, in the nightmare of tomorrow.

(1970)

Some Thoughts on Citizenship and Conscience in Honor of Don Pratt

1

The idea of citizenship in the United States seems to me to have been greatly oversimplified. It has become permissible to assume that all one needs to do to be a good citizen is to vote and obey and pay taxes, as if one can be a good citizen without being a citizen either of a community or of a place. As if citizenship is merely a matter of perfunctory dutifulness, a periodic deference to the organizations, beyond which it is every man for himself.

Because several years ago I became by choice a resident of the place I am native to, which I know intimately and love strongly, I have begun to understand citizenship in more complex terms. As I have come to see it, it requires devotion and dedication, and a certain inescapable bewilderment and suffering. It needs all the virtues, all of one's attention, all the knowledge that one can gain and bring to bear, all the powers of one's imagination and conscience and feeling. It is the complete action. Rightly understood, its influence and concern permeate the whole society, from the children's bedroom to the capitol.

But it begins at home. Its meanings come clearest, it is felt most intensely in one's own house. The health, coherence, and meaningfulness of one's own household are the measure of the success of the government, and not the other way around.

My devotion thins as it widens. I care more for my household than for the town of Port Royal, more for the town of Port Royal than for the County of Henry, more for the County of Henry than for the State of Kentucky, more for the State of Kentucky than for the United

States of America. But I *do not* care more for the United States of America than for the world.

I must attempt to care as much for the world as for my household. Those are the poles between which a competent morality would balance and mediate: the doorstep and the planet. The most meaningful dependence of my house is not on the U.S. government, but on the world, the earth. No matter how sophisticated and complex and powerful our institutions, we are still exactly as dependent on the earth as the earthworms. To cease to know this, and to fail to act upon the knowledge, is to begin to die the death of a broken machine. In default of man's personal cherishing and care, now that his machinery has become so awesomely powerful, the earth must become the victim of his institutions, the violent self-destructive machinery of man-in-the-abstract. And so, conversely, the most meaningful dependence of the earth is not on the U.S. government, but on my household – how I live, how I raise my children, how I care for the land entrusted to me.

These two poles of life and thought offer two different points of view, perspectives that are opposite and complementary. But morally, because one is contained within the other and the two are interdependent, they propose the same consciousness and the same labor. To attempt to interpose another moral standard between these two, which I take to be absolute and ultimately the same, is to prepare the way for a power that is arbitrary and tyrannical. To assert that a man owes an allegiance that is antecedent to his allegiance to his household, or higher than his allegiance to the earth, is to invite a state of moral chaos that will destroy both the household and the earth.

Since there is no government of which the concern or the discipline is primarily the health either of households or of the earth, since it is in the nature of any state to be concerned first of all with its own preservation and only second with the cost, the dependable, clear response to man's moral circumstance is not that of law, but that of conscience. The highest moral behavior is not obedience to law, but obedience to the informed conscience even in spite of law. The government will be the *last* to see the moral implications of man's dependence on the earth, and the *last* to admit that wars can no longer be fought in behalf of some men but only against all men. Though these realizations have entered the consciences and the lives of certain persons, they have not yet superseded the self-interest of any government.

As law without conscience is hollow, so law that is not willingly preceded and shaped by conscience is tyrannical; the state is deified, and men are its worshipers, obeying as compulsively and blindly as ants. The law is no defense against the greatest ills of our time, for power, as always, subverts the law. Only the consciences of persons can be depended upon to take the stand that is unequivocally moral, and to make the clear, complete refusal.

I do not mean to support, and I do not respect, any act of civil disobedience that is violent, or that is obstructive of the rights of other people. Such overbearing zeal is as fearful to me in the service of peace and brotherhood as in the service of war and hate. But I do support and respect those peaceable acts of disobedience by which conscience withholds itself from the contamination of acts antithetical to it, as when a believer in the sixth commandment refuses to kill or to support a policy of killing even when legally required to do so. Such an act is no mere vagary. It is the basis and essence of political liberty, defining the true nature of government as only such acts can define it – asserting, as it has been necessary time and again to assert in the history both of our country and of our species, that the government governs by the consent of the people, not by any divine or inherent right.

To hear the boasts and the claims of some of our political leaders, one would think that we all *lived* in the government. The lower order of our politicians no doubt do so, and they no doubt exhibit the effects. But though I am always aware that I live in my household and in the world, I wish to testify that in my best moments I am not aware of the existence of the government. Though I respect and feel myself dignified by the principles of the Declaration and the Constitution, I do not remember a day when the thought of the government made me happy, and I never think of it without the wish that it might become wiser and truer and smaller than it is.

2

Nothing in my education or experience prepared me even to expect the horror and anxiety and moral bewilderment that I have felt during these years of racism and disintegration at home and a war of unprecedented violence and senselessness abroad. The attempt to keep meaning in one's life at such a time is a continuous strain, and perhaps ultimately futile: there is undoubtedly a limit to how long private integrity can hold out in the face of, and within, public disintegration. The conflict is plainly seeded with madness and death.

Even in our sleep some critical part of our attention is held by the descending roar of a machine bigger than the world – a society so automated and bureaucratized, so stuffed with the rhetoric of self-righteousness, that it is seemingly no longer capable of a moral or a human response. With the world in our power and our power assigned to the moral authority of those who will profit most by its misuse, we continue to bless and congratulate ourselves upon the boyhood honesty of George Washington. And so the machine descends. We are already suffocating in its fumes.

Slowly America wakens to the tragedy of her history, the unquieted ghosts of her martyrs brooding over her in the night, her forfeited visions, the plundered and desecrated maidenhood of her lands and forests and rivers. I write a little more than a week after the death of Martin Luther King, who lived as only the great live, in humble obedience to the highest ideals, in proud defiance of men and laws that would have required him to abide by a narrower vision and to dream a narrower dream. He stood for the American hope in its full amplitude and generosity. His martyrdom is the apparition of the death of that hope in racism and violence.

And today I live with the sorrow and shame that one of the finest young men of the university where I teach is in jail. He is in jail because he refuses to co-operate in the prosecution of a war that he believes to be unjust and unnecessary and immoral, because he insists upon living by the sixth commandment and the Golden Rule, because he does not believe that a wrong is any less a wrong when committed with the government's sanction and by the government's order. He is in jail because he will not acknowledge, because he cannot see, any difference between public morality and private morality. This young man's name is Don Pratt, a citizen of Lexington, Kentucky, a student of the University of Kentucky, one of the exemplary men of Kentucky. I acknowledge myself deeply indebted to him. His sacrifice and his fate have become a clarifying pain in my consciousness. His nobility is one of the reasons I have – and they are not abundant – to continue to hope for the future of my species. He and the other young men who have taken the stand he has taken are among the most precious moral resources of our country. Because they have not only believed in our highest ideals, but have also acted as they believed, the world is whole before them, and they are whole before the world.

There is, as Thoreau said, a great shame in going free while good men are in jail because of their goodness. Perhaps there is also shame in only going to jail while innocent people are dying or burning alive by the 'accidents' of our technological warfare. There is shame in the inheritance of ancestral wrong, in the realization of how deliberately for how many years we have lived by the exploitation and waste of the earth and of one other. To open one's consciousness to the world as we have made it is to receive the sleepless anguish of this shame. To feel it is one of the costs to our kind of being morally alive.

And so, the sense of shame deep in me, and full of craving for moral clarity, I ask myself why it is that *I* am not in jail. And I answer, with much uncertainty, that I have not yet been faced with going to jail as an inescapable obligation – an obligation, that is, which would cancel out such other obligations as that of keeping together my family and household.

My life, as I have made it and as I understand it, is turned against what I consider the evils of our society – its suicidal wish to become a machine, its lethargic assumption that a mythologized past can serve as some kind of moral goal that can effectively discipline the present. My aim is to imagine and live out a decent and preserving relationship to the earth. I am determined to cling to this effort as long as I can maintain some meaning in it. But I know, the events of recent years make it clear, that there may come a time when it will be necessary to give it up, when to hold to it will be more destructive of it than to let it go. If I should be required in the name of the law to place my life in the service of the machinery of man's destructiveness and hate, then I hope for the courage to refuse in the name of conscience.

3

But wait. I am about to cross over into too much solemnity, a useless shame. Let me step aside from crowds – even the crowd of those whose opinions I share – and stand up finally in the place, and among the concerns, of my own life. I wish to speak no further except out of the few acres of hillside and woods and riverbank near Port Royal, Kentucky, that I hope to have made mine for life. I accept the meanings of that place, for the time I will be there, as my meanings, accepting also that my life and its effects belong ineradicably to that place. I am occupied there with a small orchard, vines and berry bushes, henyard and garden and pasture – with increasing the richness and the abundance and the meaningfulness of that part of the earth for my family and myself, and for those who will live there after us. This effort has given me many hours of intense pleasure, both in itself and in the sense of what it means as a human possibility. It holds out to me in the most immediate way the hope of peace, the ideal of harmlessness, the redeeming chance that a man can live so as to enhance and enlarge the possibility of life in the world, rather than to diminish it. I do not acknowledge the pleasure I take in this part of my life with shame, though I know that while I have felt this pleasure much of the world has been miserable.

The solemnity and ostentatious grief of some implies that there is a mystical equation by which one man, by suffering enough guilt, by a denial of joy, can atone or compensate for the suffering of many men. The logical culmination of this feeling is self-incineration, which only removes one from the problem without solving it. Because so many are hungry, should we weep as we eat? No child will grow fat on our tears. But to eat, taking whatever satisfaction it gives us, and then to turn again to the problem of how to make it possible for another to eat, to undertake to cleanse ourselves of the great wastefulness of our society, to seek alternatives in our own lives to our people's thoughtless squandering of the world's goods – that promises a solution. That many are cold and the world is full of hate does not mean that one should stand in the snow for shame or refrain from making love. To refuse to admit decent and harmless pleasures freely into one's own life is as wrong as to deny them to someone else. It impoverishes and darkens the world.

My impression is that the great causes of peace and brotherhood are being served these days with increasing fanaticism, obsessiveness, self-righteousness, and anger. As if the aim is to turn the world into a sort of Protestant heaven, from which all nonmembers have been eliminated, and in which the principal satisfaction is to go around looking holy. In short, the supporters of these causes are becoming specialists, like preachers and generals, and I think that is a very bad sign. Such specialists, it seems to me, are the enemies of their cause. Too many are now expending themselves utterly in the service of political abstractions, and my guess is that this is because of a growing sense of guilt and a growing belief that this guilt can be expiated in political action. I do not believe it, nor do I believe very much in the efficacy of political solutions. The political activist *sacrifices* himself to politics; though he has a cause, he has no life; he has become the driest of experts. And if he narrows and desiccates his life for the sake of the future of his ideals, what right has he to hope that the success of his ideals will bring a fuller life? Unsubstantiated in his own living, his motives grow hollow, puffed out with the blatant air of oratory.

What is happening now is that most public people, from government officials and political candidates to student activists, are involved in an ever-intensifying contest of self-righteous rhetoric. No one can feel certain he will be believed until he has said something more extreme than has been said before, and this both proceeds from and promotes the sense that the speaker is absolutely right and unimpeachably virtuous. There is no possibility of intelligence in it.

And pacifists and peaceworkers especially should be aware of its enormous potential of violence. The problems of violence cannot be solved on public platforms, but only in people's lives. And to give the matter over to the processes of public rhetoric is to forgo the personal self-critical moral intelligence that is essential to any hope for peace, and that can only function in the daily life of individuals. That I have abjured violence in principle does not mean that I have shrugged off the history of violence that I descend from, or the culture of violence that I have grown used to, or the habits and reflexes of violence in my body and mind, or the prejudices that preserve violence and justify it, or the love of violence. And this suggests to me that I can speak of my commitment to the cause of peace only with hesitance and with the greatest circumspection, and that I should avoid any rhetoric that might lead me to offer myself as a model.

4

What one does can originate nowhere but in his life. If his life is organizational and abstract, dependent on the support and passion of crowds, full of the fervor of allegiance rather than the fervor of personal love and independence, then his love of peace is a hollow specialization. His hope is liable to be obscured by his cause. He is apt to find himself marching in protest against militarism and shouting or shoving in protest against force. The next step is only to join the militarists in making war in protest against war, soaring in self-righteousness, condemning and slurring all who do not agree. A tyranny of fanatical peace lovers is as credible to me as a tyranny of militarists, and I don't think there would be any difference.

It seems to me inescapable that before a man can usefully promote an idea, the idea must be implemented in his own life. If he is for peace he must have a life in which peace is possible. He must be peaceable. To be a peaceable man is to be the hope of the world. To be only an agitator for peace is to be a specialist, one in a swarm of random particles, destructive in implication, however pacific by intention. How can a man hope to promote peace in the world if he has not made it possible in his own life and his own household? If he is a peaceable man, then he has assured a measure of peace in the world, though he may never utter a public word.

I am struggling, amid all the current political uproar, to keep clearly in mind that it is *not* merely because our policies are wrong that we are so destructive and violent. It goes deeper than that, and is more troubling. We are so little at peace with ourselves and our neighbors because we are not at peace with our place in the world, our land. American history has been to a considerable extent the history of our warfare against the natural life of the continent. Until we end our violence against the earth – a matter ignored by most pacifists, as the issue of military violence is ignored by most conservationists – how can we hope to end our violence against each other? The earth, which we all have in common, is our deepest bond, and our behavior toward it cannot help but be an earnest of our consideration for each other and for our descendants. To corrupt or destroy the natural environment is an act of violence not only against the earth but also against those who are dependent on it, including ourselves. To waste the soil is to cause hunger, as direct an aggression as an armed attack; it is an act of violence against the future of the human race.

The American disease is the assumption that when a man has exploited and used up the possibilities of one place, he has only to move on to another place. This has made us a nation of transients, both physically and morally, and as long as we remain so I think that we will inhabit the earth like a plague, destroying whatever we touch. It seems to me that our people are suffering terribly from a sort of spiritual nomadism, a loss of meaningful contact with the earth and the earth's cycles of birth, growth and death. They lack the vital morality and spirituality that can come only from such contact: the sense, for instance, of their dependence on the earth, and the sense of eternal mystery surrounding life on earth, which is its ultimate and most disciplining context.

As long as a man relates only to other men, he can be a specialist with impunity; the illusion of the morality of 'doing one's job,' no matter what the job, is still accessible to him. But if he would establish a satisfying relation to a place, the capsule of his specialization must be broken and his commitments widen *perforce*, for the needs of his place, his part of the earth, are not specialized, and are as far as possible from the artificial, purely human contexts in which specialization is imaginable as a solution to any problem. Once he is joined to the earth with any permanence of expectation and interest, his concerns ramify in proportion to his understanding of his dependence on the earth and his consequent responsibility toward it. He realizes, because the demands of the place make it specific and inescapable, that his responsibility is not merely that of an underling, a worker at his job, but also moral, historical, political, aesthetic, ecological, domestic, educational, and so on.

5

What I am attempting to say is that what has come to be the common form of protest, in the anxiety and confusion of these times, is not the *only* form of protest, and that in the long run it is probably not the *best* form. I realize, of course, that there are some who have no alternative to public gestures of protest: demonstrations or draft refusal or exile. But for others there is the possibility of a protest that is more complex and permanent, public in effect but private in its motive and implementation: they can *live* in protest. I have in mind a sort of personal secession from the encroaching institutional machinery of destruction and waste and violence. Conscientious civil disobedience is the most familiar example of this, also the most dramatic, and surely all moral men must think of it as a possibility, and prepare themselves. But it is an extreme step, and in my opinion should be thought of only as a last resort. In addition to the personal sacrifice it demands, it removes one from other forms of protest; while one is involved in it, and in its consequences, one is by necessity a specialist of a sort.

Another possibility, equally necessary, and in the long run richer in promise, is to remove oneself as far as possible from complicity in the evils one is protesting, and to discover alternative possibilities. To make public protests against an evil, and yet live in dependence on and in support of the way of life that is the source of the evil, is an obvious contradiction and a dangerous one. If one disagrees with the nomadism and violence of our society, then one is under an obligation to take up some permanent dwelling place and cultivate the possibility of peace and harmlessness in it. If one deplores the destructiveness and wastefulness of the economy, then one is under an obligation to live as far out on the margin of the economy as one is able: to be economically independent of exploitive industries, to learn to need less, to waste less, to make things last, to give up meaningless luxuries, to understand and resist the language of salesmen and public relations experts, to see through attractive packages, to refuse to purchase fashion or glamour or prestige. If one feels endangered by meaninglessness, then one is under an obligation to refuse meaningless pleasure and to resist meaningless work, and to give up the moral comfort and the excuses of the mentality of specialization.

One way to do this – the way I understand – is to reject the dependences and the artificial needs of urban life, and to go into the countryside and make a home there in the fullest and most permanent sense: that is, live on and use and preserve and learn from and enrich and enjoy the land. I realize that to modern ears this sounds anachronistic and self-indulgent, but I believe on the ground of my experience that it is highly relevant, and that it offers the possibility of a coherent and particularized meaningfulness that is beyond the reach of the ways of life of 'average Americans.' My own plans have come to involve an idea of subsistence agriculture – which does not mean that I advocate the privation and extreme hardship usually associated with such an idea. It means, simply, that along with my other occupations I intend to raise on my own land enough food for my family. Within the obvious limitations, I want my home to be a self-sufficient place.

But isn't this merely a quaint affectation? And isn't it a retreat from the 'modern world' and its demands, a way of 'dropping out'? I don't think so. At the very least, it is a way of dropping *in* to a concern for the health of the earth, which institutional and urban people have had at second hand at best, and mostly have not had at all. But the idea has other far-reaching implications, in terms of both private benefits and public meanings. It is perhaps enough to summarize them here by saying that when one undertakes to live fully on and from the land the prevailing values are inverted: one's home becomes an occupation, a center of interest, not just a place to stay when there is no other place to go; work becomes a pleasure; the most menial task is dignified by its relation to a plan and a desire; one is less dependent on artificial pleasures, less eager to participate in the sterile nervous excitement of movement for its own sake; the elemental realities of seasons and weather affect one directly, and become a source of interest in themselves; the relation of one's life to the life of the world is no longer taken for granted or ignored, but becomes an immediate and complex concern. In other words, one begins to stay at home for the same reasons that most people now go away.

I am writing with the assumption that this is only one of several possibilities, and that I am obligated to elaborate on this particular one because it is the one that I know about and the one that is attractive to me. Many people would not want to live in this way, and not wanting to seems the best reason not to. For many others it is simply not a possibility. But for those with suitable inclinations and the necessary abilities it is perhaps an obligation.

The presence of a sizable number of people living in this way would, I think, have a profound influence on the life of the country and the world. They would augment the declining number of independent small landowners. By moving out into marginal areas abandoned by commercial agriculture, they would restore neglected and impoverished lands, and at the same time reduce the crowdedness of the cities. They would not live in abject dependence on institutions and corporations, hence could function as a corrective to the subservient and dependent mentality developing among government people and in the mass life of the cities. Their ownership would help to keep the land from being bought up by corporations. Over a number of years, by trial and error, they might invent a way of life that would be modest in its material means and necessities and yet rich in pleasures and meanings, kind to the land, intricately joined both to the human community and to the natural world – a life directly opposite to that which our institutions and corporations envision for us, but one which is more essential to the hope of peace than any international treaty.

6

Though I have had many of these ideas consciously in mind for several years, I have found them extraordinarily difficult to write about. They are not new; other men have understood them better than I do. But there has not been much recent talk about them. Their language has been neglected, allowed to grow old-fashioned, so that in talking about them now one is always on the verge of sounding merely wishful or nostalgic or absurd. But they are ideas of great usefulness, and I am eager to have a hand in their revival. They have shown me a possibility and a promise beyond the dead end of going on as we are toward ever larger cities, in which ever more degraded and dependent and thwarted human beings stand in each other's way, breeding the fury of the world's end.

I am interested in the peace that is produced by politics because I believe that every day the holocaust is delayed gives the possibility that it will be delayed yet another day. But I am not exclusively interested in it, and I am not enthusiastic about it, because at best it is only temporary, and it is superficial, achieved always by expediency and always to the advantage of some and to the disadvantage of others. Political peace, like anything else political, is formed out of the collision of 'interests,' slogans, oversimplified points of view. And no matter how righteous the cause, it seems to me that a man is reduced by walking before the public with an oversimplification fastened to him. My evidence is that I have done it several times myself, and I never felt that I was doing what I was best able to do; I did not feel that there was any significant connection in what I was doing between my own life and the ideals and hopes I meant to serve. I was permitting shame to oversimplify what I thought and felt, so that I took too willingly to the crowd-comfort of slogans.

Political activity of any kind is doomed to the superficiality and temporariness of politics, able only to produce generalizations that will hold conflicting interests uneasily together for a time. But the life that attaches itself to the earth, to fulfill itself in the earth's meanings and demands, though it will certainly affect politics, will affect the earth and the earth's life even more. The land it has attached itself to will survive it, more whole for its sake. Its value will have the permanence of the earth, and be recorded in abundance.

Shame, like other hardships, must be borne. There is no handy expiation for the curious sense of guilt in having been born lucky, or in being well fed and warm and loved. To forsake life for the sake of life is to leave only a vacancy, all the old wrongs unchanged. Peaceableness and lovingness and all the other good hopes are exactly as difficult and complicated as living one's life, and can be most fully served in life's fullness.

7

And so, difficult and troubling as the times are, I must not neglect to say that even now I experience hours when I am deeply happy and content, and hours when I feel the possibility of greater happiness and contentment than I have yet known. These times come to me when I am in the woods, or at work on my little farm. They come bearing the knowledge that the events of man are not the great events; that the rising of the sun and the falling of the rain are more stupendous than all the works of the scientists and the prophets; that man is more blessed and graced by his days than he can ever hope to know; that the wildflowers silently bloom in the woods, exquisitely shaped and scented and colored, whether any man sees and praises them or not. A music attends the things of the earth. To sense that music is to be near the possibility of health and joy.

Yet, though I know these things, I am still a member of the human race, and must share in its confusion and its fate. I cannot escape the knowledge that, though men are unable to attain the grace or the beauty of the merest flower, their destructiveness is now certainly equal to the world. Though I would only study the earth and serve it, I have not learned to escape a hundred empty duties and distractions that turn me against myself and implicate me in offenses against my own cause. Though I would sleep well and rise early, I lie awake in fear of evil. There is much of my life that I am not master of and that I see going to waste in bewilderment and subservience, lost in the driving storm of events and details.

What remains I commit to the earth.

(1968)

Compromise, Hell!*

We are destroying our country – I mean our country itself, our land. This is a terrible thing to know, but it is not a reason for despair unless we decide to continue the destruction. If we decide to continue the destruction, that will not be because we have no other choice. This destruction is not necessary. It is not inevitable, except that by our submissiveness we make it so.

We Americans are not usually thought to be a submissive people, but of course we are. Why else would we allow our country to be destroyed? Why else would we be rewarding its destroyers? Why else would we all – by proxies we have given to greedy corporations and corrupt politicians – be participating in its destruction? Most of us are still too sane to piss in our own cistern, but we allow others to do so, and we reward them for it. We reward them so well, in fact, that those who piss in our cistern are wealthier than the rest of us.

How do we submit? By not being radical enough. Or by not being thorough enough, which is the same thing.

Since the beginning of the conservation effort in our country, conservationists have too often believed that we could protect the land without protecting the people. This has begun to change, but for a while yet we will have to reckon with the old assumption that we can preserve the natural world by protecting wilderness areas while we neglect or destroy the economic landscapes – the farms and ranches and working forests – and the people who use them. That assumption is understandable in view of the worsening threats to wilderness areas, but it is wrong. If conservationists hope to save even the wild lands and wild creatures, they are going to have to

---

* Written originally as a speech for the annual Earth Day celebration of the Kentucky Environmental Quality Commission at Frankfort, Kentucky, April 22, 2004.

address issues of economy, which is to say issues of the health of the landscapes and the towns and cities where we do our work, and the quality of that work, and the well-being of the people who do the work.

Governments seem to be making the opposite error, believing that the people can be adequately protected without protecting the land. And here I am not talking about parties or party doctrines, but about the dominant political assumption. Sooner or later, governments will have to recognize that if the land does not prosper, nothing else can prosper for very long. We can have no industry or trade or wealth or security if we don't uphold the health of the land and the people and the people's work.

It is merely a fact that the land, here and everywhere, is suffering. We have the 'dead zone' in the Gulf of Mexico and undrinkable water to attest to the toxicity of our agriculture. We know that we are carelessly and wastefully logging our forests. We know that soil erosion, air and water pollution, urban sprawl, the proliferation of highways and garbage are making our lives always less pleasant, less healthful, less sustainable, and our dwelling places more ugly.

Nearly forty years ago my state of Kentucky, like other coal-producing states, began an effort to regulate strip mining. While that effort has continued, and has imposed certain requirements of 'reclamation,' strip mining has become steadily more destructive of the land and the land's future. We are now permitting the destruction of entire mountains and entire watersheds. No war, so far, has done such extensive or such permanent damage. If we know that coal is an exhaustible resource, whereas the forests over it are with proper use inexhaustible, and that strip mining destroys the forest virtually forever, how can we permit this destruction? If we honor at all that fragile creature the topsoil, so long in the making, so miraculously made, so indispensable to all life, how can we destroy it? If we believe, as so many of us profess to do, that the Earth is God's property and is full of His glory, how can we do harm to any part of it?

In Kentucky, as in other unfortunate states, and again at great public cost, we have allowed – in fact we have officially encouraged – the establishment of the confined animal-feeding industry, which exploits and abuses everything involved: the land, its people, the animals, and the consumers. If we love our country, as so many of us profess to do, how can we so desecrate it?

But the economic damage is not confined just to our farms and forests. For the sake of 'job creation' in Kentucky, and in other backward states, we have lavished public money on corporations that come in and stay only so long as they can exploit people here more cheaply than elsewhere. The general purpose of the present economy is to exploit, not to foster or conserve.

Look carefully, if you doubt me, at the centers of the larger towns in virtually every part of our country. You will find that they are economically dead or dying. Good buildings that used to house needful, useful, locally owned small businesses of all kinds are now empty or have evolved into junk stores or antique shops. But look at the houses, the churches, the commercial buildings, the courthouse, and you will see that more often than not they are comely and well made. And then go look at the corporate outskirts: the chain stores, the fast-food joints, the food-and-fuel stores that no longer can be called service stations, the motels. Try to find something comely or well made there.

What is the difference? The difference is that the old town centers were built by people who were proud of their place and who realized a particular value in living there. The old buildings look good because they were built by people who respected themselves and wanted the respect of their neighbors. The corporate outskirts, on the contrary, were built by people who manifestly take no pride in the place, see no value in lives lived there, and recognize no neighbors. The only value they see in the place is the money that can be siphoned out of it to more fortunate places – that is, to the wealthier suburbs of the larger cities.

Can we actually suppose that we are wasting, polluting, and making ugly this beautiful land for the sake of patriotism and the love of God? Perhaps some of us would like to think so, but in fact this destruction is taking place because we have allowed ourselves to believe, and to live, a mated pair of economic lies: that nothing has a value that is not assigned to it by the market, and that the economic life of our communities can safely be handed over to the great corporations.

We citizens have a large responsibility for our delusion and our destructiveness, and I don't want to minimize that. But I don't want to minimize, either, the large responsibility that is borne by government.

It is commonly understood that governments are instituted to provide certain protections that citizens individually cannot provide for themselves. But governments have tended to assume that this responsibility can be fulfilled mainly by the police and the military services. They have used their regulatory powers reluctantly and often poorly. Our governments have only occasionally recognized the need of land and people to be protected against economic violence. It is true that economic violence is not always as swift, and is rarely as bloody, as the violence of war, but it can be devastating nonetheless. Acts of economic aggression can destroy a landscape or a community or the center of a town or city, and they routinely do so.

Such damage is justified by its corporate perpetrators and their political abettors in the name of the 'free market' and 'free enterprise,' but this is a freedom that makes greed the dominant economic virtue, and it destroys the freedom of other people along with their communities and livelihoods. There are such things as economic weapons of massive destruction. We have allowed them to be used against us, not just by public submission and regulatory malfeasance, but also by public subsidies, incentives, and sufferances impossible to justify.

We have failed to acknowledge this threat and to act in our own defense. As a result, our once-beautiful and bountiful countryside has long been a colony of the coal, timber, and agribusiness corporations, yielding an immense wealth of energy and raw materials at an immense cost to our land and our land's people. Because of that failure also, our towns and cities have been gutted by the likes of Wal-Mart, which have had the permitted luxury of destroying locally owned small businesses by means of volume discounts.

Because as individuals or even as communities we cannot protect ourselves against these aggressions, we need our state and national governments to protect us. As the poor deserve as much justice from our courts as the rich, so the small farmer and the small merchant deserve the same economic justice, the same freedom in the market, as big farmers and chain stores. They should not suffer ruin merely because their rich competitors can afford (for a while) to undersell them.

Furthermore, to permit the smaller enterprises always to be ruined by false advantages, either at home or in the global economy, is ultimately to destroy local, regional, and even national capabilities of producing vital supplies such as food and textiles. It is impossible to understand, let alone justify, a government's willingness to allow the human sources of necessary goods to be destroyed by the 'freedom' of this corporate anarchy. It is equally impossible to understand how a government can permit, and even subsidize, the destruction of the land or of the land's productivity. Somehow we have lost or discarded any controlling sense of the interdependence of the Earth and the human capacity to use it well. The governmental obligation to protect these economic resources, inseparably human and natural, is the same as the obligation to protect us from hunger or from foreign invaders. In result, there is no difference between a domestic threat to the sources of our life and a foreign one.

It appears that we have fallen into the habit of compromising on issues that should not, and in fact cannot, be compromised. I have an idea that a large number of us, including even a large number of politicians, believe that it is wrong to destroy the Earth. But we have powerful political opponents who insist that an Earth-destroying economy is justified by freedom and profit. And so we compromise by agreeing to permit the destruction only of parts of the Earth, or to permit the Earth to be destroyed a little at a time – like the famous three-legged pig that was too well loved to be eaten all at once.

The logic of this sort of compromising is clear, and it is clearly fatal. If we continue to be economically dependent on destroying parts of the Earth, then eventually we will destroy it all.

So long a complaint accumulates a debt to hope, and I would like to end with hope. To do so I need only repeat something I said at the beginning: our destructiveness has not been, and it is not, inevitable. People who use that excuse are morally incompetent, they are cowardly, and they are lazy. Humans don't have to live by destroying the sources of their life. People can change; they can learn to do better. All of us, regardless of party, can be moved by love of our land to rise above the greed and contempt of our land's exploiters. This of course leads to practical problems, and I will offer a short list of practical suggestions.

We have got to learn better to respect ourselves and our dwelling places. We need to quit thinking of rural America as a colony. Too much of the economic history of our land has been that of the export of fuel, food, and raw materials that have been destructively and too cheaply produced. We must reaffirm the economic value of good stewardship and good work. For that we will need better accounting than we have had so far.

We need to reconsider the idea of solving our economic problems by 'bringing in industry.' Every state government appears to be scheming to lure in a large corporation from somewhere else by 'tax incentives' and other squanderings of the people's money. We ought to suspend that practice until we are sure that in every state we have made the most and the best of what is already there. We need to build the local economies of our communities and regions by adding value to local products and marketing them locally before we seek markets elsewhere.

We need to confront honestly the issue of scale. Bigness has a charm and a drama that are seductive, especially to politicians and financiers; but bigness promotes greed, indifference, and damage, and often bigness is not necessary. You may need a large corporation to run an airline or to manufacture cars, but you don't need a large corporation to raise a chicken or a hog. You don't need a large corporation to process local food or local timber and market it locally.

And, finally, we need to give an absolute priority to caring well for our land – for every bit of it. There should be no compromise with the destruction of the land or of anything else that we cannot replace.

We have been too tolerant of politicians who, entrusted with our country's defense, become the agents of our country's destroyers, compromising on its ruin.

And so I will end this by quoting my fellow Kentuckian, a great patriot and an indomitable foe of strip mining, the late Joe Begley of Blackey: 'Compromise, hell!'

(2004)

The Way of Ignorance*

In order to arrive at what you do not know
You must go by a way which is the way of ignorance.

T. S. Eliot, 'East Coker'

Our purpose here is to worry about the predominance of the supposition, in a time of great technological power, that humans either know enough already, or can learn enough soon enough, to foresee and forestall any bad consequences of their use of that power. This supposition is typified by Richard Dawkins's assertion, in an open letter to the Prince of Wales, that 'our brains . . . are big enough to see into the future and plot long-term consequences.'

When we consider how often and how recently our most advanced experts have been wrong about the future, and how often the future has shown up sooner than expected with bad news about our past, Mr. Dawkins's assessment of our ability to know is revealed as a superstition of the most primitive sort. We recognize it also as our old friend hubris, ungodly ignorance disguised as godly arrogance. Ignorance plus arrogance plus greed sponsors 'better living with chemistry,' and produces the ozone hole and the dead zone in the Gulf of Mexico. A modern science (chemistry or nuclear physics or molecular biology) 'applied' by ignorant arrogance resembles much too closely an automobile being driven by a six-year-old or a loaded pistol in the hands of a monkey. Arrogant ignorance promotes a

* Written as a preliminary paper for a conference of the same title at the Land Institute, Matfield Green, Kansas, June 3–5, 2004. The purpose of the conference is stated in my first paragraph.

global economy while ignoring the global exchange of pests and diseases that must inevitably accompany it. Arrogant ignorance makes war without a thought of peace.

We identify arrogant ignorance by its willingness to work on too big a scale, and thus to put too much at risk. It fails to foresee bad consequences not only because some of the consequences of all acts are inherently unforeseeable, but also because the arrogantly ignorant often are blinded by money invested; they cannot afford to foresee bad consequences.

Except to the arrogantly ignorant, ignorance is not a simple subject. It is perhaps as difficult for ignorance to be aware of itself as it is for awareness to be aware of itself. One can hardly begin to think about ignorance without seeing that it is available in several varieties, and so I will offer a brief taxonomy.

There is, to begin with, the kind of ignorance we may consider to be inherent. This is ignorance of all that we cannot know because of the kind of mind we have – which, I will note in passing, is neither a computer nor exclusively a brain, and which certainly is not omniscient. We cannot, for example, know the whole of which we and our minds are parts. The English poet and critic Kathleen Raine wrote that 'we cannot imagine how the world might appear if we did not possess the groundwork of knowledge which we do possess; nor can we in the nature of things imagine how reality would appear in the light of knowledge which we do not possess.'

A part of our inherent ignorance, and surely a most formidable encumbrance to those who presume to know the future, is our ignorance of the past. We know almost nothing of our history as it was actually lived. We know little of the lives even of our parents. We have forgotten almost everything that has happened to ourselves. The easy assumption that we have remembered the most important people and events and have preserved the most valuable evidence is immediately trumped by our inability to know what we have forgotten.

There are several other kinds of ignorance that are not inherent in our nature but come instead from weaknesses of character.

Paramount among these is the willful ignorance that refuses to honor as knowledge anything not subject to empirical proof. We could just as well call it materialist ignorance. This ignorance rejects useful knowledge such as traditions of imagination and religion, and so it comes across as narrow-mindedness. We have the materialist culture that afflicts us now because a world exclusively material is the kind of world most readily used and abused by the kind of mind the materialists think they have. To this kind of mind, there is no longer a legitimate wonder. Wonder has been replaced by a research agenda, which is still a world away from demonstrating the impropriety of wonder. The materialist conservationists need to tell us how a materialist culture can justify its contempt and destructiveness of material goods.

A related kind of ignorance, also self-induced, is moral ignorance, the invariable excuse of which is objectivity. One of the purposes of objectivity, in practice, is to avoid coming to a moral conclusion. Objectivity, considered a mark of great learning and the highest enlightenment, loves to identify itself by such pronouncements as the following: 'You may be right, but on the other hand so may your opponent,' or 'Everything is relative,' or 'Whatever is happening is inevitable,' or 'Let me be the devil's advocate.' (The part of devil's advocate is surely one of the most sought after in all the precincts of the modern intellect. Anywhere you go to speak in defense of something worthwhile, you are apt to encounter a smiling savant writhing in the estrus of objectivity: 'Let me play the devil's advocate for a moment.' As if the devil's point of view will not otherwise be adequately represented.)

There is also ignorance as false confidence, or polymathic ignorance. This is the ignorance of people who know 'all about' history or its 'long-term consequences' in the future. And this is closely akin to self-righteous ignorance, which is the failure to know oneself. Ignorance of one's self and confident knowledge of the past and future often are the same thing.

Fearful ignorance is the opposite of confident ignorance. People keep themselves ignorant for fear of the strange or the different or the unknown, for fear of disproof or of unpleasant or tragic knowledge, for fear of stirring up suspicion and opposition, or for fear of fear itself. A good example is the United States Department of Agriculture's panic-stricken monopoly of inadequate meat inspections. And there is the related ignorance that comes from laziness, which is the fear of effort and difficulty. Learning often is not fun, and this is well known to all the ignorant except for a few 'educators.'

And finally there are for-profit ignorance, which is maintained by withholding knowledge, as in advertising, and for-power ignorance, which is maintained by government secrecy and public lies.

Kinds of ignorance (and there must be more than I have named) may thus be sorted out. But having sorted them out, one must scramble them back together again by acknowledging that all of them can be at work in the same mind at the same time, and in my opinion they frequently are.

I may be talking too much at large here, but I am going to say that a list of kinds of ignorance comprises half a description of a human mind. The other half, then, would be supplied by a list of kinds of knowledge.

At the head of that list let us put the empirical or provable knowledge of the materialists. This is the knowledge of dead certainty or dead facts, some of which at least are undoubtedly valuable, undoubtedly useful, but at best this is static, smallish knowledge that always is what it always was, and it is rather dull. A fact may thrill us once, but not twice. Once available, it is easy game; we might call it sitting-duck knowledge. This knowledge becomes interesting again when it enters experience by way of use.

And so, as second, let us put knowledge as experience. This is useful knowledge, but it involves uncertainty and risk. How do you know if it is going to rain, or when an animal is going to bolt or attack? Because the event has not yet happened, there is no empirical answer; you may not have time to calculate the statistical probability even on the fastest computer. You will have to rely on experience, which will increase your chance of being right. But then you also may be wrong.

The experience of many people over a long time is traditional knowledge. This is the common knowledge of a culture, which it seems that few of us any longer have. To have a culture, mostly the same people have to live mostly in the same place for a long time. Traditional knowledge is knowledge that has been remembered or recorded, handed down, pondered, corrected, practiced, and refined over a long time.

A related kind of knowledge is made available by the religious traditions and is not otherwise available. If you premise the falsehood of such knowledge, as the materialists do, then of course you don't have it and your opinion of it is worthless.

There also are kinds of knowledge that seem to be more strictly inward. Instinct is inborn knowledge: how to suck, bite, and swallow; how to run away from danger instead of toward it. And perhaps the prepositions refer to knowledge that is more or less instinctive: up, down, in, out, etc.

Intuition is knowledge as recognition, a way of knowing without proof. We know the truth of the Book of Job by intuition.

What we call conscience is knowledge of the difference between right and wrong. Whether or not this is learned, most people have it, and they appear to get it early. Some of the worst malefactors and hypocrites have it in full; how else could they fake it so well? But we should remember that some worthy people have believed conscience to be innate, an 'inner light.'

Inspiration, I believe, is another kind of knowledge or way of knowing, though I don't know how this could be proved. One can say in support only that poets such as Homer, Dante, and Milton seriously believed in it, and that people do at times surpass themselves, performing better than all you know of them has led you to expect. Imagination, in the highest sense, is inspiration. Gifts arrive from sources that cannot be empirically located.

Sympathy gives us an intimate knowledge of other people and other creatures that can come in no other way. So does affection. The knowledge that comes by sympathy and affection is little noticed – the materialists, I assume, are unable to notice it – but in my opinion it cannot be overvalued.

Everybody who has done physical work or danced or played a game of skill is aware of the difference between knowing how and being able. This difference I would call bodily knowledge.

And finally, to be safe, we had better recognize that there is such a thing as counterfeit knowledge or plausible falsehood.

I would say that these taxonomies of mine are more or less reasonable; I certainly would not claim that they are scientific. My only assured claim is that any consideration of ignorance and knowledge ought to be at least as complex as this attempt of mine. We are a complex species – organisms surely, but also living souls – who are involved in a life-or-death negotiation, even more complex, with our earthly circumstances, which are complex beyond our ability to guess, let alone know. In dealing with those circumstances, in trying 'to see into the future and plot long-term consequences,' the human mind is neither capacious enough nor exact nor dependable. We are encumbered by an inherent ignorance perhaps not significantly reducible, as well as by proclivities to ignorance of other kinds, and our ways of knowing, though impressive within human limits, have the power to lead us beyond our limits, beyond foresight and precaution, and out of control.

What I have said so far characterizes the personal minds of individual humans. But because of a certain kind of arrogant ignorance, and because of the gigantic scale of work permitted and even required by powerful technologies, we are not safe in dealing merely with personal or human minds. We are obliged to deal also with a kind of mind that I will call corporate, although it is also political and institutional. This is a mind that is compound and abstract, materialist, reductionist, greedy, and radically utilitarian. Assuming as some of us sometimes do that two heads are better than one, it ought to be axiomatic that the corporate mind is better than any personal mind, but it can in fact be much worse – not least in its apparently limitless ability to cause problems that it cannot solve, and that may be unsolvable. The corporate mind is remarkably narrow. It claims to utilize only empirical knowledge – the preferred term is 'sound science,' reducible ultimately to the 'bottom line' of profit or power – and because this rules out any explicit recourse to experience or tradition or any kind of inward knowledge such as conscience, this mind is readily susceptible to every kind of ignorance and is perhaps naturally predisposed to counterfeit knowledge. It comes to its work equipped with factual knowledge and perhaps also with knowledge skillfully counterfeited, but without recourse to any of those knowledges that enable us to deal appropriately with mystery or with human limits. It has no humbling knowledge. The corporate mind is arrogantly ignorant by definition.

Ignorance, arrogance, narrowness of mind, incomplete knowledge, and counterfeit knowledge are of concern to us because they are dangerous; they cause destruction. When united with great power, they cause great destruction. They have caused far too much destruction already, too often of irreplaceable things. Now, reasonably enough, we are asking if it is possible, if it is even thinkable, that the destruction can be stopped. To some people's surprise, we are again backed up against the fact that knowledge is not in any simple way good. We have often been a destructive species, we are more destructive now than we have ever been, and this, in perfect accordance with ancient warnings, is because of our ignorant and arrogant use of knowledge.

Before going further, we had better ask what it is that we humans need to know. We need to know many things, of course, and many kinds of things. But let us be merely practical for the time being and say that we need to know who we are, where we are, and what we must do to live. These questions do not refer to discreet categories of knowledge. We are not likely to be able to answer one of them without answering the other two. And all three must be well answered before we can answer well a further practical question that is now pressing urgently upon us: How can we work without doing irreparable damage to the world and its creatures, including ourselves? Or: How can we live without destroying the sources of our life?

These questions are perfectly honorable, we may even say that they are perfectly obvious, and yet we have much cause to believe that the corporate mind never asks any of them. It does not care who it is, for it is not anybody; it is a mind perfectly disembodied. It does not care where it is so long as its present location yields a greater advantage than any other. It will do anything at all that is necessary, not merely to live, but to aggrandize itself. And it charges its damages indifferently to the public, to nature, and to the future.

The corporate mind at work overthrows all the virtues of the personal mind, or it throws them out of account. The corporate mind knows no affection, no desire that is not greedy, no local or personal loyalty, no sympathy or reverence or gratitude, no temperance or thrift or self-restraint. It does not observe the first responsibility of intelligence, which is to know when you don't know or when you are being unintelligent. Try to imagine an official standing up in the high councils of a global corporation or a great public institution to say, 'We have grown too big,' or 'We now have more power than we can responsibly use,' or 'We must treat our employees as our neighbors,' or 'We must count ourselves as members of this community,' or 'We must preserve the ecological integrity of our work places,' or 'Let us do unto others as we would have them to do unto us' – and you will see what I mean.

The corporate mind, on the contrary, justifies and encourages the personal mind in its worst faults and weaknesses, such as greed and servility, and frees it of any need to worry about long-term consequences. For these reliefs, nowadays, the corporate mind is apt to express noisily its gratitude to God.

But now I must hasten to acknowledge that there are some corporations that do not simply incorporate what I am calling the corporate mind. Whether the number of these is increasing or not, I don't know. These organizations, I believe, tend to have hometowns and to count themselves as participants in the local economy and as members of the local community.

I would not apply to science any stricture that I would not apply to the arts, but science now calls for special attention because it has contributed so largely to modern abuses of the natural world, and because of its enormous prestige. Our concern here has to do immediately with the complacency of many scientists. It cannot be denied that science, in its inevitable applications, has given unprecedented extremes of scale to the technologies of land use, manufacturing, and war, and to their bad effects. One response to the manifest implication of science in certain kinds of destruction is to say that we need more science, or more and better science. I am inclined to honor this proposition, if I am allowed to add that we also need more than science.

But I am not at all inclined to honor the proposition that 'science is self-correcting' when it implies that science is thus made somehow 'safe.' Science is no more safe than any other kind of knowledge. And especially it is not safe in the context of its gigantic applications by the corporate mind. Nor is it safe in the context of its own progressivist optimism. The idea, common enough among the universities and their ideological progeny, that one's work, whatever it is, will be beneficently disposed by the market or the hidden hand or evolution or some other obscure force is an example of counterfeit knowledge.

The obvious immediate question is, How *soon* can science correct itself? Can it correct itself soon enough to prevent or correct the real damage of its errors? The answer is that it cannot correct itself soon enough. Scientists who have made a plausible 'breakthrough' hasten to tell the world, including of course the corporations. And while science may have corrected itself, it is not necessarily able to correct its results or its influence.

We must grant of course that science in its laboratories may be well under control. Scientists in laboratories did not cause the ozone hole or the hypoxic zones or acid rain or Chernobyl or Bhopal or Love Canal. It is when knowledge is corporatized, commercialized, and applied that it goes out of control. Can science, then, make itself responsible by issuing appropriate warnings with its knowledge? No, because the users are under no obligation to heed or respect the warning. If the knowledge is conformable to the needs of profit or power, the warning will be ignored, as we know. We are not excused by the doctrine of scientific self-correction from worrying about the influence of science on the corporate mind, and about the influence of the corporate mind on the minds of consumers and users. Humans in general have got to worry about the origins of the permission we have given ourselves to do large-scale damage. That permission is our problem, for by it we have made our ignorance arrogant and given it immeasurable power to do harm. We are killing our world on the theory that it was never alive but is only an accidental concatenation of materials and mechanical processes. We are killing one another and ourselves on the same theory. If life has no standing as mystery or miracle or gift, then what signifies the difference between it and death?

To state the problem more practically, we can say that the ignorant use of knowledge allows power to override the question of scale, because it overrides respect for the integrity of local ecosystems, which respect alone can determine the appropriate scale of human work. Without propriety of scale, and the acceptance of limits which that implies, there can be no form – and here we reunite science and art. We live and prosper by form, which is the power of creatures and artifacts to be made whole within their proper limits. Without formal restraints, power necessarily becomes inordinate and destructive. This is why the poet David Jones wrote in the midst of World War II that 'man as artist hungers and thirsts after form.' Inordinate size has of itself the power to exclude much knowledge.

What can we do? Anybody who goes on so long about a problem is rightly expected to have something to say about a solution. One is expected to 'end on a positive note,' and I mean to do that. But I also mean to be careful. The question, What can we do? especially when the problem is large, implies the expectation of a large solution.

I have no large solution to offer. There is, as maybe we all have noticed, a conspicuous shortage of large-scale corrections for problems that have large-scale causes. Our damages to watersheds and ecosystems will have to be corrected one farm, one forest, one acre at a time. The aftermath of a bombing has to be dealt with one corpse, one wound at a time. And so the first temptation to avoid is the call for some sort of revolution. To imagine that destructive power might be made harmless by gathering enough power to destroy it is of course perfectly futile. William Butler Yeats said as much in his poem 'The Great Day':

> Hurrah for revolution and more cannon shot!
> A beggar upon horseback lashes a beggar on foot.
> Hurrah for revolution and cannon come again!
> The beggars have changed places, but the lash goes on.

Arrogance cannot be cured by greater arrogance, or ignorance by greater ignorance. To counter the ignorant use of knowledge and power we have, I am afraid, only a proper humility, and this is laughable. But it is only partly laughable. In his political pastoral 'Build Soil,' as if responding to Yeats, Robert Frost has one of his rustics say,

> I bid you to a one-man revolution –
> The only revolution that is coming.

If we find the consequences of our arrogant ignorance to be humbling, and we are humbled, then we have at hand the first fact of hope: we can change ourselves. We, each of us severally, can remove our minds from the corporate ignorance and arrogance that is leading the world to destruction; we can honestly confront our ignorance and our need; we can take guidance from the knowledge we most authentically possess, from experience, from tradition, and from the inward promptings of affection, conscience, decency, compassion, even inspiration.

This change can be called by several names – change of heart, rebirth, metanoia, enlightenment – and it belongs, I think, to all the religions, but I like the practical way it is defined in the Confucian *Great Digest*. This is from Ezra Pound's translation:

The men of old wanting to clarify and diffuse throughout the empire that light which comes from looking straight into the heart and then acting, first set up good government in their own states; wanting good government in their states, they first established order in their own families; wanting order in the home, they first disciplined themselves; desiring self-discipline, they rectified their own hearts; and wanting to rectify their hearts, they sought precise verbal definitions of their inarticulate thoughts [the tones given off by the heart]; wishing to attain precise verbal definitions, they set to extend their knowledge to the utmost.

This curriculum does not rule out science – it does not rule out knowledge of any kind – but it begins with the recognition of ignorance and of need, of being in a bad situation.

If the ability to change oneself is the first fact of hope, then the second surely must be an honest assessment of the badness of our situation. Our situation is extremely bad, as I have said, and optimism cannot either improve it or make it look better. But there is hope in seeing it as it is. And here I need to quote Kathleen Raine again. This is a passage written in the aftermath of World War II, and she is thinking of T. S. Eliot's poem *The Waste Land*, written in the aftermath of World War I. In *The Waste Land*, Eliot bears unflinching witness to the disease of our time: we are living the death of our culture and our world. The poem's ruling metaphor is that of a waterless land perishing for rain, an image that becomes more poignant as we pump down the aquifers and dry up or pollute the rivers.

But Eliot [Kathleen Raine said] has shown us what the world is very apt to forget, that the statement of a terrible truth has a kind of healing power. In his stern vision of the hell that lies about us . . . , there is a quality of grave consolation. In his statement of the worst, Eliot has always implied the whole extent of the reality of which that worst is only one part.

•

Honesty is good, then, not just because it is a virtue, but for a practical reason: it can give us an accurate description of our problem, and it can set the problem precisely in its context.

Honesty, of course, is not a solution. As I have already said, I don't think there are solutions commensurate with our problems. I think the great problems call for many small solutions. But for that possibility to attain sufficient standing among us, we need not only to put the problems in context but also to learn to put our work in context. And here is where we turn back from our ambitions to consult both the local ecosystem and the cultural instructions conveyed to us by religion and the arts. All the arts and sciences need to be made answerable to standards higher than those of any art or science. Scientists and artists must understand that they can honor their gifts and fulfill their obligations only by living and working as human beings and community members rather than as specialists. What this may involve may not be predictable even by scientists. But the best advice may have been given by Hippocrates: 'As to diseases make a habit of two things – to help, or at least, to do no harm.'

The wish to help, especially if it is profitable to do so, may be in human nature, and everybody wants to be a hero. To help, or to try to help, requires only knowledge; one needs to know promising remedies and how to apply them. But to do no harm involves a whole culture, and a culture very different from industrialism. It involves, at the minimum, compassion and humility and caution. The person who will undertake to help without doing harm is going to be a person of some complexity, not easily pleased, probably not a hero, probably not a billionaire.

The corporate approach to agriculture or manufacturing or medicine or war increasingly undertakes to help at the risk of harm, sometimes of great harm. And once the risk of harm is appraised as 'acceptable,' the result often is absurdity: we destroy a village in order to save it; we destroy freedom in order to save it; we destroy the world in order to live in it.

The apostles of the corporate mind say, with a large implicit compliment to themselves, that you cannot succeed without risking failure. And they allude to such examples as that of the Wright brothers. They don't see that the issue of risk raises directly the issue of scale. Risk, like everything else, has an appropriate scale. By propriety of scale we limit the possible damages of the risks we take. If we cannot control scale so as to limit the effects, then we should not take the risk. From this, it is clear that some risks simply should not be taken. Some experiments should not be made. If a Wright brother wishes to risk failure, then he observes a fundamental decency in risking it alone. If the Wright airplane had crashed into a house and killed a child, the corporate mind, considering the future profitability of aviation, would count that an 'acceptable' risk and loss. One can only reply that the corporate mind does not have the householder's or the parent's point of view.

I am aware that invoking personal decency, personal humility, as the solution to a vast risk taken on our behalf by corporate industrialism is not going to suit everybody. Some will find it an insult to their sense of proportion, others to their sense of drama. I am offended by it myself, and I wish I could do better. But having looked about, I have been unable to convince myself that there is a better solution or one that has a better chance of working.

I am trying to follow what T. S. Eliot called 'the way of ignorance,' for I think that is the way that is appropriate for the ignorant. I think Eliot meant us to understand that the way of ignorance is the way recommended by all the great teachers. It was certainly the way recommended by Confucius, for who but the ignorant would set out to extend their knowledge to the utmost? Who but the knowingly ignorant would know there is an 'utmost' to knowledge?

But we take the way of ignorance also as a courtesy toward reality. Eliot wrote in 'East Coker':

> The knowledge imposes a pattern, and falsifies,
> For the pattern is new in every moment
> And every moment is a new and shocking
> Valuation of all we have been.

•

This certainly describes the ignorance inherent in the human condition, an ignorance we justly feel as tragic. But it also is a way of acknowledging the uniqueness of every individual creature, deserving respect, and the uniqueness of every moment, deserving wonder. Life in time involves a great freshness that is falsified by what we already know.

And of course the way of ignorance is the way of faith. If enough of us will accept 'the wisdom of humility,' giving due honor to the ever-renewing pattern, accepting each moment's 'new and shocking / Valuation of all we have been,' then the corporate mind as we now have it will be shaken, and it will cease to exist as its members dissent and withdraw from it.

(2004)

The Future of Agriculture*

Our fundamental problem is world-destruction, caused by an irreconcilable contradiction between the natural world and the engineered world of industrialism. This conflict between nature and human interest may have begun with the first tools and weapons, but only with the triumph of industrialism has it become absolute. By now the creaturely world is absolutely at the mercy of industrial processes, which are doing massive ecological damage. How much of this damage may be repairable by economic and cultural changes remains to be seen.

Industrial destructiveness, anyhow, is our disease. Most of our most popular worries – climate change, fossil fuel addiction, pollution, poverty, hunger, and the various forms of legitimated violence – are symptoms. If, for example, we were somehow granted a limitless supply of cheap, clean energy, we would continue, and even accelerate, our destruction of the world by agricultural erosion, chemical poisoning, industrial war, industrial recreation, and various forms of 'development.'

And there is no use in saying that if we can invent the nuclear bomb and fly to the moon, we can solve hunger and related problems of land use. Epic feats of engineering require only a few brilliant technicians and a lot of money. But feeding a world of people year to year for a long time requires cultures of husbandry fitted to the nature of millions of unique small places – precisely the kind of cultures that industrialism has purposely disvalued, uprooted, and destroyed.

Hard as it may be for a dislocated, miseducated, consumptive society to accept, and for its pet economists to believe, the future of food

* A speech for the Future of Food Conference at Georgetown University, Washington, D.C., on May 4, 2011.

is not distinguishable from the future of the land, which is indistinguishable in turn from the future of human care. It depends ultimately on the health, not of the financial system, but of the ecosphere. In the interest of that health, we will have to bring all the disciplines, all the arts and sciences, into conformity with the nature of places. Like other species, we will have to submit to the necessity of local adaptation. I am sure that somebody will wish to remind me of the migrations of birds, animals, and insects, and also of migrations by humans from earliest times. Did these involve local adaptation? Yes, except for those of industrial humans using fossil fuel, all of these migrations have been made under the rule of local adaptation. The hummingbird successfully crossing the Gulf of Mexico is adapted, mile by mile, to the distance; it does not exceed its own mental and physical capacities; and it makes the trip, exactly like pre-industrial human migrants, on contemporary energy. For humans, local adaptation is not work for a few financiers and a few intellectual and political hotshots. This is work for everybody, requiring everybody's intelligence. It is work inherently democratic.

What must we do?

First, we must not work or think on a heroic scale. In our age of global industrialism, heroes too lightly risk the lives of people, places, and things they do not see. We must work on a scale proper to our limited abilities. We must not break things we cannot fix. There is no justification, ever, for permanent ecological damage. If this imposes the verdict of guilt upon us all, so be it.

Second, we must abandon the homeopathic delusion that the damages done by industrialization can be corrected by more industrialization.

Third, we must quit solving our problems by 'moving on.' We must try to stay put, and to learn where we are geographically, historically, and ecologically.

Fourth, we must learn, if we can, the sources and costs of our own economic lives.

Fifth, we must give up the notion that we are too good to do our own work and clean up our own messes. It is not acceptable for this work to be done for us by wage slavery or by enslaving nature.

Sixth, by way of correction, we must make local, locally adapted economies, based on local nature, local sunlight, local intelligence, and local work.

Seventh, we must understand that these measures are radical. They go to the root of our problem. They cannot be performed for us by any expert, political leader, or corporation.

This is an agenda that may be undertaken by ordinary citizens at any time, on their own initiative. In fact, it describes an effort already undertaken all over the world by many people. It defines also the expectation that citizens who by their gifts are exceptional will not shirk the most humble services.

(2011)

The Rise

We put the canoe in about six miles up the Kentucky River from my house. There, at the mouth of Drennon Creek, is a little colony of summer camps. We knew we could get down to the water there with some ease. And it proved easier than we expected. The river was up maybe twenty feet, and we found a path slanting down the grassy slope in front of one of the cabins. It went right into the water, as perfect for launching the canoe and getting in as if it had been worn there by canoeists.

To me that, more than anything else, is the excitement of a rise: the unexpectedness, always, of the change it makes. What was difficult becomes easy. What was easy becomes difficult. By water, what was distant becomes near. By land, what was near becomes distant. At the water line, when a rise is on, the world is changing. There is an irresistible sense of adventure in the difference. Once the river is out of its banks, a vertical few inches of rise may widen the surface by many feet over the bottomland. A sizable lagoon will appear in the middle of a cornfield. A drain in a pasture will become a canal. Stands of beech and oak will take on the look of a cypress swamp. There is something Venetian about it. There is a strange excitement in going in a boat where one would ordinarily go on foot – or where, ordinarily, birds would be flying. And so the first excitement of our trip was that little path; where it might go in a time of low water was unimaginable. Now it went down to the river.

Because of the offset in the shore at the creek mouth, there was a large eddy turning in the river where we put in, and we began our drift downstream by drifting upstream. We went up inside the row of shore trees, whose tops now waved in the current, until we found an opening among the branches, and then turned out along the channel. The current took us. We were still settling ourselves as if in preparation, but our starting place was already diminishing behind us.

There is something ominously like life in that. One would always like to settle oneself, get braced, say 'Now I am going to begin' – and then begin. But as the necessary quiet seems about to descend, a hand is felt at one's back, shoving. And that is the way with the river when a current is running: once the connection with the shore is broken, the journey has begun.

We were, of course, already at work with the paddles. But we were ahead of ourselves. I think that no matter how deliberately one moved from the shore into the sudden fluid violence of a river on the rise, there would be bound to be several uneasy minutes of transition. It is another world, which means that one's senses and reflexes must begin to live another kind of life. Sounds and movements that from the standpoint of the shore might have come to seem even familiar now make a new urgent demand on the attention. There is everything to get used to, from a wholly new perspective. And from the outset one has the currents to deal with.

It is easy to think, before one has ever tried it, that nothing could be easier than to drift down the river in a canoe on a strong current. That is because when one thinks of a river one is apt to think of *one* thing – a great singular flowing that one puts one's boat into and lets go. But it is not like that at all, not after the water is up and the current swift. It is not one current, but a braiding together of several, some going at different speeds, some even in different directions. Of course, one *could* just let go, let the boat be taken into the continuous mat of drift – leaves, logs, whole trees, cornstalks, cans, bottles, and such – in the channel, and turn and twist in the eddies there. But one does not have to do that long in order to sense the helplessness of a light canoe when it is sideways to the current. It is out of control then, and endangered. Stuck in the mat of drift, it can't be maneuvered. It would turn over easily; one senses that by a sort of ache in the nerves, the way bad footing is sensed. And so we stayed busy, keeping the canoe between the line of half-submerged shore trees and the line of drift that marked the channel. We weren't trying to hurry – the currents were carrying us as fast as we wanted to go – but it took considerable labor just to keep straight. It was like riding a spirited horse not fully bridle-wise: we kept our direction *by intention*; there could be no dependence on habit or inertia; when our minds wandered the river took over and turned us according to inclinations of its own. It bore us like a consciousness, acutely wakeful, filling perfectly the lapses in our own.

But we did grow used to it, and accepted our being on it as one of the probabilities, and began to take the mechanics of it for granted. The necessary sixth sense had come to us, and we began to notice more than we had to.

There is an exhilaration in being *accustomed* to a boat on dangerous water. It is as though into one's consciousness of the dark violence of the depths at one's feet there rises the idea of the boat, the buoyancy of it. It is always with a sort of triumph that the boat is realized – that it goes *on top of the water*, between breathing and drowning. It is an ancient-feeling triumph; it must have been one of the first ecstasies. The analogy of riding a spirited horse is fairly satisfactory; it is mastery over something resistant – a buoyancy that is not natural and inert like that of a log, but desired and vital and to one's credit. Once the boat has fully entered the consciousness it becomes an intimate extension of the self; one feels as competently amphibious as a duck, whose feet are paddles. And once we felt accustomed and secure in the boat, the day and the river began to come clear to us.

It was a gray, cold Sunday in the middle of December. In the woods on the north slopes above us we could see the black trunks and branches just faintly traced with snow, which gave them a silvery, delicate look – the look of impossibly fine handwork that nature sometimes has. And they looked cold. The wind was coming straight up the river into our faces. But we were dressed warmly, and the wind didn't matter much, at least not yet. The force that mattered, that surrounded us, and inundated us with its sounds, and pulled at or shook or carried everything around us, was the river.

To one standing on the bank, floodwater will seem to be flowing at a terrific rate. People who are not used to it will commonly believe it is going three or four times as fast as it really is. It is so all of a piece, and so continuous. To one drifting along in a boat this exaggerated impression of speed does not occur; one is going the same speed as the river then and is not fooled. In the Kentucky when the water is high a current of four or five miles an hour is about usual, I would say, and there are times in a canoe that make that seem plenty fast.

What the canoeist gets, instead of an impression of the river's speed, is an impression of its power. Or, more exactly, an impression of the *voluminousness* of its power. The sense of the volume alone has come to me when, swimming in the summertime, I have submerged mouth and nose so that the plane of the water spread away from the lower eyelid; the awareness of its bigness that comes then is almost intolerable; one feels how falsely assuring it is to look down on the river, as we usually do. The sense of the power of it came to me one day in my boyhood when I attempted to swim ashore in a swift current, pulling an overturned rowboat. To check the downstream course of the boat I tried grabbing hold of the partly submerged willows along the shore with my free hand, and was repeatedly pulled under as the willows bent, and then torn loose. My arms stretched between the boat and the willow branch might have been sewing threads for all the holding they could do against that current. It was the first time I realized that there could be circumstances in which my life would count for nothing, absolutely nothing – and I have never needed to learn that again.

Sitting in a canoe, riding the back of the flooding river as it flows down into a bend, and turns, the currents racing and crashing among the trees along the outside shore, and flows on, one senses the volume and the power all together. The sophistications of our age do not mitigate the impression. To some degree it remains unimaginable, as is suggested by the memory's recurrent failure to hold on to it. It can never be remembered as wild as it is, and so each new experience of it bears some of the shock of surprise. It would take the mind of a god to watch it as it changes and not be surprised.

These long views that one gets coming down it show it to move majestically. It is stately. It has something of the stylized grandeur and awesomeness of royalty in a Sophoclean tragedy. But as one watches, there emanates from it, too, an insinuation of darkness, implacability, horror. And the nearer look tends to confirm this. Contained and borne in the singular large movement are hundreds of smaller ones: eddies and whirlpools, turnings this way and that, cross-currents rushing out from the shores into the channel. One must simplify it in order to speak of it. One probably simplifies it in some way in order to look at it.

There is something deeply horrifying about it, roused. Not, I think, because it is inhuman, alien to us; some of us at least must feel a kinship with it, or we would not loiter around it for pleasure. The horror must come from our sense that, so long as it remains what it is, it is not subject. To say that it is indifferent would be wrong. That would imply a malevolence, as if it could be aware of us if only it wanted to. It is more remote from our concerns than indifference. It is serenely and silently not subject – to us or to anything else except the other natural forces that are also beyond our control. And it is apt to stand for and represent to us all in nature and in the universe that is not subject. That is its horror. We can make use of it. We can ride on its back in boats. But it won't stop to let us get on and off. It is not a passenger train. And if we make a mistake, or risk ourselves too far to it, why then it will suffer a little wrinkle on its surface, and go on as before.

That horror is never fully revealed, but only sensed piecemeal in events, all different, all shaking, yet all together falling short of the full revelation. The next will be as unexpected as the last.

A man I knew in my boyhood capsized his motorboat several miles upriver from here. It was winter. The river was high and swift. It was already nightfall. The river carried him a long way before he drowned. Farmers sitting in their houses in the bottoms heard his cries passing down in the darkness, and failed to know what to make of them. It is hard to imagine what they could have done if they had known.

I can't believe that anyone who has heard that story will ever forget it. Over the years it has been as immediate to me as if I had seen it all – almost as if I had *known* it all: the capsized man aching and then numb in the cold water, clinging to some drift log in the channel, and calling, seeing the house lights appear far off across the bottoms and dwindle behind him, the awful power of the flood and his hopelessness in it finally dawning on him – it is amazingly real; it is happening to him. And the families in their lighted warm kitchens, eating supper maybe, when the tiny desperate outcry comes to them out of the darkness, and they look up at the window, and then at each other.

'Shh! Listen! What was that?'

'By God, it sounded like somebody hollering out there on the river.'

'But it *can't* be.'

But it makes them uneasy. Whether or not there *is* somebody out there, the possibility that there *may* be reminds them of their lot; they never know what may be going by them in the darkness. And they think of the river, so dark and cold.

The history of these marginal places is in part the history of drownings – of fishermen, swimmers, men fallen from boats. And there is the talk, the memory, the inescapable *feeling* of dragging for the bodies – that terrible fishing for dead men lost deep in the currents, carried downstream sometimes for miles.

Common to river mentality, too, are the imaginings: step-offs, undertows, divers tangled in sunken treetops, fishermen hooked on their own lines.

And yet it fascinates. Sometimes it draws the most fearful to it. Men must test themselves against it. Its mystery must be forever tampered with. There is a story told here of a strong big boy who tried unsuccessfully to cross the river by walking on the bottom, carrying an iron kettle over his head for a diving bell. And another story tells of a young man who, instead of walking under it, thought he would walk *on* it, with the help of a gallon jug tied to each foot. The miracle failing, of course, the jugs held his feet up, and his head under, until somebody obliged him by pulling him out. His pride, like Icarus', was transformed neatly into his fall – the work of a river god surely, *hybris* being as dangerous in Henry County as anywhere else.

To sense fully the power and the mystery of it, the eye must be close to it, near to level with the surface. I think that is the revelation of George Caleb Bingham's painting of trappers on the Missouri. The painter's eye, there, is very near the water, and so he sees the river as the trappers see it from their dugout – all the space coming down to that vast level. One feels the force, the aliveness, of the water under the boat, close under the feet of the men. And there they are, isolated in the midst of it, with their box of cargo and their pet fox – men and boat and box and animal all so strangely and poignantly coherent on the wild plain of the water, a sort of island.

But impressive as the sights may be, the river's wildness is most awesomely announced to the ear. Along the channel, the area of the most concentrated and the freest energy, there is silence. It is at the shore line, where obstructions are, that the currents find their voices. The water divides around the trunks of the trees, and sucks and slurs as it closes together again. Trunks and branches are ridden down to the surface, or suddenly caught by the rising water, and the current pours over them in a waterfall. And the weaker trees throb and vibrate in the flow, their naked branches clashing and rattling. It is a storm of sound, changing as the shores change, increasing and diminishing, but never ceasing. And between these two storm lines of commotion there is that silence of the middle, as though the quiet of the deep flowing rises into the air. Once it is recognized, listened to, that silence has the force of a voice.

After we had come down a mile or two we passed the house of a fisherman. His children were standing on top of the bank, high at that place, waiting for him to come in off the river. And on down we met the fisherman himself, working his way home among the nets he had placed in the quieter water inside the rows of shore trees. We spoke and passed, and were soon out of sight of each other. But seeing him there changed the aspect of the river for us, as meeting an Arab on a camel might change the aspect of the desert. Problematic and strange as it seemed to us, here was a man who made a daily thing of it, and went to it as another man would go to an office. That race of violent water, which would hang flowing among the treetops only three or four days, had become familiar country to him, and he sunk his nets in it with more assurance than men sink wells in the earth. And so the flood bore a pattern of his making, and he went his set way on it.

And he was not the only creature who had made an unexpected familiarity with the risen water. Where the drift had matted in the shore eddies, or caught against trees in the current, the cardinals and chickadees and titmice foraged as confidently as on dry land. The rise was an opportunity for them, turning up edibles they would have found with more difficulty otherwise. The cardinals were more irresistibly brilliant than ever, kindling in the black-wet drift in the cold wind. The sight of them warmed us.

The Kentucky is a river of steep high banks, nearly everywhere thickly grown with willows and water maples and elms and syca-mores. Boating on it in the summer, one is enclosed in a river-world, moving as though deep inside the country. One sees only the river, the high walls of foliage along the banks, the hilltops that rise over the trees first on one side and then the other. And that is one of the delights of this river. But one of the delights of being out on a winter rise is in seeing the country, and in seeing it from a vantage point that one does not usually see it from. The rise, that Sunday, had lifted us to the bank tops and higher, and through the naked trees we could look out across the bottoms. It was maybe like boating on a canal in Holland, though we had never done that. We could see the picked cornfields, their blanched yellow seeming even on that cloudy day to give off a light. We could see the winter grain spiking green over the summer's tobacco patches, the thickly wooded hollows and slews, the backs of houses and farm buildings usually seen only by the people who live there.

Once, before the man-made floods of modern times, and before the automobile, all the river country turned toward the river. In those days our trip would probably have had more witnesses than it did. We might have been waved to from house windows, and from barn doors. But now the country has turned toward the roads, and we had what has come to be the back view of it. We went by mostly in secret. Only one of the fine old river houses is left on this side of the river in the six miles of our trip, and it is abandoned and weathering out; the floods have been in it too many times in the last thirty-five years, and it is too hard to get back to from the road. We went by its blank windows as the last settlers going west passed the hollow eyes of the skulls of their predecessors' oxen.

The living houses are all out along the edges of the valley floor, where the roads are. And now that all the crops had been gathered out of the bottoms, men's attention had mostly turned away. The land along the river had taken on a wildness that in the summer it would not have. We saw a pair of red-tailed hawks circling low and unafraid, more surprised to see us than we were to see them.

Where the river was over the banks a stretch of comparatively quiet water lay between the trees on the bank top and the new shore line. After a while, weary of the currents, we turned into one of these. As we made our way past the treetops and approached the shore we flushed a bobwhite out of a brush pile near the water and saw it fly off downstream. It seemed strange to see only one. But we didn't have to wait long for an explanation, for presently we saw the dogs, and then the hunters coming over the horizon with their guns. We knew where their bird had gone, but we didn't wait to tell them.

These men come out from the cities now that the hunting season is open. They walk in these foreign places, unknown to them for most of the year, looking for something to kill. They wear and carry many dollars' worth of equipment, and go to a great deal of trouble, in order to kill some small creatures that they would never trouble to know alive, and that means little to them once they have killed it. If those we saw had killed the bobwhite they would no doubt have felt all their expense and effort justified, and would have thought themselves more manly than before. It reminds one of the extraordinary trouble and expense governments go to in order to kill men – and consider it justified or not, according to the 'kill ratio.' The diggers among our artifacts will find us to have been honorable lovers of death, having been willing to pay exorbitantly for it. How much better, we thought, to have come upon the *life* of the bird as we did, moving peaceably among the lives of the country that showed themselves to us because we were peaceable, than to have tramped fixedly, half oblivious, for miles in order to come at its death.

We left the hunters behind and went down past a green grainfield where cattle were grazing and drinking at the waterside. They were not disturbed that the river had come up over part of their pasture, no more troubled by the height of today's shore line than they were by the height of yesterday's. To them, no matter how high it was, so long as the ground was higher it was as ordinary as a summer pond. Surely the creatures of the fifth day of Creation accepted those of the sixth with equanimity, as though they had always been there. Eternity is always present in the animal mind; only men deal in beginnings and ends. It is probably lucky for man that he was created last. He would have got too excited and upset over all the change.

Two mallards flew up ahead of us and turned downriver into the wind. They had been feeding in the flooded corn rows, reminding us what a godsend the high water must be for ducks. The valley is suddenly full of little coves and havens, so that they can scatter out and feed safer and more hidden, and more abundantly too, than they usually can, never having to leave the river for such delicacies as the shattered corn left by the pickers. A picked cornfield under a few inches of water must be the duck Utopia – Utopia being, I assume, more often achieved by ducks than by men.

If one imagines the shore line exactly enough as the division between water and land, and imagines it rising – it comes up too slowly for the eye usually, so one *must* imagine it – there is a sort of magic about it. As it moves upward it makes a vast change, far more than the eye sees. It makes a new geography, altering the boundaries of worlds. Above it, it widens the freehold of the birds; below it, that of the fish. The land creatures are driven back and higher up. It is a line between boating and walking, gill and lung, standing still and flowing. Along it, suddenly and continuously, all that will float is picked up and carried away: leaves, logs, seeds, little straws, bits of dead grass.

And also empty cans and bottles and all sorts of buoyant trash left behind by fishermen and hunters and picnickers, or dumped over creek banks by householders who sometimes drive miles to do it. We passed behind a house built on one of the higher banks whose back-yard was simply an avalanche of kitchen trash going down to the river. Those people, for all I know, may be champion homebodies, but their garbage is well traveled, having departed for the Gulf of Mexico on every winter rise for years.

It is illuminating and suitably humbling to a man to recognize the great power of the river. But after he has recognized its power he is next called upon to recognize its limits. It can neither swallow up nor carry off all the trash that people convenience themselves by dumping into it. It can't carry off harmlessly all the sewage and pesticides and industrial contaminants that we are putting into it now, much less all that we will be capable of putting into it in a few years. We haven't accepted – we can't really believe – that the most characteristic product of our age of scientific miracles is junk, but that is so. And we still think and behave as though we face an unspoiled continent, with thousands of acres of living space for every man. We still sing 'America the Beautiful' as though we had not created in it, by strenuous effort, at great expense, and with dauntless self-praise, an unprecedented ugliness.

The last couple of miles of our trip we could hear off in the bottoms alongside us the cries of pileated woodpeckers, and we welcomed the news of them. These belong to the big trees and the big woods, and more than any other birds along this river they speak out of our past. Their voices are loud and wild, the cries building strongly and then trailing off arrhythmically and hesitantly as though reluctant to end. Though they never seemed very near, we could hear them clearly over the commotion of the water. There were probably only a pair or two of them, but their voices kept coming to us a long time, creating beyond the present wildness of the river, muddy from the ruin of mountainsides and farmlands, the intimation of another wildness that will not overflow again in *our* history.

The wind had finally made its way into our clothes, and our feet and hands and faces were beginning to stiffen a little with the cold. And so when home came back in sight we thought it wasn't too soon. We began to slant across the currents toward the shore. The river didn't stop to let us off. We ran the bow out onto the path that goes up to my house, and the current rippled on past the stern as though it were no more than the end of a stranded log. We were out of it, wobbling stiff-legged along the midrib on our way to the high ground.

With the uproar of the water still in our ears, we had as we entered the house the sense of having been utterly outside the lives we live as usual. My warm living room was a place we seemed to have been away from a long way. It needed getting used to.

(1969)

Acknowledgments

The essays in this book were originally published in the following:

'A Native Hill': *The Hudson Review*, Vol. 21, No. 4 (winter 1968–9)

'The Making of a Marginal Farm': *Recollected Essays, 1965–1980* (North Point Press, 1981)

'Think Little': *Whole Earth Catalog* (September 1970)

'Nature as Measure': *Bringing it to the Table: On Farming and Food* (Counterpoint Press, 2010)

'The Total Economy': first published as 'The Idea of a Local Economy' in *Orion Magazine* (winter 2000)

'Writer and Region': *The Hudson Review*, Vol. 40, No. 1 (spring 1987)

'Damage': *What Are People For?* (North Point Press, 1990); first published as a pamphlet by the Iowa Humanities Lecture Series Board.

'The Work of Local Culture': *What Are People For?* (North Point Press, 1990)

'The Unsettling of America': *The Unsettling of America: Culture and Agriculture* (Sierra Club Books, 1977)

'The Agrarian Standard': *Orion Magazine* (summer 2002)

'The Pleasures of Eating': *What Are People For?* (North Point Press, 1990)

'Horse-Drawn Tools and the Doctrine of Labor Saving': *The New Farm* (1987)

'Getting Along with Nature': *Home Economics: Fourteen Essays* (North Point Press, 1987)

'A Few Words for Motherhood': *The New Farm* (1980)

'Two Minds': *Citizenship Papers* (Counterpoint Press, 2003)

'The Prejudice Against Country People': *The Progressive* magazine (2001)

'Faustian Economics': *Harper's Magazine* (May 2008)

'Quantity versus Form': *Southern Arts Journal* (2004)

'Word and Flesh': *What Are People For?* (North Point Press, 1990)

'Why I Am Not Going to Buy a Computer': *Harper's Magazine* (May 1987)

'Feminism, the Body, and the Machine': *What Are People For?* (North Point Press, 1990)

'Family Work': *Home Food Systems* (Rodale Press, 1981)

'Rugged Individualism': *Playboy* (2004)

'Economy and Pleasure': *What Are People For?* (North Point Press, 1990)

'In Distrust of Movements': *Orion Magazine* (summer 1999)

'In Defense of Literacy': *A Continuous Harmony* (Harvest/HBJ, 1975)

'Some Thoughts on Citizenship and Conscience in Honor of Don Pratt': *The Long-Legged House* (Harcourt, Brace & World, 1969)

'Compromise, Hell!': first published as 'People Can't Survive if the Land is Dead' in *Lexington Herald Leader*, and then, under its present title, in *Orion Magazine* (November/December 2004)

'The Way of Ignorance': *New Letters* (summer 2005)

'The Future of Agriculture': originally a speech for the Future of Food Conference at Georgetown University, Washington, D.C., on May 4, 2011

'The Rise': *The Long-Legged House* (Harcourt, Brace & World, 1969)

The essays have also been published in the following North Point and Counterpoint Press editions:

The Art of the Commonplace: The Agrarian Essays of Wendell Berry (Counterpoint Press, 2002): 'A Native Hill,' 'The Unsettling of America,' 'The Pleasures of Eating,' 'Feminism, the Body, and the Machine,' 'Economy and Pleasure'.

Recollected Essays, 1965–1980 (North Point Press, 1981): 'The Making of a Marginal Farm'.

A Continuous Harmony: Essays Cultural and Agricultural (Counterpoint Press, 2012): 'Think Little,' 'In Defence of Literacy'.

Bringing it to the Table: On Farming and Food (Counterpoint Press, 2009): 'Nature as Measure'.

What Matters? Economics for a Renewed Commonwealth (Counterpoint Press, 2010): 'The Total Economy,' 'The Work of Local Culture,' 'Faustian Economics'.

What Are People For? (Counterpoint Press, 2010): 'Writer and Region,' 'Damage,' 'Word and Flesh,' 'Why I Am Not Going to Buy a Computer'.

Citizenship Papers (Counterpoint Press, 2003): 'The Agrarian Standard,' 'Two Minds,' 'The Prejudice Against Country People,' 'In Distrust of Movements'.

The Gift of Good Land: Further Essays Cultural and Agricultural (Counterpoint Press, 1981): 'Horse-Drawn Tools and the Doctrine of Labor Saving,' 'A Few Words for Motherhood,' 'Family Work'.

Home Economics: Fourteen Essays (Berkeley, Counterpoint Press, 1987): 'Getting Along with Nature'.

The Way of Ignorance (Counterpoint Press, 2005): 'Quantity versus Form,' 'Rugged Individualism,' 'Compromise, Hell!,' 'The Way of Ignorance'.

The Long-Legged House (Counterpoint Press, 2012): 'Some Thoughts on Citizenship and Conscience in Honor of Don Pratt,' 'The Rise'.

It All Turns on Affection: The Jefferson Lecture and Other Essays (Counterpoint Press, 2012): 'The Future of Agriculture'.

WENDELL BERRY, an essayist, novelist, and poet, has been honored with the T. S. Eliot Prize for Poetry, the Aiken Taylor Award for Modern American Poetry, the John Hay Award of the Orion Society, and the Richard C. Holbrooke Distinguished Achievement Award of the Dayton Literary Peace Prize, among others. In 2010, he was awarded the National Humanities Medal by Barack Obama, and in 2016, he was the recipient of the Ivan Sandrof Lifetime Achievement Award from the National Book Critics Circle. He is also a fellow of the American Academy of Arts and Sciences. Berry lives with his wife, Tanya Berry, on their farm in Henry County, Kentucky.